The Equal Opportunities Handbook

To the many people whose ideas, suggestions and time has enabled me to compile this guide a simple word of thanks is hopelessly inadequate; but here it is anyway. Special thanks to Chris, Dave, Ed, Teresa, Joan, Gary, Nicola, Andrew, Sean, Rob, Raj, Jackie, Richard, Ray, Jeanette, Mel, Hazel, Yvonne, Jayshree, Kala, Hamid, Miguel, Gabriella, and to Anya Palmer from the Stonewall Group. Also, last but not least, many thanks to Richard Burton and Jenny Tyler from Blackwell for their enthusiasm, encouragement and inspirational editing.

This book is dedicated to Chris and Rob – with love.

The Equal Opportunities Handbook

A Guide to Law and Best Practice in Europe

HELEN COLLINS

First published 1992

Blackwell Publishers
108 Cowley Road
Oxford OX4 1JF
UK

238 Main Street
Suite 501
Cambridge
MA 02142
USA

British Library Cataloguing in Publication Data

A CIP catalogue record for this book is available from the British Library.

Library of Congress Cataloging-in-Publication Data

Collins, Helen.
The equal opportunities handbook : a guide to law and best practice in Europe / Helen Collins.
p. cm.
Includes bibliographical references and index.
ISBN 0–631–18648–4
(PB : acid-free paper)
1. Discrimination in employment – Law and legislation – European Economic Community countries. 2. Affirmative action programs – Law and legislation – European Economic Community countries. 3. Discrimination in employment – Law and legislation – Great Britain. 4. Affirmative action programs – Law and legislation – Great Britain.
I. Title.
KJE2942.C65 1992
344.4′01133 – dc20
[344.041133] 92–10369
CIP

Typeset in 11 on 13 pt Plantin
by Graphicraft Typesetters Ltd., Hong Kong
Printed in Great Britain by TJ Press (Padstow) Ltd., Padstow, Cornwall

This book is printed on acid-free paper

Contents

Part IV A Way Forward

Preface

Staff are the key factor that determine the success or failure of any organization. Managers, personnel and trainers must realize that investment in human resource is every bit as important as investment in manufacturing. Equal opportunities is about changing people's prejudices and habits, to facilitate the discovery of increased potential in every member of a workforce. This increase can be realized and profitably utilized without vast expenditure in capital equipment – by breaking down the barriers of prejudice that serve as obstacles to economic progress.

At the heart of human resource management and development lies equality of opportunity. In the current ever-changing economic climate, 'equality management' is rather akin to 'crisis management'. That is, it is an attempt to restore, as best one can, order, logic and direction to a situation where demographic changes, declining birth rates, a reduction in school leavers, skill shortages, increasing international competition and the establishment of a Single European Market, to mention just a few of the factors, are altering the structure of employment and the labour market in a dramatic way never previously envisaged. These difficulties and the changing face of the labour market have an immediate and direct impact upon employers; and the issues facing employers will in turn jeopardize the national economy unless suitable equal opportunities strategies are successfully established in the near future.

This book will guide any professional involved in human resource issues through the questions that affect his or her workforce in light of the many changes currently occurring in the labour market. Bringing equal opportunities into a firm involves the firm's ability to react to changes in the labour market purposefully, quickly and systematically. The challenges created by changes in the labour market can only be met by company heads who are convinced of the importance of human resources and the need for equal opportunities in order to exploit the full potential of each member of their workforce. Companies can only survive in such a changing environment if this need is recognized early and corresponding strategies for action are developed and implemented. Dynamic development requires active and creative (rather than reactive) personnel management. Thus, increased investment in human capital is essential for building up a strong economic base. Nowadays equal opportunities cannot simply be left to the natural course of events; it must be sought in an organized way, stimulated and directed so that it can be incorporated into the firm quickly, fully and decisively.

The introduction of the Opportunity 2000 campaign and the EC equal opportunities action programmes affirm the potential of the vast resources waiting to be exploited through equal opportunities. Good equal opportunities practices demand a flexibility which can take full account of the range of human resources available to a company. It is important to state at the outset that an equal opportunities programme is not static, but must develop. Management must communicate its long-term plans and aims with enthusiasm. Motivation will spring from the commitment of each member of the workforce, and also from the degree of delegation and autonomy granted to those involved in establishing the framework of good equal opportunities practice within the organization. There is no miraculous substitute for commitment to equality, commitment that can only be brought about through training, awareness-raising, staff participation and good internal communications.

An equal opportunities policy has to be integrated into all other aspects of business practice within an organization. The procedures introduced by policy implementation (for example, monitoring, evaluation, positive-action measures), which are recognized nowadays as a major factor in the equality process, always modify this process to some degree, in some cases radically, since they call into question conventional working habits, activities and methods. In promoting equality, everyone goes at their own pace, depending on their starting point and their readiness to accept the changes brought about by good equal opportunities policies. Within the area of equality of opportunity in the 1990s, ongoing innovation is central to the existence and development of an organization. Given the rapid progress of economic and technological change in the UK and European manufacturing environment and market, efficient human resource management is the only way to adapt and assume a leading position. For any large organization, equality management must be seen as a state of mind, a permanent attitude to be continuously renewed. Apart from the general ideas which have been incorporated into employment during the spate of equality legislation generated in the 1970s, there is still little real know-how in the field. And with the major changes currently taking place in the demographic make-up of the workforce, the acquisition of such know-how is now more imperative than ever before. Not a little modesty and great circumspection should be exercised before we satisfy ourselves with the results of our equal opportunities procedures.

Finally, 'the proof of the pudding is in the eating'. Evidence shows that in the majority of firms, a dynamic equal opportunities policy is an extremely efficient means of promoting motivation and encouraging high staff-retention rates, low rates of absenteeism and high morale, which in turn lead to greater productivity and innovation. This is because in firms which are committed to equality, those who are responsible for personnel ensure that an employee's ability and outlook is continuously upgraded, not only in the production field, important though that is, but also in all the associated fields which jointly ensure industrial and commercial success and strengthen the overall image of the firm.

List of Abbreviations

ACAS	Advisory Conciliation and Arbitration Service
ADEA	Age Discrimination in Employment Act (USA)
AIDS	Acquired Immune Deficiency Syndrome
BBC	British Broadcasting Corporation
BITC	Business in the Community
BPW	Business and Professional Women
CAADE	Campaign Against Age Discrimination in Employment
CEDP	Committees for the Employment of Disabled People
CHE	Campaign for Homosexual Equality
COIT	Central Office of Industrial Tribunals
CRE	Commission for Racial Equality
DAS	Disablement Advisory Service
DPA	Disabled Persons Act
DRO	Disablement Resettlement Officer
EC	European Community
ECJ	European Court of Justice
ECU	European Currency Unit
EOC	Equal Opportunities Commission
EPA	Equal Pay Act
ERS	Employment Rehabilitation Service
ESF	European Social Fund
ET	Employment Training
EWC	Expected Week of Confinement
GLF	Gay Liberation Front
GOQ	Genuine Occupational Qualification
HELIOS	Handicapped People Living Independently in an Open Society

HIV	Human Immunodeficiency Virus
ICCPR	International Covenant on Civil and Political Rights
ICESCR	International Covenant on Economic, Social and Cultural Rights
IFA	International Federation on Ageing
IL	Independent Living
IT	Industrial Tribunal
JES	Job Evaluation Study
LAGER	Lesbian and Gay Employment Rights
MENCAP	The Royal Society for Mentally Handicapped Children and Adults
MIND	The National Association for Mental Health
NACRO	National Association for the Care and Resettlement of Offenders
NADPAS	National Association of Discharged Prisoners' Aid Societies
NAVH	National Association of Voluntary Hostels
NBC	National Black Caucus
NCCL	National Council for Civil Liberties
NOP	National Opinion Poll
NOW	New Opportunities for Women
PACT	Placing Assessment and Counselling Team
PRA	Pre-Retirement Association
PSI	Policy Studies Institute
QW	Qualifying Week
RADAR	The Royal Association for Disability and Rehabilitation
RDP	Registered Disabled Person
RNIB	Royal National Institute for the Blind
RNID	Royal National Institute for the Deaf
ROW	Rights of Women
RRA	Race Relations Act
RREAS	Race Relations Employment Advisory Service
SDA	Sex Discrimination Act
SEPACS	Sheltered Employment Procurement and Consultancy Services
SMP	Statutory Maternity Pay
SPS	Sheltered Placement Scheme
TEC	Training and Enterprise Council
TIDE	Telecommunications and Information Technology for Elderly People

TUC	Trades Union Congress
UDHR	Universal Declaration of Human Rights
UN	United Nations
WASH	Women Against Sexual Harassment
WLM	Women's Liberation Movement
YT	Youth Training

Guide to the Major Types of EC and UN Laws and Measures

EC Directive A Directive is a European Community law binding on each of the 12 Member States. In most cases this requires national legislation to be approved by the parliament of each Member State in accordance with the customs and procedures of that Member State. The end result to be achieved is the legally binding aspect of a Directive; the choice of method as to how it is to be achieved is left for each Member State parliament to decide independently. Businesses affected by a Directive have to take account of national legislation as well as the Directive itself. There can be a substantial time gap between approval of a Directive by the Council of Ministers and its being implemented into all member countries. Implementation is by no means uniform or consistent throughout the Twelve.

EC Regulation A Regulation is a law. Regulations are binding in their entirety and are immediately applicable to all Member States.

EC Decision Decisions can be issued by the Council of Ministers or the European Commission. They are only binding on those to whom they are addressed, unlike Directives, which are binding on all Member State parliaments. No national implementing legislation is required with a Decision. A Decision may be addressed to a Member State, to an employer or to an individual. A Decision taken which involves financial penalties or other similar obligations is enforceable in national courts.

EC Recommendation or Opinion Neither Recommendations nor Opinions have any legally binding effect upon national parliaments.

They are not laws. They merely state the view of the organization which issues them (in general the European Commission). Recommendations and Opinions can be issued by both the Council of Ministers and the European Commission.

UN Human Rights Treaties The issue of human rights was enshrined in the UN Universal Declaration of Human Rights (UDHR) which was adopted in 1948. It did not have the force of law, however, and in 1966 the General Assembly of the United Nations adopted the International Covenant on Civil and Political Rights (ICCPR) and the International Covenant on Economic, Social and Cultural Rights (ICESCR), both of which came into force in 1976. Not all UN members have ratified the Covenants; ratification establishes a legal obligation to honour their Articles. A signature is not legally binding. The Convention on the Elimination of All Forms of Discrimination against Women was adopted by the General Assembly in 1979. To date, only about a third of United Nations members have ratified it.

Part I

Equal Opportunities Issues

1

Equal Opportunities – The Background

Introduction

What is equal opportunities all about? The purpose of this book is to explain and highlight all of the topics that come under the rubric of 'equal opportunities'. Basically, equal opportunities is about treating everybody fairly and equally regardless of their background or lifestyle. The laws which govern equal opportunities try to ensure that people are treated equally on the basis of individual need. The context in which people experience unfairness and inequality is usually in relation to employment, housing, education and training – although it can and does also happen on a more general everyday level. This book will show how equal opportunities *can* work, by examining equal opportunities policies and good practices.

In order to ensure that everyone from all walks of life gains equal access to jobs, housing, education and training, various laws have been introduced in the UK with governing organizations to control their implementation. The legislation which tries to combat all forms of discrimination is examined in detail in chapter 2. Translating the legal theory into working practice became the role of commissions set up under Acts of Parliament. The two commissions established were the Equal Opportunities Commission (EOC) in 1975, which covers equal opportunities in general, though with emphasis on sex discrimination, and the Commission for Racial Equality (CRE) in 1976, which, as the name suggests, deals with racial discrimination. Other organizations have grown to cater for the needs of other minority groups. They include the National Association for the Care and Resettlement of Offenders (NACRO), which began operating as a registered charity in 1966, and the Disablement Advisory Service (DAS), set up in 1983, which deal respectively with ex-offenders and disabled persons. From 1992 the DAS is in the process of being integrated with the Employment Rehabilitation Service (ERS) to form a single organization called a Placing Assessment and Counselling Team (PACT). These are just a few. There are many more groups, both local and national, public and voluntary. Addresses for most of them can be found in appendix 3 of this guide.

Listed below are issues generally associated with equal opportunities:

- Sex discrimination
- Racial discrimination
- Disability
- Age discrimination
- Sexual orientation/Sexuality
- Ex-offenders.

The question of human rights is receiving more world-wide attention today than at any time before. This is not because more violations of rights may be occurring today than in the past, but because of several new developments on both a European and a global scale. First, the impact of television, radio and newspapers has increased our awareness of events not just locally but internationally. Furthermore, an increase in world transport has created an upswing in mobility which in turn has led to a greater increase in the involvement of nations in each others' political, economic and social affairs. Human rights have received a much higher profile through the work of several organizations, most notably, the United Nations (UN). United Nations treaties and principles (see appendix 1, table 7) are accepted as necessary by most countries – even though many governments world-wide do not adhere to them. With the exception of a nuclear war, nothing is likely to make these developments disappear. Human rights are at the very centre of the structure of the United Nations. All member states of the UN claim to uphold the purposes of the United Nations Charter, which calls for 'universal respect for', and observance of, 'Human rights and fundamental freedoms for all without distinction as to race, colour, sex, language or religion'. Unfortunately, the fact remains that the overwhelming majority of member countries fall short of fulfilling that obligation, and it remains in essence an ideal. This highlights the clear difference that exists in rights and equality on paper as against a genuine commitment to human rights and equal opportunities in practice. Traditions die hard, and even their ghosts tend to linger on for decades; well-established customs and entrenched beliefs defy quick solutions or overnight improvements.

Is it sufficient to accept that if equality is a constitutional right then it is also a fact? – Or at least that there is an adequate safeguard against the inevitable shortfalls in human nature? Why are laws and policies on equal opportunities required in order to protect human rights? For centuries, throughout the world minority groups have rapidly become disadvantaged groups at the hands of the majority population, and have suffered discrimination in employment, education, housing and training, as well as in every other conceivable type of social or economic right. Such discrimination is manifested today in unequal pay, poorer promotion prospects, inadequate vocational guidance, bad housing conditions and unemployment. Frequently, discrimination is not even 'allowed' to occur, since its equally insidious twin, 'prejudice', has already paved the way to ensure that a woman of childbearing age, for instance, is rejected even before the job interview – because the employer does not relish the potential prospect of contributing to her maternity pay. Needless to say, the real reasons for her rejection are heavily disguised by 'acceptable' alternative reasons.

If we assume that everyone is entitled to equal opportunities, then that is entirely compatible with the belief that inequalities exist. Only if by some supernatural miracle of abstraction was there no particular identity, in terms of race, sex, class, language, sexuality, ethnicity, disability, nationality, religion, etc, would there be no need for equal opportunities, since there would be no inequalities to redress. However, each of us belongs to groups in society which both distinguish and subject us to each other. Further, no single identity can be isolated from another. Take, for example, a registered disabled person who falls readily within the category of the disability equality issue. That person is also male or female, black or white, homosexual or heterosexual, etc. Clearly, although it is always easier to see how privilege or deprivation affect others than ourselves, the insights to be gained risk becoming lost if 'we' cannot imagine that 'we' are anything like those others.

The implication of the existence of difference among, for example, women makes it very difficult to talk with any degree of accuracy about 'women in general' or even 'people in general'. It is generally incorrect to insist on the separability of gender, sexuality, race, age, etc., essentially because the indubitable effects of each as a discriminator are so common. The discrimination encountered by a Asian woman with a disability in trying to enter the labour market – which is overwhelmingly prejudiced against disabled workers anyway – is compounded by her sex and race.

Finally, before moving on to examine each equality issue separately, let us consider the fact that in the UK, for example, the large majority of people actually fall into a minority group, or (more specifically) into a disadvantaged group: women (over 50 per cent of the population), gays and lesbians (10 per cent of the population), ethnic minority groups (5 per cent of the population) and many others such as people with disabilities, housewives, ex-offenders, older people, etc. Equal opportunities policies are therefore, in fact, to the benefit of the majority population, not, as is commonly espoused, to that of the minority.

The Single European Market will have an enormous social impact and effect on all of us. As the final stages in establishing the single market are entered into, attention needs to be focused on the imbalances in equality that exist between Member States. Social reforms and standards vary widely among the 12 member countries. Since its foundation over 30 years ago, the European Community has grown into one of the most prosperous economic areas in the world. In the course of those 30 years the Community has witnessed a 100 per cent rise in the overall standard of living. This has been reflected in several areas; most especially in employment, health service provision and social security schemes. However, the distribution of economic wealth is far from even. Social benefits are far greater in countries in the north of the Community, in Denmark, Belgium and Germany, than they are in, for instance, Portugal and Greece in the south of the Community.

Sex Discrimination

Equal opportunities is a subject which has increased in popularity over the last decade or so. Why this increase in the level of interest has come about could be given a number of explanations. Over the last 20 to 30 years there are more women working in paid employment outside the home than at any time before. Women now represent two-thirds of the world's total workforce; yet as a collective group they receive far less income than men.

Many events converged in the 1960s to spark the interest in equality for women. The development of the contraceptive pill and the Abortion Act 1967 gave women more control over their lives, and their freedom and choices increased. The 1970s saw the introduction of government legislation (see chapter 2) aimed at abolishing the discrimination that women had suffered.

During the 1960s the women's liberation movement gradually emerged; women in many countries as well as Britain and America formed groups to put pressure on their governments for an end to oppression. Women who had previously been isolated and restricted within their homes gained mutual support and understanding through these groups. The purpose of the women's liberation movement was for women to recognize their own position and status within their communities and to take action themselves to eliminate the discrimination.

Race Relations and Racial Discrimination

Around the same time as the birth of the women's movement, Britain became a nation of many races. During the 1950s and 1960s people from as far apart as Bangladesh and Trinidad immigrated to the UK. Most came from the Indian subcontinent, Bangladesh and Pakistan, and from the West Indies. Other groups came from China, parts of Africa, and southern and eastern Europe. Today, ethnic minorities in Britain account for approximately 5 per cent of the population. Many immigrants feel bitter that they accepted the invitation to come to Britain to work and on arrival suffered harshly from discrimination. Shortage of labour after the Second World War which had left many jobs in Britain unfilled is the main reason why people predominantly from the former colonies of India and the West Indies were invited to Britain. Many new immigrants were recruited by the public service industries, which were experiencing a shortage of labour. There is no doubt that they made and continue to make a vital contribution to these industries – to Britain's railway network, to London's underground and bus services, and to the National Health Service, to name but a few. Pressure was put on the government to ensure that ethnic minority groups were given the same treatment and opportunities as whites. Eventually, the first Race Relations Act (see chapter 2) was passed in 1965, making it unlawful to discriminate against someone because of her or his ethnic origin. However, declaring it unlawful did not abolish prejudice and discrimination.

Disability

Equal opportunities legislation and practice also attempt to work together in the fair treatment of people with disabilities. Efforts have been made over the past 20 years to increase the opportunities within employment and education for people with disabilities and special needs. It is often felt, however, that while people with special needs are reasonably well catered for from 5 to 16 in special schools or units outside of mainstream schooling, upon reaching adulthood very little is available to them in the labour market or through further training. The voluntary sector and many charities deserve applause for their practical approach to this issue; they (and often they alone) have provided work placements, specialized training, as well as such practical facilities as ramps for wheelchair access, tapes for the blind, and skills workshops. What is clearly lacking is a working partnership between the government, voluntary organizations and charities, in the public and private sectors, to improve the working lives of people handicapped in some way by a disability. It is not enough to rely on government legislation such as the Disabled Persons Act to provide all of the answers.

Age Discrimination

Discrimination against older people seems to be increasing at almost the same rate as the number of people reaching retirement age. In the next 25 years, the number of people in Britain over 65 is expected to increase by 20 per cent, and the number of people over 84 to increase by 47 per cent. As yet, however, there is little prospect of the massive rise in numbers being met by a similar increase in resources. Old age is often perceived by society, with help from the media in a succession of negative images with corresponding terminology. Few, if any, older people occupy prominent positions in key television programmes in order to redress the negative imagery associated with old age. It is perhaps interesting to note that although quite a high percentage of Members of Parliament are aged over 60, there is scarcely any legislation of a similar nature to the Sex Discrimination Act or Race Relations Act to protect against the damaging effects of ageism. Age discrimination is virtually endemic in British society, but has yet to attract the same degree of attention as other areas of discrimination from government legislators and the general public.

Offenders and Ex-Offenders

Offenders and ex-offenders are a group which some, but by no means all, organizations endorse within their equal opportunities policy. NACRO exists to enable young people who have committed an offence to gain qualifications, training and work experience in a 'sheltered' environment where they will not be treated unfairly because of their past offences. Many ex-offenders experience discrimination during the very first stages in job-hunting; that is, during the recruitment and selection stages for employment. If more organizations' equal opportunities policies were to include ex-offenders alongside other minority groups, more ex-offenders would be able to experience a wider range of opportunities in the world of work.

Sexuality: Equal Opportunities for Gays and Lesbians

The final area this guide is concerned with is perhaps the most controversial issue within equal opportunities, and is noticeable in its absence from many (otherwise excellent) equal opportunities policies. This topic is sometimes referred to as 'sexual orientation', and covers the fair treatment of homosexuals (gays and lesbians). The fact that many people are perhaps afraid of homosexuality, and address the issue by ignoring it, is evident in the lack of information and legislation available on the issue. Earlier, reference was made to the women's liberation movement (WLM) and its aims to encourage women to take action themselves to eliminate their oppression. This is highly relevant to the homosexual community; as they – perhaps more than other minority groups – have had to group together to give themselves a political and social voice. In contrast to other oppressed groups, there is no government-funded body actively attempting to eliminate prejudice against gays and lesbians. Legislation which addresses the issue is usually very negative, and reduces rather than increases gay and lesbian rights. Due to this lack of a national political response, the gay community is very fragmented; indeed since the 1960s and 1970s when the Gay Liberation Front (GLF) was active, very little in the way of government resources has been directed towards the issue.

It is estimated that one in every ten people is homosexual. This means that if we say the population of Britain is 55 million, about five million are gay or lesbian. If equal opportunities is about treating everyone equally, without doubt these five million people deserve far more recognition on a national level – especially within the arena of political legislation and government funding. A national organization similar to the EOC, CRE and PACTs would be ideal, and would enable people to gain advice, support and information, as well as act as a forum for handling cases of discrimination. Such an organization would be able to collate regional information and act as a signposting service. This type of centralized activity could serve to lessen the isolation that many people in minority groups experience.

The power of politics is very clear in the case of homosexuals. It is often only through a national voice, be it either the government or the media, that we are made aware of what is happening in the world. If the government or a political party debates or introduces an Act of Parliament or a new law (for example, the compulsory wearing of seat belts), over a very short period of time everyone is aware of their duty. In contrast, if an issue is never raised, people never become aware of it. One of the fundamental ways of changing attitudes is through information. All too often, negative attitudes are based on misinformation. Individual attitude change can be reinforced by organizational commitment to positive attitudes. The lack of political recognition of homosexuals does not mean that these five million people do not exist. Overt or direct discrimination in employment is common, despite the fact that discriminatory practices in the workplace limit both the individual's freedom to work and the organization's freedom to employ the best person for the job. If more equal opportunities policies were to incorporate sexual orientation into their statements and guidelines alongside the better established sex and racial discrimination, the better it would be for all of us. The effect of such a move would be twofold: it would enable the equal treatment of homosexuals and heterosexuals to become common practice, and it would reduce the ignorance manifesting itself in fear, prejudice and discrimination within society, which in time would bring about acceptance of this five-million-strong minority group.

Part II

Law and Practice in the UK

2

Equal Opportunities – The Law

Sex Equality Legislation

It is important to stress that the laws governing sex discrimination between men and women are not straightforward. (For a summary, see appendix 1, table 1). In fact, even the Amendment Regulations such as the Equal Pay (Amendment) Regulations 1983 are highly complex and subject to much criticism. During the House of Lords debate on them they were described by Lord Denning as 'beyond compare . . . no ordinary lawyer would be able to understand them'. This prediction has been largely fulfilled. The Regulations have given rise to major problems of legal interpretation and serious delay in the processing of complaints.

There are many examples of sex discrimination in employment. It is important to remember that each case is decided on its own merits. If an employee considers that she or he has been unfairly treated, expert advice and opinion should be sought. If necessary, the Equal Opportunities Commission can give advice on preparing a case for an industrial tribunal. In order to apply to an industrial tribunal, an 'ITI' form must be completed and sent to the Central Office of Industrial Tribunals (COIT). These forms may be obtained from the EOC, a job centre or any unemployment benefit office. Addresses of the EOC and COIT offices are given in appendix 3.

The Sex Discrimination Act

The Sex Discrimination Act (SDA) came into force on 29 December 1975. The SDA 1986 broadened the scope of the Act in many areas. To reflect the realities of discrimination, most people refer to the victim of discrimination as a woman, but the law equally protects a man. The SDA states that it is 'unlawful to treat anyone on the grounds of sex, less favourably than a person of the opposite sex is or would be treated in the same circumstances'.

Sex discrimination is not allowed in:

- Employment
- Education
- The provision of housing, goods and services
- Advertising.

Sex discrimination can be divided into two kinds of discrimination:

Direct discrimination involves treating a woman less favourably than a man because she is a woman; for example, offering her less pay or holidays than a man. This also covers only employing single (unmarried) people for some jobs.

Indirect discrimination means that conditions are applied to everyone (both men and women) but favour one sex more than the other and cannot be justified. Examples include stating that candidates must be six-foot tall in recruiting for clerical positions; or recruiting only people capable of lifting 50 pounds in weight where this is not justifiable for the demands of the job. In both these cases men are more likely to fulfil the criteria than women.

Sex discrimination in employment

It is against the law to discriminate on the grounds of sex in:

- Recruitment and selection
- Advertisement of jobs
- Access to promotion and training facilities.

In employment, it is also unlawful to discriminate against married persons. Since 7 November 1987 the scope of the Act has been extended to include employers who employ five persons or less. Amendments have been introduced in order to bring the Act in line with EC equality legislation, namely the Equal Treatment Directive and the Directive on Equal Pay. Employers must ensure that they do not discriminate against or in favour of men or women or against married people. Equal treatment is now also required by law in respect of any term or condition relating to retirement. This is necessary if the matter concerns the promotion, demotion, training or transfer of personnel on the basis of retirement.

Sex discrimination in education

Co-educational schools, polytechnics, colleges and universities must not discriminate in their provision of courses or in their admission to such courses or other services. It is unlawful, for example, to refuse a girl admission to a craft design and technology course or a motor mechanics course because she is a girl. Similarly, it is unlawful to refuse a boy admission to a nursery nursing/child care or domestic science class because he is a boy. This is extended to include the careers service, which must not discriminate in the advice and information it offers to girls and boys. For example, a girl requesting information on a non-traditional female subject or job such as motor mechanics must be offered the same guidance and information as a boy requesting similar information.

Single sex schools may, of course, restrict admission to one sex only, but this should not lead to the provision of a restricted or more traditional curriculum. For instance, a girl attending an all girls' school should have the same or very similar access to non-traditional subjects as she would have in a co-educational or mixed school.

Sex discrimination in housing, goods and services

With a very few exceptions, no one providing housing, goods or services to the general public can lawfully discriminate on the grounds of sex. For example, it is unlawful to advertise a property to rent as 'only suitable for a young professional lady'. Undoubtedly, many readers will nevertheless have seen advertisements which dictate the 'type' of lodger they are seeking. For instance, many local newspapers or newsagents' windows display accommodation notices or have adverts for 'a respectable retired gentleman' or a 'young professional lady'. The very fact that these are so commonplace serves as a reminder of how difficult it is to monitor or check all advertisements, and thus how difficult it is to ensure that the Act is working as it should. It refers, in fact, to everything to do with the buying or renting of accommodation. In addition, a hotel, guest house or restaurant may not refuse accommodation to an individual on the basis of her or his sex. Facilities and services such as banks, building societies or credit brokers must offer credit, for example a mortgage or loan, on the same terms to men and to women.

Sex discrimination in advertising

Unlawful sex discrimination in advertising addresses all the issues discussed earlier: employment, education, housing, goods and services. It is necessary, bar a very few exceptions, to word an advertisement such that it is open to both sexes equally. It is recommended in the case of illustrated advertisements (that is, where people are shown actually carrying out a job) that both sexes should be represented equally, both in number and prominence. As referred to earlier, the same rules apply in the advertising of premises to rent for accommodation, when it would be unlawful for a landlady, landlord or estate agent to advertise premises as suitable for a 'respectable gentleman' or a 'retired lady only'.

There are, however, some exceptions where discrimination is lawful; though it must be emphasized that these situations are rare and are considerably outnumbered by instances of discrimination which are unlawful. Sex discrimination is allowed when a person's sex is a Genuine Occupational Qualification (GOQ) for a job (see definition in appendix 2). It is sufficient to note at this stage that a GOQ allows discrimination on the grounds of sex only and not of marital status, and the GOQ exception does not apply where the employer has enough staff already who could perform the duties required without undue inconvenience.

Case procedure – sex discrimination in employment

If an employee feels that s/he has been treated unfairly because of her or his sex, the Sex Discrimination Act provides the right to take the complaint to a county court in England or Wales, or a sheriff court in Scotland. This applies if the unfair treatment occurred in the context of education, advertising (housing, or premises) or the provision of goods and services such as in banks, building societies and credit companies. If the grievance is to do with employment, it may be taken to an industrial tribunal. It is important to keep detailed notes of any interviews which take place about the complaint between employer and employee (or would-be employee, since the Act applies to advertising and interviewing for posts as well as all other employment processes), as reference may be made to such notes if a subsequent tribunal takes place. Employers should note that they may also be held liable by an industrial tribunal for discriminatory acts by their employees, if reasonable steps to ensure that discrimination is not occurring are not taken.

The steps to take in bringing a case are explained below.

1 It is crucial to remember that in order to enforce the law by taking a case to an industrial tribunal the case must be presented to the tribunal no later than three months after the act happened. In other words, if it is a complaint about an event which happened on 1 March the application must be in by 31 May.
2 In general, it is obviously better to handle the situation internally if possible. First of all, use the existing procedure for handling grievances. Written details of the procedure ought to be available on request.
3 Contact the relevant trade union representative or, alternatively, get in touch with a member of the equal opportunities monitoring committee if there is one in the organization. In addition, contact the Equal Opportunities Commission, who can give advice free of charge – and in certain cases financial assistance for legal representation before an industrial tribunal.
4 If a complaint cannot be settled internally by agreement then the complainant may bring the case before an industrial tribunal. To help decide whether to start a case a special questionnaire (entitled 'Sex Discrimination Act 1975 – The Questions Procedure') is available from the Equal Opportunities Commission or from any local job centre or employment office. The form is to be completed by the person whose conduct is the subject of the complaint. It provides the opportunity to find out the reasons for the treatment and can help clarify whether an employee was discriminated against. These requests may also be made by ordinary letter. The questionnaire may be used in either of two ways:

   - Before making the initial claim to an industrial tribunal, provided it is completed within the three-month time limit from the date on which the particular event occurred; or
   - Within three weeks after the day on which the claim was sent to the tribunal.

   It is important to note that there is no obligation on a respondent to reply. If a reply is provided, the answers may be admissible as evidence in a tribunal or court. If a reply is not provided, this too may be used as evidence against a respondent at any subsequent sitting of an industrial tribunal. If the answers given are vague or ambiguous the industrial tribunal in any subsequent hearing may draw a just conclusion, including an inference that discrimination did actually occur.
5 A copy of the complaint will automatically be sent from the appropriate COIT office (see address in appendix 3) to the Advisory, Conciliation and Arbitration Service (ACAS). ACAS will contact the

complainant to establish whether the case can be resolved without the need for a hearing at an industrial tribunal. A conciliation officer from ACAS may be called in by either party. It is important to remember that it is always best to think very carefully before agreeing to any settlement, since if an agreement is reached, subsequent rights to take any further legal proceeding become void.

6 If there is no settlement, the complainant may take the complaint to an industrial tribunal. No information supplied to a conciliation officer from ACAS may be divulged to a tribunal without the prior consent of the person involved. In order to start legal proceedings, obtain a form called an 'ITI' either from the Equal Opportunities Commission or any local job centre, unemployment benefit office or employment office.

7 The tribunal will also send a copy of the complaint to the other party concerned and in due course will send copies of the employer's response to both the complainant and the conciliation officer.

8 Burden of proof: At an industrial tribunal it is for the applicant (complainant) to provide *prima facie* evidence to prove that s/he has been discriminated against. If the respondent (person whom the complaint is about) claims that the treatment was not unlawful because of an exception from the Sex Discrimination Act, he or she has to prove that the exception applies. Next, it is up to the tribunal to decide whether or not unlawful sex discrimination actually occurred.

9 If the tribunal finds in the complainant's favour it can do any or all of the following:

- Make an order declaring the complainant's rights or the rights of both parties.
- Award compensation which could include expenses, loss of earnings, damages for injuries to feelings, or damages for potential loss of future earnings. There is an overall statutory limit to such an award up to a present maximum of £8,500.
- Recommend that the person or organization (or a combination of each) against whom the complaint is made, take within a specified time limit a particular course of action to stop the effect of any discrimination (for example, to consider the complainant for promotion within the next 12 months, or to guarantee a place on a training course). If the recommendation is not complied with, the tribunal may increase the amount of compensation awarded.

10 If the tribunal goes against the complainant, he or she may appeal to the Employment Appeal Tribunal if it is felt that the law has been wrongly interpreted. Appeals to the Employment Appeal Tribunal must be lodged within 42 days of the date on which the industrial tribunal decision was registered. The decisions of these tribunals are

legally binding on industrial tribunals. If a case reaches this stage, it is advisable to consult a solicitor.

11 Cost: Assistance from the Equal Opportunities Commission costs nothing. Tribunals sit in most areas of the country and in general no costs or fees are payable by applicants. In fact, even if the case is lost, a complainant will not normally be asked to pay any costs provided that he or she has acted reasonably and has gone about the procedure in good faith. However, it should be borne in mind that tribunals do have the power to award costs against applicants who bring unreasonable or vexatious cases to them.

Sexual harassment

Sexual harassment is not actually defined in the Sex Discrimination Act. However, since 1985 when the first successful claim of sexual harassment was won, behaviour has been challenged under section 1 of the Act. This section enables employees to claim they have received less favourable treatment on the grounds of sex. In the landmark case of Porcelli v Strathclyde Regional Council, the Scottish Court of Appeal ruled that a woman who complained of sexual harassment had suffered unlawful discrimination. She won her case against her employer under the Sex Discrimination Act. Since 1985 there have been a number of sexual harassment cases under the Sex Discrimination Act covering a range of different kinds of conduct, ranging from relatively minor to very serious.

At a tribunal the claimant has to prove that she or he was dismissed, forced to resign, or endured some other 'serious detriment' as a direct result of the alleged harassment. A detriment is a disadvantage of some kind. For example, the conduct causes the person to resign, or it affects her or his health. Under the Sex Discrimination Act, employers are not only responsible for their own conduct but are also liable for any discriminatory acts committed by their employees in the course of employment – whether or not committed with the employer's knowledge or approval. An employer will avoid such liability only if he or she can prove that he or she took such steps as were reasonably practicable to prevent the employee doing the act or acts complained of.

The Equal Pay Act 1970 and the Equal Pay (Amendment) Regulations 1983

The Equal Pay Act applies equally to men and women of all ages. It applies whether a person is working full-time or part-time, in a large firm or a small organization and even if she or he has been employed by a firm for only a short time. There is no minimum period of employment before the Equal Pay Act applies as there is under some other employment legislation. The Act does not give anyone a right to claim equal pay with another person of the same sex: individuals must always compare their work with a member of the opposite sex employed by the same employer (or an associated employer, for example, a head office or a subsidiary office, if common terms and conditions apply at both establishments or to the two jobs being compared). The main change introduced by the 1983 amendments is that women performing jobs in which traditionally few men have been employed (for example, secretaries, canteen staff, receptionists, cleaners, sewing machinists) are now within the scope of the Act. Previously many women discovered that the Equal Pay Act could not assist them, however low-paid their job in relation to male colleagues, because there was no man at their workplace on the same or broadly similar work and because no job-evaluation study (JES) had been carried out. One of the first realizations that equal pay legislation had no effect on women in many low-paid jobs was brought home to women's groups who got involved in attempting to unionize night cleaners, first in London and then in other major cities. The Equal Pay Act 1970 did not benefit the cleaners because broadly speaking it applied only to women doing the same or similar work as men working for the same organization.

The 1983 Equal Pay (Amendment) Regulations which amended the Equal Pay Act 1970 were implemented as a result of proceedings against the UK government by the European Commission. In 1981, it was alleged specifically that the UK had failed to enact any measures to enable an employee to claim equal pay for work of equal value free of sex discrimination. Therefore it was in breach of its obligations under Article 119 of the Treaty of Rome, and the Equal Pay (Amendment) Regulations 1983 were implemented to bring it in line with the Equal Pay Directive.

The aim of the Equal Pay Act is to eliminate discrimination between men and women in pay and other terms of their employment contracts such as bonus payments, piecework, sick leave and holidays. It seeks to achieve this aim in two main ways:

1 By giving a woman the right to equal pay in the terms of her contract when she is employed:

- On like work, that is, work of the same or of a broadly similar nature to that of a man.
- In a job which, though different from that of a man, has been given an equal (or equivalent) value under a job-evaluation study, unless her employer can show a material difference in pay. A material difference is one not based on sex, but simply to do with what an individual brings to the job; for example, a degree or specialist experience in a particular field. It is important to remember that what constitutes a material difference in one instance may be irrelevant in another; it all depends on the facts of each case. Job evaluation is a method of assessing the relative value of different jobs within a company under such headings as effort, responsibility, skill, decision-making and working conditions. Employers are not required by law to undertake a job-evaluation study, but in cases where a valid one already exists its findings can be used as the basis of a claim. In fact, even if a job-evaluation study reveals that the jobs are not equal, the claimant may still bring a claim if she can show grounds for suspecting discrimination in the study. For instance, a job evaluation could be shown to have discriminated indirectly against a woman if a high value has been attached to a job, such as HGV driver, carried out by a man, but a low value to light machining work carried out by a woman: this is on the face of it discriminatory and a claim could be pursued. A woman could bring her claim by highlighting that if not for the discriminatory way in which the job elements were 'weighted', her job would have been valued as equivalent. Whether a claim is being made on the basis that the work is the same or broadly similar or whether the claim is based on equal value, the burden of proof is on the employer to show that there are no material factors within the realm of the Act which justify the difference in treatment.
- (From 1 January 1984) On work of equal value; that is, in a job which is equal in value to that of a man in terms of the demands made on her under such headings as skill, effort and decision-making. There is no requirement that the job is the same or broadly similar; neither is a job-evaluation study required.

2 The second way the Equal Pay Act seeks to achieve its purpose is by providing for the Central Arbitration Committee to eliminate discrimination in collective agreements, employers' pay structures and statutory wages orders which contain any provisions that apply specifically to women only or to men only.

The Equal Opportunities Commission is not alone in wanting improvements to both the Equal Pay and Sex Discrimination Acts. The EOC has recommended several amendments to the Acts that are of considerable importance. Crucial among these is a recommendation to unravel the complications associated with the practices of the Acts. In 1988 the Commission presented formal proposals to the Secretary of State for Home Affairs for strengthening the legislation, which included a recommendation that the Sex Discrimination and the Equal Pay Acts should be replaced by a new law called the Equal Treatment Act. The new statute, if enacted, would cover the same ground as both existing Acts and take into account the requirements of European Community law, and act as a single comprehensive and accessible statute. At the heart of the new law would be the principle that women have an absolute right to equal treatment, as opposed to merely having the right not to be discriminated against.

In spite of the presence of an Equal Pay Act for over two decades, there is still a substantial gap between the salaries and wages of woman and men in the UK. Over a 14-year period from 1977 to 1991 the gap has narrowed by only 2.8 per cent. Meanwhile, women make up 68 per cent of the five million employees earning less than the Low Pay Unit threshold. The complexity of rules and procedures, the numerous tribunal and court hearings and months of delay that cases often entail, mean that applicants need a lot of stamina. The 1983 Equal Pay (Amendment) Act has not been widely used by women; only 20 equal value claims on average were decided each year between 1984 and 1989.

In 1990 the Equal Opportunities Commission published a document containing formal proposals for improving the effectiveness of the Acts, and eliminating much of the confusion over their legal interpretation. Entitled 'Equal Pay for Men and Women, Strengthening the Acts', it contained over 25 proposals for change. The report focused on the urgent need to set up a legal framework and straightforward procedures to facilitate rather than impede an individual's access to judicial determination. Also, it included recommendations for tackling sources of inequality in pay structures and collective agreements. To date, few of the recommendations have been acted upon.

The Employment Act 1989

This Act, which received Royal Assent on 16 November 1989, extends to England, Scotland and Wales, but not to Northern Ireland. The 1989 Employment Act provides an illustration of the way in which UK employment law can be heavily affected by EC legislation. In order to comply with the requirements of the EC Equal Treatment Directive and Article 119 of the Treaty of Rome, the Act repeals much of the UK's legislation restricting the employment of women, and amends the UK's statutory redundancy scheme. The points below highlight the major changes brought in by this latest law:

1 The Act narrows the exemption which makes an act of sex discrimination lawful. In order to bring UK law into line with the Equal Treatment Directive, the Act restricts the scope of the blanket exemption up to then provided by the Sex Discrimination Act 1975 for acts of discrimination done under statutory authority. Under the SDA it is lawful to discriminate on the basis of sex in the areas of employment, education and training if it is necessary to do so to comply with a requirement of existing legislation (that is, an Act passed by Parliament before the SDA). Since the Employment Act was introduced the emphasis has been shifted, so that with effect from January 1990 any provision of existing laws has been void to the extent that it imposes a requirement to do an act which would constitute direct or indirect sex discrimination in vocational training or employment.
2 With regard to justifying indirect discrimination, the Act requires that in any legal proceedings where the legality of a statutory requirement is at issue, the onus of proving the requirement is justifiable will fall on the person applying the requirement (in practice, the employer or a respondent/discriminator, in an industrial tribunal hearing).
3 Section 2 of the Act gives the Secretary of State the power to amend, repeal or revoke by order any existing legislation on discrimination in the fields of employment or vocational training, but before doing so he must consult with the Equal Opportunities Commission.
4 The Act removes the majority of the restrictions on the employment of women and young persons, except in cases where restrictions are necessary on health and safety grounds.
5 The Act provides for industrial tribunals to be amended, to enable a tribunal to give preliminary consideration to a case by conducting a 'pre-hearing review'. The Act also provides for regulations which enable a tribunal to order the inspection of documents on its own initiative rather than merely, as in the past, on the request of a party to the proceedings.
6 The Act amends the statutory redundancy scheme, so that all employees will be entitled to a redundancy payment up to their normal retirement age or to the age of 65. This gives women the right to receive statutory redundancy payments up to the age of 65 and thus puts them on an equal footing with men.

7 The Act makes it lawful to discriminate in favour of lone parents in respect of training.
8 The Act repeals some Genuine Occupational Qualifications repealed. Under one of the GOQ exceptions of the SDA, it was lawful to discriminate on the grounds of sex in recruitment, promotion or training for a job, if the job needed to be held by a man due to restrictions imposed by the laws regulating the employment of women. Because of the amendments to the SDA brought in by the Employment Act, this exception is now redundant and so has been repealed. As such this section is of major importance with regard to equal opportunities for women in employment. The new section restricts permitted discrimination in employment and vocational training to situations where it is necessary to comply with statutory requirements enacted prior to the SDA 1975, where the purpose of the protection is for women in relation to pregnancy or maternity or other particular risks women run because of their childbearing capacity. The relevant provisions include the prohibition from employment of a woman in a factory within four weeks of her expected date of confinement, and the restrictions on the employment of women in manufacturing processes which involve the use of lead and the use of ionising radiations. It is therefore lawful to discriminate in order to comply in these situations with the Factories Act 1961 and the Ionising Radiations Regulations 1985 respectively.

Parental Rights

Paid maternity leave is guaranteed under the Social Security Act 1986. The principal eligibility requirement is that the claimant must have been continuously employed for at least two years before the expected week of confinement, and must work at least 16 hours a week. In cases where the applicant works between 8 and 15 hours a week, five years' continuous employment is required for eligibility. The law allows a pregnant employee the right to reasonable time off to receive antenatal care; no length of service qualification is required.

Pregnant women receive 18 weeks maternity leave pay: six weeks in total at 90 per cent followed by 12 weeks at a lower rate of state maternity pay. A further 22 weeks off is allowed, but the woman receives a lump-sum maternity allowance only for the first 18 weeks of this period, while the remaining period is unpaid.

There are no statutory provisions for paternity leave. The majority of UK employers expect their employees to use holiday entitlements. Parental leave in the UK is regulated only through negotiation or custom or practice. There are no statutory rights to leave for family reasons. Companies adopt a wide variety of approaches to special leave. National agreements rarely contain clauses on special leave other than for bereavement.

Childcare

Compulsory primary schooling begins at age five, but many four-year-olds attend primary school on a voluntary basis. Services for children (excluding schools) are the responsibility of local authority welfare departments and the Department of Health. A new Children's Act was introduced in 1989. The Act covers many aspects of the law affecting children, including childcare services. It requires local authorities to review the whole range of childcare services in their area every three years. However, although it *permits* local authorities to provide services for any child, it only *requires* them to provide services for children 'in need', excluding any statutory role in provision of services for children with employed parents. A growing number of employers are examining the potential for family/employer partnerships in developing childcare services. For example, Midland Bank have embarked on a programme of 300 nurseries for children of staff.

Race Relations Legislation

The Race Relations Act 1976

In Britain there are no laws (such as apartheid or slavery laws) which expressly discriminate against people on the basis of their race, colour or ethnic origin. In theory, members of all races can enjoy the benefits of public transport, education and training opportunities, employment and housing. The Race Relations Act is necessary, however, to protect those who are liable to be treated less favourably in all of these situations because of their race or colour. Under Section 71 of the Race Relations Act local authorities have a duty to carry out their functions with due regard to the need to eliminate racial discrimination and to promote good race relations in their areas.

The Race Relations Act 1976 makes racial discrimination in the fields of employment, education, training, the provision of goods and services and the allocation of premises unlawful. In the context of employment, it is unlawful to discriminate against job applicants in each of the following areas:

- In recruitment; for example, in the advertising of job vacancies or in the supply of job details to the careers service, to a recruitment agency or an employment agency, by making discriminatory arrangements for recruitment, such as asking to be sent only white clerical assistants.
- In terms and conditions of employment; for instance, sickness pay, holiday entitlement, wages, access to occupational pension schemes, etc.
- In the day-to-day treatment of employees, and in the provision of access to training courses, promotion, career development programmes, welfare at work schemes, etc.

The Act defines two kinds of racial discrimination – direct and indirect.

Direct racial discrimination consists of treating a person on racial grounds less favourably than others are or would be treated in the same or similar circumstances. (Racial grounds means any of the following grounds: colour, race, nationality (including citizenship) or ethnic or national origins.)

Indirect racial discrimination consists of applying (in any circumstances covered by the Act) a requirement or condition which, although applied equally to persons of all racial groups, is such that:

1 A considerably smaller proportion of a particular racial group can comply with it than the proportion of people not of that group who can comply.
2 It is to the detriment of the person because he or she cannot comply with it; and
3 It cannot be shown by the discriminator to be justifiable irrespective of the race, colour, nationality or ethnic or national origins of the person to whom it is applied.

Possible examples are:

- A ruling about clothing or uniforms which disproportionately disadvantages a particular racial group (which for religious or cultural reasons may be unable to comply) and cannot be justified.

- An employer who requires higher language standards than are needed for safe and effective performance of a job, for example, stating in a job description that perfect spoken and written English are required for the post, when a person could do the job perfectly adequately without such prerequisites.

The Act also provides for protection against victimization: individuals are thus protected from any kind of victimization which ensues as a result of asserting their rights under the Act (the definition of victimization is set out in appendix 2). This provision was introduced in order to counteract the notion that an individual who asserted his or her rights under the Act would fall prey to further discrimination or retaliation from his or her employer. The omission of protection from victimization had been seen to be one of the main drawbacks of the 1968 Race Relations Act.

Racial discrimination which is allowed by law

Positive action The Race Relations Act 1976 introduced the concept of positive action. It should be noted that the Act does not allow for 'reverse discrimination'; that is, it would be unlawful to discriminate in favour of a particular racial group in the processes of recruitment or promotion on the sole basis that members of that group have in the past been disadvantaged. However, the Act does allow for specific forms of positive action in appropriate circumstances. Positive action may also operate in favour of the majority ethnic population, but is more usual for it to be employed for minority ethnic groups. The provisions are outlined in Section 38 of the Act.

The procedures which must be borne in mind if an employer wishes to consider or implement positive-action measures are as follows:

- If at any time during the previous 12 months there were no persons of a given racial group doing particular work, it is lawful under the Act to encourage and help members of that particular group to enter and thus undertake such work. Such action taken may include specific training courses to assist participants to gain a wider experience and knowledge of a specific form of work. Although employers may discriminate positively by providing special training courses for particular racial groups, or by encouraging them to apply for certain jobs, they cannot discriminate positively in the recruitment process; that is, recruitment itself must be based on ability to do the job, not on racial criteria.
- In assessing whether a particular racial group is proportionately

underrepresented in a given area of work, or at a given level, comparisons may be made in either of the following two ways:

- With the total proportion of employees of that racial group within the whole organization. A survey might reveal, for example, that the proportion of employees from a particular racial group at a given level in the workforce is smaller than the proportion of persons of that racial group employed as a whole. For instance, if 60 per cent of workers in a factory are Asian but only 10 per cent of the supervisors are Asian, then the proportion of Asians who are supervisors is smaller than the proportion of Asians employed in total.
- With the total proportion of that racial group within the 'catchment area' from which the organization could expect to draw its workforce. This would apply, for instance, if a factory in a predominantly black area had hardly any black employees.

Genuine Occupational Qualification (GOQ) Employers may lawfully discriminate in recruitment or in giving workers the chance for promotion or training only if it can be shown that membership of a particular racial group is a requirement for a job. Within the scope of the Race Relations Act there are only four circumstances in which an employer can claim that being of a particular racial group constitutes a 'genuine occupational qualification'.

1. In the realms of dramatic work or the entertainment world in general, if the job is to play a given role in a play or film which requires the person to be of a particular racial group for reasons of authenticity. Thus, it would be lawful for a theatre company to audition only black actors when looking for someone to play Martin Luther King or black actresses to play the role of Maya Angelou or Winnie Mandela, or for a company to look for a white actress to play Margaret Thatcher.
2. The post involves working as an artist's or photographer's model which requires the person to be of a particular racial group, again for reasons of authenticity.
3. The post involves working in a cafe or restaurant, the setting of which requires a person of a particular racial group to work in it, for similar reasons of authenticity. For example, in the case of a Chinese or Greek restaurant, Chinese or Greek assistants may be required in order to provide an authentic ambience.
4. In the provision of personal services to a particular racial group, whereby the job can be most effectively undertaken by a person of the same racial group. For example, it is lawful for an Asian women's drop-in centre or hostel for battered wives to employ Asian workers on the grounds that the Asian women would find it easier to relate to and communicate with persons of the same racial group.

Racial equality law amendments (under the Employment Act 1989)

The Employment Act 1989 (section II) has introduced an exemption for Sikhs from the requirement to wear a safety helmet when on a building site. Orthodox Sikhs are under a religious obligation to wear a turban, yet may also be required under relevant health and safety law to wear a safety helmet. In recognition of this dilemma the Employment Act provides that as from November 1989, any legal requirement to wear a safety helmet does not apply to a Sikh on a building site when he is wearing a turban. Thus, the operation of the Race Relations Act is also affected, so that if an employer requires a Sikh to wear a safety helmet on a site and has no reasonable grounds to believe that the Sikh would not wear a turban at all times when on a site, that the requirement will by inference be presumed to be unjustifiable and therefore constitute an act of indirect racial discrimination.

Also, under the 1989 Employment Act, section 37 of the Race Relations Act has been broadened. Previously, this section had permitted positive action to be undertaken by specified training bodies in providing encouragement or access to training to racial groups which were underrepresented in particular work. From 16 January 1990, it is lawful for 'any person' to discriminate in this way. Furthermore, organizations who wish to provide training under the Race Relations Act no longer have to get designation from central government. The Commission for Racial Equality hopes that these changes will lead to more employers making use of the training provisions of the Act.

How the Race Relations Act is enforced

The Race Relations Act is enforced in two ways:

- By individuals. The 1976 Act gives the aggrieved party direct access to civil courts or tribunals in order to seek redress.
- By the CRE, which has various powers to enforce the law in the public interest.

If an individual feels that s/he has a justifiable case the following points should be considered.

Advice If the alleged discrimination is in the field of employment an individual can take the complaint to an industrial tribunal. Advice about handling the complaint can be sought from the Commission for Racial Equality, a citizen's advice bureau or a law centre. In addition, for individuals who belong to a trade union, a union official or shop steward may be able to assist in the preparation of the case and represent a complainant at any subsequent hearing. Further, solicitors can provide free, or subsidized, advice under a scheme known as the 'green form' scheme. However, the scheme does not cover the solicitor to represent at a tribunal; s/he cannot therefore provide free representation, but can nevertheless provide advice on the merits of a case and help in filling out appropriate forms.

Time As with proceedings under the Sex Discrimination Acts, the three-month period also applies here. Thus, if the act of discrimination being complained about occurs on 5 January, the application must be received by the appropriate COIT office on the 4th of April at the very latest.

The questions procedure In much the same way as the grievance procedure under the Sex Discrimination Act works, a standard form called the 'Questionnaire of Person Aggrieved' can be obtained free of charge from the CRE, any local job centre or employment office or from any Community Relations Council. Standard forms are available on which:

- The aggrieved person may ask questions to the person s/he considers responsible for the unfavourable treatment; such questions should relate to the reasons why the particular treatment has occurred.
- The respondent (the discriminator) can reply with an account of the events and reasons for the behaviour.

The sorts of questions that may be appropriate include:

- Asking whether the discriminator agrees with your version of the facts and, if not, in what respect does s/he disagree?
- Asking whether it is felt that the treatment did constitute unlawful discrimination.
- If a job applicant feels that a job application was rejected or interview was unsuccessful because of racial criteria, the applicant is entitled to ask questions pertaining to the other applicants and their racial origins.

The questions that are asked and the replies that are given may be used as evidence in any subsequent hearing. If the respondent does not reply to the questions or gives answers which are vague or ambiguous then the tribunal may conclude from that whatever inference it wishes. In some cases, it may well infer that the person concerned has indeed committed an act of unlawful discrimination. It is important to use the questionnaire procedure, not least as it helps a complainant focus on the complaint and clarify any outstanding uncertainties. Further, once respondents have given particular reasons in writing about their alleged discriminatory behaviour, they are stuck with those reasons. If at any subsequent hearing they change their version of the events or give different reasons for their behaviour, this may lead to the conclusion that they are being untruthful and have indeed discriminated unlawfully.

Settlements Agreeing to a settlement means in practice accepting a sum of money offered by the discriminator and hence ending the proceedings before the case goes to an industrial tribunal. A settlement is an agreement which usually involves a joint statement signed by the two parties. Prior to deciding whether or not to accept a settlement, legal advice should be sought as to the strength of the case and the amount of damages that any tribunal is likely to award. Any financial figure that a discriminator advances is, it should be remembered, open to further negotiation from the complainant, who should consider all aspects of the case including:

- Loss of earnings
- Loss of potential earnings
- Expenses
- Injury to feelings.

If an individual is involved in discussions relating to a settlement s/he should attempt to negotiate for as high a sum as possible. If it is felt that there is a very strong case and the discrimination is easy to prove the respondent may well be willing to offer more money than the tribunal eventually would. In some cases, discriminators are more concerned about negative publicity than they are about the money that they have to give.

Burden of proof Unfortunately, a complainant has the burden of proving discrimination. In a case involving direct discrimination the complainant has to provide adequate evidence to show that s/he has been treated less favourably than another person. It is then up to the respondent to challenge this evidence. In order to prove cases of indirect discrimination it is necessary to prove three things:

1 That the discriminator has imposed a particular condition or requirement (in practice, in the workplace, this means a 'must' – that is, something which has to be complied with).
2 That the complainant cannot comply with it. For example, a factory has a rule that all shop floor workers must wear a particular helmet. One employee, an orthodox Sikh, wears long hair under a turban; he, therefore, cannot comply with this rule, and as a result he is dismissed or suspended from his job. Unless the factory can provide evidence that this rule is justifiable, the employee has indeed suffered indirect discrimination.
3 The proportion of a racial group who can comply with it is substantially smaller than the proportion of people from other racial group who can comply with it. Statistical evidence or self-evidence should provide an accurate picture here.

Industrial tribunals Once a complainant has proved these three elements, it is up to the respondent to show that the condition or requirement (the 'must') was justifiable. If s/he cannot do so, the complainant will succeed in the claim. As it is up to the complainant to prove discrimination, either s/he or a representative will open the case and bring the evidence in first. 'Opening a case' simply means providing an outline of the situation. Following this, any supporting witnesses with evidence may be called. Next, it will be the turn of the other party to call witnesses to give evidence and the complainant will be entitled to cross-examine them. If the tribunal decides that discrimination has occurred, it may do one of two things:

1 Recommend that the discriminator take a certain course of action to reduce or remove the negative effect which the discrimination has had on the complainant. For instance, if a tribunal discovers that promotion to a particular job was not offered because of race discrimination, they may specifically recommend that such promotion is offered as soon as a vacancy arises. If the respondent (in practice, that is, the employer) does not abide by the recommendation the tribunal may well increase the compensation.
2 An industrial tribunal may award compensation up to £8,500. However, most cases where discrimination was proved only result in nominal awards for injury to feelings. Such amounts are usually within the region of £200–£300. Needless to say, such amounts are derisory, and operate neither as a deterrent nor as an appropriate compensation for the discrimination that a complainant has endured.

Work permits

If an individual wishes to come and work in the UK, s/he will have to apply for a work permit before departure. The employer concerned needs to apply to the Department of Employment for permission to employ a foreign worker. Work permits are valid for four years and only apply to the job an individual originally applied to do. Since work-permit holders are not in theory 'freely available for work' there is no access to income support or other benefits if for any reason the job is lost. A wife (but not a husband), and any children under 18, of a permit holder may be allowed to enter the UK to join her husband, so long as they can be fully supported without recourse to public money. After four years, a permit holder can qualify to settle in the UK. Once a holder has been allowed to settle there are no further immigration restrictions on what he or she may do. Some jobs do not require a work permit, including missionaries, foreign journalists and ministers of religion. In addition, people with capital of £150,000 or more may enter the UK regardless of whether they have a specific job to start.

Although the European Community has torn down the barriers that stop, for example, an Italian working in Ireland or a Greek working in Spain, multinational companies still find it difficult to move their staff in and out of EC countries. Over the next few years governments around the world will be urged by the International Bar Association to improve their procedures for issuing work permits to the staff of large companies. In fact, in the UK, new rules were introduced in 1991 by the Department of Employment to make the work permit scheme more responsive to employers' needs.

The history of race relations law in the UK

Political strategies on race relations have been pursued by both Conservative and Labour governments in the UK since 1965. The Parliament of the UK agreed to legislation directly about race relations on three separate occasions. The Race Relations Acts (as they were called) were introduced over a ten-year period, in 1965, 1968 and 1976 (see appendix 1, table 2). The very fact that it took a decade to implement appropriate legislation highlights the inadequacies of the first attempts. All three Acts have been received with a large amount of controversy and wide-ranging opposition from several angles. Opposition is polarized between, on the one hand, those who see the Acts as an attempt to give more favourable

Table 2.1 Legislation on immigration and race relations since 1965

Year	*Law*
1965	Race Relations Act
1966	Local Government Act
1968	Commonwealth Immigrants Act
1968	Race Relations Act
1969	Immigration Appeals Act
1971	Immigration Act
1976	Race Relations Act
1981	British Nationality Act
1988	Immigration Act

treatment to blacks and Asians above whites in the contexts of housing, employment and education, etc.; and those who consider the Acts to be inadequate, largely symbolic and a token gesture on behalf of governments to encourage ethnic minorities to assimilate into wider society, an assimilation expected to occur without much positive intervention by the central government. The current levels of racial discrimination and persistent inequality make the latter view more credible.

As immigration from the West Indies and the Indian subcontinent grew in the late 1950s, white consciousness of and competition with immigrants increased. Widespread opposition to free entry for new Commonwealth immigrants grew rapidly. The period from 1965 to 1968 was a time when the government tried with some success to redirect and 'settle' white opinion, by introducing two Race Relations Acts to promote good race relations. The government itself soon realized that the provisions of the 1965 Race Relations Act were insufficient and of very limited effect. Many people had stated all along that an Act which penalized discrimination only in public places like hotels, restaurants or bars was grossly inadequate and needed to be thoroughly expanded. It is worth noting that the first two Acts were preceded by extensive research in North America by the British government. Evidently, there was a genuine attempt to learn from others; though it might have been more useful to visit some of the ex-colonies to examine racism in practice and learn from direct experience.

Table 2.1 shows the chronology of legislation on immigration and race relations since 1965. As can be seen, the first attempts to deal with potential racial conflict can be traced back a quarter of a century to the mid-sixties. These Acts sought to do two things: first, to provide, if necessary by legal constraint, for non-discrimination in such areas as housing, employment, insurance, education and training, etc. Second, to set up welfare agencies to institute enquiries into racially based practices as well as to handle complaints. In 1965 a Race Relations Board came into existence and was given 'teeth' through the institution of special county courts. At the time of the 1968 Act a Community Relations Commission was created to promote positive steps in the building of a multi-racial society. An additional part of their remit ensured that they had a major role to play in educating the population as a whole about race relations issues. Conciliation Committees and Community Relations Officers were locally established in cities and major towns throughout the UK, particularly in areas where it was thought there was most need. A growing tendency towards the belief that laws cannot change attitudes and that education alone could tackle prejudice began to be seen during that period. Laws may indeed remove the 'right' to discriminate but ultimately education alone can remove the tendency to pre-judge. It has already been pointed out that the initial Acts were partly based on American systems. Interestingly, the UK Acts eventually came under the same criticisms as their American equivalents, in so far as their operation and impact was hampered right from the start by inadequate financial support. A lack of sufficient funding suggests that in reality race relations issues were quite far down the political agenda at the time.

By the early 1970s critics of the earlier Acts were calling for updated and more effective strategies with greater all-round impact. It was increasingly evident that race discrimination had to be dealt with much more effectively if its occurrence was going to subside, particularly at all levels within education and employment. Research that had previously taken place highlighted that persistently high levels of prejudice and discrimination existed, despite the efforts of successive governments since 1965. Arguments put on the political timetable focused on the need to widen the scope of the previous Acts. The most important of these debates included the need to refine the definition of discrimination used in the 1965 and 1968 Acts. It was stated that discrimination had to be regarded as referring to (and differentiating between) institutionalized, unintended, direct or indirect discrimination. A single definition covering every conceivable type of discrimination based on racial criteria was seen to be grossly inadequate and needing to be refined far more.

The ineffectiveness of the governing groups also came under criticism, and central government's lack of formal support was highlighted as the main cause of the problem. It was believed that the government had to strengthen all the powers of the Race Relations Board in order to make it more answerable to the groups it had been designed to serve. All these measures therefore necessitated a more interventionist and less marginal stance from central government and the policymakers, as well as the cooperation of local authorities.

The most significant innovations of the 1976 Act were an extension of the aims of the law to include not only intentional or direct discrimination but also racial discrimination brought about by indirect forms of behaviour. Another development was the reorganization of the Race Relations Board and the Community Relations Commission into a joint organization which was called the Commission for Racial Equality. In addition, a new procedure for dealing with complaints of discrimination was implemented under the 1976 Act. From that time they were to be handled directly by industrial tribunals; which in theory meant that, with the added support and weight of a tribunal procedure, they were to be taken more seriously.

The introduction of the concept of indirect discrimination was partly based on the American experience of affirmative-action measures against institutionalized forms of race discrimination. The second innovation, the establishment of the Commission for Racial Equality, came about as a result of the problems associated with organizational management of anti-discrimination legislation in the previous decade. The new 'combined' agency was seen as progressing towards a more coherent and structured implementation of the law as well as supporting equal opportunities and good race relations.

The Commission for Racial Equality has contributed enormously to defending employment rights as well as initiating moves to protect the basic rights of minorities in employment. It has encouraged employers to work with the trade unions towards achieving equal opportunities in both industrial and service sectors. In 1984, the CRE published a Code of Practice which highlighted what further measures needed to be pursued in order to combat discrimination in the labour market. It conducted research which pointed out the need to develop formalized equal opportunities policies beyond standard promises and lip-service. The Code emphasized the crucial nature of the monitoring process as a way of assessing the distribution of employees and of evaluation as a means of redressing any imbalance in the position of minorities. It also pointed out the need for positive-action programmes as a method of increasing the number of minorities in areas of employment where they were underrepresented. In summary, the Commission's Code actively encouraged all organizations to adopt a practical policy, pointing out that formal measures represent an important safeguard for minorities in protecting basic rights in situations involving race relations issues.

The progress of the new and improved legislation on race relations introduced in 1976 has been by no means perfect. In 1981, five years after its introduction, the Scarman Report on urban unrest showed clearly that the policies had actually had limited impact on the causes of racial disadvantage and discrimination. Admittedly, although the Act was quite radical in promise, transferring its aims into practice has been difficult. The 1976 Act has been criticized from three main angles: first, that the stated policies have not produced the anticipated results; second, that the administration set up to implement the Act has largely, through no fault of its own, not functioned effectively enough and third, and perhaps most significant of all, that the intended policies fall well short of meeting the expectations of ethnic minority communities. Moreover, in practice, discriminatory practices are almost as much the norm today as they were a decade and a half ago when the Act was implemented. The CRE has not received the financial and political support from government it requires in challenging entrenched racist attitudes at collective and institutional levels.

During the 1980s a number of groups including the CRE campaigned for a major reorganization of the management of race relations policies and for a more progressive stance and support from central government. Several proposals have been drafted, including a wider definition of the law to allow for more effective positive action to undo the effects of past and current discrimination. Unfortunately, positive action has often been as unpopularly received as contract compliance (see definition in appendix 2). In order to implement positive action at street-level, strengthening the penalties against employers found to be contravening the Act is necessary. Race relations in the UK could benefit from emulating the German approach to the Quota system on employment of people with disabilities, whereby a fine is charged to those organizations which fail to comply. The UK, too, has a quota system for the employment of people with disabilities but it is not strictly enforced. Potentially, collected funds could be directed towards anti-discrimination training and awareness-raising which would serve to educate against, challenge and combat institutional racism.

Politicians on all sides have recognized the importance of establishing race policy and advisory bodies to deal with race issues. The 1987 general election witnessed the reappearance of Britain's first ethnic minority MPs for almost 60 years. The black 'section' within the Labour Party represents fundamental (albeit limited) progress. Organized and autonomous black power via an independent black political party – as against 'sectioning' within mainstream political parties – remains the subject of both interesting and controversial debate. The National Black Caucus (NBC) is an organization which has been set up to unite black voters, and use the black vote for political power in major cities. Suffice to say that although many attempts have been made, mainstream politics have generally failed overall to respond positively enough to the needs of minority groups.

The first survey of racial attitudes in almost ten years was conducted in 1991 by National Opinion Polls (NOP), in conjunction with the Runnymede Trust for the *Independent on Sunday* newspaper. The Runnymede Trust is a non-party-political race-relations research organization. Before that, the last survey about attitudes was conducted in 1982 by the Policy Studies Institute (PSI). The 1991 poll highlighted a number of key topics, many of which showed that there had been a slight improvement in public racial attitudes nationally. The topics for the survey included voting intentions at the next general election; perceptions of ethnic minority candidates at a general election; and attitudes to various racial stereotypes, and to immigration, multiculturalism and race relations. The poll involved face-to-face questioning, and targeted a balanced and representative sample of black, Asian and white people over the age of 18. One of the most significant findings of the survey was the opinion of different racial groups on just how racist British society actually is; with a substantially higher number of blacks than whites considering Britain to be a racist society, while fewer Asians than whites thought it to be so. All ethnic groups were inclined to overestimate the numbers of black and Asian people living in Britain. The latest official estimate figure is 2.6 million; most people thought the number to be at least double the official figure. The most striking tendency highlighted by the poll was that most people consider themselves as individuals to be fair-minded; with racism being seen by many as the fault of institutions, most notably the police and the criminal justice system, as well as major employers.

Stronger action initiated and supported by central government is required to force compliance on employers who are prejudiced in their recruitment and selection methods against minority members. Ultimately, employers who are not doing enough to monitor and recruit ethnic minorities should be penalized, both financially by industrial tribunals and by the withdrawal of contracts and incentives. However, the government is likely to object to a proposal to take action against prejudiced employers. Positive action and enforced quotas have never been popular with any political party.

For many black and Asian people the problems of living in a racist society are compounded by other types of discrimination, in addition to racial discrimination. As has already been shown, the status of any minority group in society depends heavily on the social context in which people live. This is made apparent by the wide variety of patterns in different ethnic, geographic and social subcultures. In short, anyone who falls within two or more minority groups (which are both by tradition and by definition socially disadvantaged groups) is likely to suffer from a wider range of prejudices and increased discrimination.

The situation, for example, of older people from ethnic minority communities can be characterized by acts of discrimination based on racism and compounded by ageism, or vice versa. Not only do such individuals become the easy victims in a society which readily dismisses older people, but they are equally likely to fall prey to negative racial attitudes in the wider society. The situation is often exacerbated by inaccurate and ill-thought-out Western assumptions about the care older people automatically receive from within their own cultures and communities. In turn, this can lead to unnecessary and otherwise avoidable suffering of a financial and emotional nature.

Young black people in either care or detention face the dual likelihood of enduring discrimination both because they are black and because, in the case of the latter, they have committed an offence. Institutional racism is endemic in many of the major governing organizations in the UK, which renders an already disadvantaged individual even more vulnerable.

The British gay scene is predominantly white; in many areas the social and cultural needs of black and most notably Asian gays and lesbians have been overlooked. As in most other walks of life, racist assumptions and stereotypes have been carried over into the gay sub-culture. In short, evidence shows that the ultimate choice is between being gay or being black; with very little cultural mix in between to enable a gay Asian male, for instance, to develop both of his cultural identities. Minority ethnic gay groups have to cope with effects of both racism and homophobia. Western gay culture is overwhelmingly based on American and British white gay lives and experiences, and cultural representation has been difficult to establish for gays and lesbians from ethnic minority communities. This has led in part to a separatist tendency, and to the existence of minorities within minorities. In part, the growth of such groups is a response to the feeble attempts on the part of the white majority representation towards integration and assimilation. In the 1990s, in a climate where the gay movement is attempting to reclaim its own identity and history, it is essential that it endorse all ethnic cultures.

For black women the situation can be equally daunting. Frequent harassment of a sexist and racist nature is quite widespread. Many black and Asian women have had to work doubly hard and excel in their achievements in order to receive an equivalent status to their white peers. Black women are scarcely represented at all in politics or the legal profession, due to the combined effects of racism and sexism. Interestingly, a labour force survey carried out between 1987 and 1989 showed that a higher percentage of black women qualified beyond 'A' level than white women and than black or white men.

In summary, it seems that the presence of a Race Relations Act and any amount of anti-race-discrimination policies can only have a limited effect when they are as unenforceable as our current legislation. What is needed is a tightening of the laws and the kind of strong political will that has put environmental issues on the agenda. Britain could lead the way, as the only European Community country with established race laws, and help to change the face of Europe.

Disability Legislation

There are several laws which make reference to disability and the treatment of people with disabilities (for a summary see appendix 1, table 3), though they are not exclusively about the employment of people with disabilities. Laws such as the Factories Acts and the Health and Safety at Work Act, and measures it has introduced, affect disabled as well as non-disabled workers equally. (Similarly, the Employment Protection Act is relevant to all employees, but it has insufficient direct implications on equal opportunities to warrant special discussion in this chapter.)

A number of EC measures also relate both generally and specifically to disability issues. In 1991 the European Commission announced a proposal for a Council Directive on Mobility. The Directive lays down minimum requirements to improve the mobility and the safe transport to work for people with reduced mobility. Ultimately, making it easier for disabled people to travel is an essential prerequisite for any programme which seeks to improve the employment and training prospects for workers with disabilities. The proposed Directive is part of the Commission's implementation of the European Charter of Fundamental Social Rights (referred to as the 'Social Charter'). A Council Directive has the effect, once adopted, of requiring Member States to enact legislation. The HELIOS programme adopted by the Council of Ministers in 1988 represents a practical response to the needs and ambitions of the 30 million Community nationals whose lives are affected by some form of long-term disability. This programme established for the first time in the EC a framework for the development of policy to promote the full integration and independent way of life of all people with disabilities. In addition, there is a general Recommendation which states that suitable measures to 'provide fair opportunities for disabled people in the fields of employment and vocational training' should be taken by each Member State. However, a Recommendation is not a law, so it does not have any binding or enforceable effect. The purpose of the Recommendation is to urge Member States to take appropriate action to improve the situation. The British government is not alone in having so far failed to act upon it.

One of the major criticisms made by disabled people about disability legislation is that it fails to meet their needs because it is formed in the main by non-disabled people. Clearly, non-disabled policymakers are less informed about the real needs of disabled people and can only speculate about the experience of disability. Such speculation has led to the development of theories which are largely academic in nature. There has also been a tendency to consider disability as a charity issue rather than an important legislative issue. This has had the effect of marginalizing disability, which in turn has caused a complacency in attitude and lack of public and political attention. Moreover, associating disability with charity has neglected the central issue of disability rights as *rights* which should not be dependent on charity. The major laws which relate to disability are outlined below.

Disabled Persons (Employment) Acts 1944 and 1958

The post-war years in Britain were a period of almost full employment which coincided with a public interest in social reform. The fact that many people had been injured in war inspired a national recognition of the inadequacies within the system for providing for the war injured of both the First and Second World Wars.

In 1943, the Tomlinson Committee prepared a report that was to become the basis of post-war policy on disability issues. The stated aim of the Committee was to secure a full share in employment for people with disabilities. A year later the recommendations of the Tomlinson Report were implemented and enacted as the Disabled Persons Act 1944, which still remains in force.

The aim of the Disabled Persons Act is to assist people who are handicapped by a disability to gain employment which is suitable and will make the best use of their skills. It has consistently been shown that the vast majority of people with disabilities can take their place alongside others in ordinary working life. Depending on the nature of an employee's disability it is important that appropriate support and, if necessary, rehabilitation support is provided. Assistance and advice on all aspects of disability can be obtained from Disablement Resettlement Officers, at local job centres or from Placing Assessment and Counselling Teams (PACTs).

The 1944 Act made provision for 87 Committees for the Employment of Disabled People (CEDPs) to be set up. Their objective was to act as advisory committees to the Secretary of State for Employment (in practice the Employment Service) on local and regional matters relating to the employment of people with disabilities. The committees perform several tasks. In addition to gathering up-to-date information on services available in the local community, they also encourage and assist employers to implement positive policies, practices and improved facilities for people with disabilities.

The Act introduced three unique opportunities for people with disabilities in order to ensure that they get their fair share of opportunities in employment. They are:

1 The Register of Disabled Persons (registration is voluntary).
2 The Quota scheme: a duty placed on employers to employ a quota (a percentage of the workforce) of registered disabled people.
3 Reserved vacancies in certain jobs for people who are registered disabled.

Even with such an Act in place for decades now, the problems associated with unemployment and education for people with disabilities still loom large. A particular problem has been about the issues of integration or segregation. In addition, problems over definitions and their impact on certain disabilities have created widespread confusion over what actually constitutes disability. The type of disability and in particular the level of severity are at risk of subjective assessment. Policies have tended to be very erratic in effect, and the special needs of women with disabilities have been largely overlooked by the policymakers. Since wars are traditionally fought by men, the post-war origins of much disability legislation have been steeped in sexist assumptions.

The Chronically Sick and Disabled Persons Act 1970

The Chronically Sick and Disabled Persons Act was introduced in 1970 and offered a framework of opportunity for people with disabilities. For the first time, local authorities had the legal foundation on which to build. The Act promised to open up the community more for people with disabilities in a number of practical ways. Issues about accessibility, mobility and transport were debated, and guidelines issued relating to their impact on public buildings and transportation. The main criticism of the Act is that leaving the obligations at local authority level has resulted in wide variations in both the standard and availability of provision. Put simply, the services that disabled people receive depend far more on geographical criteria than on the adherence to a single principle of equity.

Companies (Employment of Disabled Persons) Regulations 1980 and the Companies Act 1985

These regulations (incorporated into the Companies Act introduced in 1985) require that companies employing over 250 people must contain in their Annual Directors' Report a policy statement about the measures they have taken to recruit, train and promote workers with disabilities. The report must contain a clear statement about the policies which have applied during the previous financial year. The Act makes it an offence not to comply with these requirements. Although public sector employers are exempt from the statutory requirements, they are nevertheless advised by the Department of Trade and Industry to apply the rules. The specific implications for employers with regard to personnel are:

- To give full and fair consideration to people with disabilities applying for jobs.
- To continue the employment of workers who become disabled during the course of working for the company. Whenever possible, suitable training courses should be arranged for newly disabled employees.
- To arrange for some form of ongoing training and career development of employees with disabilities so as to assist their career development and promotion prospects.

All organizations which are affected by this legislation may get help with, for example, drawing up a policy, offering appropriate training courses, or obtaining general information on the employment of people with disabilities, from the local Placing Assessment and Counselling Team, which can be contacted through local job centres. It should be noted that unlike the Quota scheme, which applies only to those who are registered as disabled, the Companies Act applies to all workers with disabilities, registered or not.

The Disabled Persons Act 1981

This Act deals in the main with the issues of accessibility to premises and adaptation of buildings to cater for workers with mobility problems. Under this Act, providers of premises are obliged to make suitable provision for access to buildings; for example, installing wheelchair ramps, widening doorways, demolishing kerbs or any other obstructive artefact. The provisions which employers adopt must conform to the standards set by the Code of Practice for Access for the Disabled in Buildings (BSI). The Act also applies to public highways and imposes a duty on highway authorities and planning departments to have full regard (in the design and implementation of roads) to the needs of disabled and blind persons. This also applies to other companies carrying out construction work on public highways. Finally, the Act also requires the Secretary of State to report to Parliament with proposals for improvements in access to public buildings and all buildings which are commonly used by the public.

What became law in 1992

Two important laws were enacted by Parliament before it broke up for the 1992 general election.

The Further and Higher Education Act removes further education colleges and sixth-form colleges from local education authority control and sets up funding councils. The councils must find a suitable course for students up to the age of 25 with learning difficulties. They also have to provide independent living and communication skills courses which lead to a vocational or academic course.

The Education (Schools) Act 1992 has introduced a league table to compare schools' examination performance and increases the power of Her Majesty's Inspectorate (HMI). All inspections will include someone with expertise in special needs.

Employers' Agenda on Disability – Ten Points for Action

In 1992, the Employers' Forum on Disability launched an Employers' Agenda on Disability: Ten Points for Action, to promote the recognition, recruitment and career development of people with disabilities. The agenda is backed by 21 leading UK employers including Anglia Television, B&Q, Barclays Bank, Boots, British Rail, National Westminster Bank and the Post Office, all of whom are members of the Forum. It also has the support of the Prime Minister, John Major. The 21 companies who have agreed to support the initiative will build the points for action into their equal opportunities policies. It is the first step to creating a blueprint for best practice, which the companies intend to promote throughout the business community.

The key elements of the agenda are:

- Making a positive effort to attract people with disabilities and, once employed, to develop their careers to the benefit of the companies and the individuals themselves.
- Changing attitudes within the workplace through training and awareness programmes.
- Monitoring progress in implementing the agenda through an annual audit of performance, reviewed at board level. Achievements and

objectives will be communicated to employers and published in UK annual reports.

The members of the Employers' Forum on Disability are working to create increased opportunities for disabled people within their own companies. Historically, equal opportunities have been influenced by the legislation focused on women and ethnic minorities, while people with disabilities have very often been overlooked. There are some six million adults in Great Britain, of whom 2.6 million are of working age. Only 36 per cent of disabled men and 31 per cent of disabled women are in employment. These figures represent an enormous waste of talent and resource. Very often, employers do not necessarily discriminate from ill will and prejudice as much as from simply not knowing what needs to be done.

The ten points for action are:

1 Equal opportunities policy and procedures statement
The employment of people with disabilities will form an integral part of all equal opportunities policies and practices.
2 Staff training and disability awareness
The company will take specific measures to raise awareness of disability throughout the organization.
3 The working environment
The company will take all reasonable steps to ensure the working environment does not prevent disabled people from taking up positions for which they are suitably qualified.
4 Recruitment
The company will review and develop recruitment procedures which encourage applications from people with disabilities.
5 Career development
The company will take specific steps to ensure that disabled people have the same opportunity as other staff to develop their full potential within the organization.
6 Retention, retraining and redeployment
Any employee who becomes disabled will be given the fullest support to return to a role appropriate to his or her experience and ability within the organization.
7 Training and work experience
The company will ensure that disabled people are involved in work experience and education/industry links as well as all manners of vocational training which are appropriate.
8 People with disabilities in the wider community
The company will respond to disabled people as customers, suppliers, shareholders, and members of the wider community in general.

9 Involvement of disabled people
When implementing the ten points for action, the company will encourage the full participation of disabled employees to ensure that employment practices reflect and meet their needs.

10 Monitoring performance
The company will monitor its progress in implementing the ten key points. There will be an annual audit of performance which will be reviewed at board level.

For further information on joining the Employers' Agenda for Disability contact the Employers' Forum on Disability (see address in appendix 3). The Forum is a non-profit-making organization funded by its 50 member companies, and works in association with the Prince of Wales' Advisory Group on Disability.

Code of Good Practice on the Employment of Disabled People

This Code was first introduced in 1984 and was revised in 1988. It was issued by the Department of Employment, and copies are available from the Department or from the Disablement Advisory Service (or the Placing Assessment and Counselling Teams, PACTs). The Code is a response to such issues as how and why people with disabilities should be treated fairly in all employment-related matters, and answers the concerns employers may have about what to do to ensure that this happens in their company. It is divided into two parts. Part I of the Code is addressed to directors and senior managers, and concentrates on the importance for all companies to have a positive approach coupled with a specific policy towards employing, retaining and promoting workers with disabilities. Part II of the Code is designed to be used as a reference or guide for all employers and employees alike. It covers the following areas:

- The legislation relating to disability and implications for employers.
- The characteristics of workers with disabilities and what this means for employers.
- A critical analysis of some of the concerns employers may have about recruiting people with disabilities.
- How to adopt good-practice measures in the recruitment and selection processes in respect of applicants with disabilities.
- A look at some good practices in relation to people with disabilities, such as training programmes, promotion and career development.
- A look at the various options that may be considered for employees who become disabled during the course of working for a company.

- Considerations about the design of good policy and coordinating policy.
- A look at further help which is available to employers in drawing up a policy and ensuring its successful implementation.
- Sources of financial and other practical types of help (for example, on adaptations to premises, special aids for visually handicapped people, rehabilitation courses, etc.).

Thus, part I of the Code is concerned with day-to-day employment-matters of any organization, and how to bring together all activities in order to develop good practices in the field of disability. The Code also contains a substantive address-list of all the relevant organizations which are concerned with specific disabilities, as well as addresses of the offices of Opportunities for People with Disabilities. Opportunities for People with Disabilities is an employers' organization funded by caring employers. All senior staff are on secondment from industry or commerce. There are 11 offices in England (addresses are available in appendix 3 of this guide).

Disability – the symbol

The Employment Service has introduced the symbol as a simple-to-use, effective way for employers to show publicly that they are committed to the creation of good policies and practices in the employment and training of workers with disabilities. The symbol applies to all organizations, whatever their size or sector. Furthermore, it is related to all forms of disability. Where employers use the symbol it means that they endorse and are willing to practice the policies set out in the Code of Good Practice on the Employment of Disabled People. This will convey a positive message to workers and would-be workers about an organization's recruitment practices; they can expect that employers who use the symbol will be likely to give them a fair consideration for posts, training and career development.

The symbol may be used in a variety of ways including:

- On the top or bottom of letterheads.
- On application forms.
- In recruitment literature.
- In job advertisements.
- In reception areas or other publicly accessible places.
- In personnel departments.
- At conferences, exhibitions and employer conventions.

Manager checklist for use of the symbol and the employment of workers with disabilities

The preliminary steps to take:

- Adopt and implement an effective policy (use the guidelines which are available in the Code of Practice, available free from your local DAS, PACT or job centre).
- Involve employees with disabilities in developing and maintaining a good-policy and good-practice procedure. Involve them in every stage of decision-making processes.
- Provide equal opportunities for training and promotion for workers with disabilities. Whenever possible, seek to meet the specific needs of workers (ask, don't guess, what the needs are), utilizing external advice and help as appropriate.
- Be flexible: think about modifying a job or arranging for retraining; consider all employees on the basis of ability to do a job, not on the basis of disability.

During recruitment processes:

- Ensure that you know the facts about a particular disability. Brief yourself about a disability by reference to the Code of Practice, or contact one of the specific organizations (for example, RNIB, RNID, the Spastics Society, etc.).
- Plan the interview with special regard to access, sanitary arrangements, seating and mobility.

During an interview:

- Focus on the applicant's abilities, not on the disability.
- Try not to make assumptions, or fall prey to subjective impressions or feelings based on prejudices, about a person's capacity to do the job.
- Discuss openly the effects of the disability from the applicant's perspective. Ask how s/he sees her or himself integrating into the workforce, and about any special difficulties foreseen and ideas about how to overcome them.

During an induction process:

- Prepare and involve all colleagues. As much workforce participation as possible in the implementation of the Code of Practice and in the use of the symbol is crucial to sustain commitment.
- Make any important adjustments to the workplace (before the new recruit's start date if possible). Involve him or her from the outset in all

decisions which are going to have a direct bearing on his or her working life.

For career development (leading to increased job satisfaction):

- Get to know the special wishes of the employee concerned, in respect of job fulfilment and development, and any particular plans or aspirations s/he may have.
- Encourage and support a worker with a disability no less than you would support a non-disabled worker. Similarly, treat his or her ambitions on an equal footing as all other workers' ambitions.
- Monitor and assess progress at negotiated intervals; and
- If any problems arise during the review, try to iron them out as soon as possible to avoid such problems getting worse.
- Ensure equal access to training courses and promotion prospects at all levels throughout the entire organization.
- Become familiar with any special training offered through the local TEC and through any EC action programme for people with disabilities such as HELIOS.
- Liaise with the Disablement Advisory Service in order to keep up to date on schemes, information and any special grants which may be available.

Disability: what else is needed

A number of measures are needed to fully integrate people with disabilities into the labour market and society at large. The existing framework of the Quota system needs to incorporate in-built penalties and sanctions for non-compliance. An increase in Sheltered Placement Schemes (see definition in appendix 2) is essential to cater for the wide-ranging needs of people with a whole range of disabilities. Within mainstream employment more grants and financial incentives are necessary to encourage employers to recruit more widely from the Register of Disabled Persons.

Anti-discrimination legislation such as exists in the US is needed to instigate formal procedures. Anti-discrimination legislation would establish a far more purposeful and universal framework against which to measure services and provision. Few would disagree with the 1975 United Nations Declaration of Rights of Disabled Persons that they should have the right to become 'as self-reliant as possible' and to 'participate in all social, creative or recreational activities'.

Age Discrimination

There are no statutory rules against ageist practices – no equivalent of the Sex Discrimination Act or the Rehabilitation of Offenders Act (see appendix 1). As has already been discussed, legislation alone will not end any form of discrimination; but it does bring the issue into the limelight, and go some way towards re-evaluating current practices. A number of existing laws apply to older people at work as much as to younger people: the Health and Safety at Work Act, the Factories Acts, the Employment Protection Act, the Equal Pay Act, the Race Relations Act, etc. But partly because of the lack of specific legal measures, older people are the target of a great deal of discrimination. Poverty is very common in this group. State pensions have remained set at subsistence levels. Interestingly, the maximum social security payments for older people residing in care are lower than for younger people with physical handicaps. This reflects the negative assumptions that older people are immobile and have fewer needs.

Pensions and retirement

The British government has decided that the statutory retirement age should be the same for men and women. Since November 1987 employers can no longer set different compulsory retirement ages for men and women in comparable positions. At present women receive the state pension at 60 and men at 65. But government Ministers still have to decide how the changes should be made in this. The change in statutory retirement age follows a European Court ruling in 1990, discussed below, that a man working in the British insurance industry had been unfairly discriminated against by having to wait until 65 before receiving his occupational pension. Clearly, this move affects the lives of millions of older people whose income mainstay is linked to the success of occupational pension funds.

The Barber Decision The retirement age is not the same in all countries. For example, in the UK women may qualify for the state retirement pension at age 60 and men at 65. (Incidentally, this does not breach the Equality Directives as state pension age is specifically excluded from the scope of the Directives. Women do not have to retire at 60, but they may do so and get a retirement pension.)

The European Commission is planning the harmonization of pension ages between men and women in Member States where pension ages differ, such as the UK, Belgium, Greece, Italy and Portugal. In the meantime, the European Court of Justice has established that although different states can set different pension ages, men and women should normally be able to work until the same age. In the case of private occupational pensions men and women must be given equal benefits at the same age.

While Community law permits Member States to have different ages for men and women to receive a state pension, the European Court of Justice has established that public sector employers, such as health authorities and schools, cannot oblige women to retire at a different age to men.

Also, even though state pensions may be payable at different ages, pensions under private company schemes must be paid to men and women at the same age. The same is true for all redundancy payments. This principle applies equally to men, so that they are guaranteed the same treatment on redundancy as women of the same age.

In one British case (Barber, case 262/88), the ECJ ruled that a man aged 55, who was not eligible for a pension on redundancy under a company's rules concerning a private pension scheme before normal retirement age, was entitled to a pension, because a woman of the same age would have been eligible under the same scheme. The judgement in 1990 in the case of Barber and the Guardian Royal Exchange had direct implications for the occupational pension system. The European Court decided that occupational pension schemes are pay for the purposes of Article 119 of the Treaty of Rome, which requires that men and women should receive equal pay for equal work. Prior to this decision it was commonly accepted that sex discrimination in occupational pension schemes, particularly in different ages for men and women, was permissible until the European Commission made further proposals on equal treatment in this area. The Barber judgement exploded this view and has catapulted UK private pension schemes into an environment of equality, with complicated and often startling consequences. Some of these consequences provide the government with a difficult choice. The costs of reducing the pensionable age for men from 65 to 60 would be extremely high. The political implications of increasing the official retirement age for women are equally daunting. A number of methods could be adopted; a new retirement age of 63 for both sexes is one option which some ministers believe is the most workable. The Labour Party is already committed to a 'flexible decade of retirement' under which both men and women would be free to choose retirement at any age from 60 on a full pension, or go on working up to 70 if they prefer. Conservative Ministers believe that in practice this would be all but equivalent to equalized retirement at 60 and that would be prohibitively expensive. Further, there is some irritation among policymakers in the UK that the 1990 ruling appeared to take little account of the fact that Britain would be worst affected because it has the largest and most sophisticated occupational pension system, although Germany and the Netherlands are also likely to be seriously affected. The UK government recognizes that it will ultimately be impossible to sustain indefinitely a non-equalized state pension system if the occupational system has already been changed by law.[1]

Just how the pension systems will change, and what specific effects the Barber judgement will have, are difficult to assess precisely. This is because there are still many questions of detail which have to be resolved by the ECJ.

Employment (Age Limits) Bill

A Bill was introduced in 1989 called the Employment (Age Limits) Bill; but was too late for the House of Commons at that session. If accepted the Bill would have brought Britain into line with North America in that it would have made age discrimination unlawful. There has not been any further progress on this bill since 1989.

Protection under existing laws

The 1989 Employment Act provides a further illustration of the way in which UK employment law can be affected by EC legislation. In order to comply with the Equal Treatment Directive and Article 119 of the Treaty of Rome, the 1989 Employment Act has amended the

[1] On 4 August 1992 the Social Security Advisory Committee published its response to the consultation document issued in December 1991 by the Department of Social Security, *Options for Equality in State Pension Age*. The response proposes that pension ages should be gradually equalized at 65 over a period of 15 years starting in 2,000 and that the estimated £3 billion savings should be used to improve pension provision for vulnerable groups – many of whom are women – who may, at the moment, endure inadequate pension provision.

UK's statutory redundancy scheme. Until 1989, men were entitled to a statutory redundancy payment until they reached the age of 65, whereas women ceased to be entitled to a redundancy payment at 60. The Employment Act has put an end to this uncertainty for future redundancy payments by equalizing the age limits for men and women.

All employees now cease to be entitled to a payment once they reach the normal retiring age for employees holding the position which they held at their workplace. However, if the normal retiring age is higher than 65 or has, unlawfully, been set at a different level for men and women, then the age limit will be 65.

Mandatory retirement is not illegal under British law. There are wide variations in pensionable ages throughout all sort of occupations and industries. In general, they bear little relation to individual preferences. The consequences of an inflexible retirement-age system fall especially hard on women as they currently have a lower pension age, and have probably worked for fewer years due to family responsibilities. The House of Commons Social Services Committee acknowledged this in 1982, and recommended that the age limit for employment protection for women should be 65. This was incorporated and has been achieved via the Employment Protection Act 1989.

Age issues in equal opportunities policies and practices

An increasing number of supermarkets and do-it-yourself shops have recognized the potential of older workers and actively recruited people aged over 55. Tesco, for example, have positively welcomed applications from older workers. Sainsbury's are also very progressive in that field. However, still too many companies resist the move and merely pay lip-service to the demographic changes which are already taking place. Many people are no doubt familiar with the phrase 'Demographic Time Bomb' which is being used increasingly often. Yet in far too many quarters little attention is paid to its implications. The doors of recruitment campaigns, the Careers Service and most employment agencies are rarely even ajar for older workers. Not even the most highly skilled bomb-disposal expert will be able to prevent the explosion that is underway. A combination of anti-age-discrimination legislation, positive-action strategies and age-awareness-raising campaigns is necessary to encourage both older people and employers to recognize and develop their potential.

It is doubtful that the introduction of the Single European Market in 1992 will improve the status of older people, since virtually no European country has a training policy dedicated to older workers. In 1967 the United States Government introduced the Age Discrimination in Employment Act (ADEA). The purpose of the Act was to protect older workers from discriminatory practices. Some of the practices it sought to control included age-based discrimination in recruitment and dismissal. Subsequent amendments to the Act have now abolished mandatory retirement ages for most occupational groups. Introducing a similar Act in Britain would, at the very least, focus public attention on the issue.

Legislative safeguards are needed in several areas to protect the rights of older people, not least of which is in employment. For example, fundamental changes are required in the manner in which jobs are advertised and in the recruitment process. Indirect or covert discrimination often occurs by placing unwritten and unnecessary age restrictions on vacancies. Compulsory retirement ages should be abolished and replaced by optional schemes. Finally, in order to raise the profile of older workers, representatives should be appointed to oversee organizational practices and promote positive action.

Other measures

The Pre-Retirement Association of Great Britain and Northern Ireland (PRA) is a non-profit-making organization that has been successfully staging pre-retirement courses throughout the country since the mid 1960s. The courses cover several related issues from the angle of financial and emotional well-being. There are also some individual employers who conduct similar courses for employees approaching retirement. Unfortunately, however, with very few exceptions it is a case of too little too late. In fact, it is estimated that almost 10,000 people retire each week in the UK alone, yet it is believed that little more than 5 per cent of the figure receive any pre-retirement preparation planning. Therefore the true picture for the remaining nine and a half thousand is particularly bleak.

Sexuality

As has already been pointed out in chapter 1, legislation on this issue is very sparse. Specific laws which have been introduced in respect of homosexuality have reduced rather than increased gay and lesbian rights (see appendix 1, table 5). Homosexuals have almost no legal rights with regards to employment, other than within particular organizations which include sex orientation in their Equal Opportunities Policies while at the same time introducing practical measures to recruit and promote homosexuals, and offering them equal access to training within the workplace. In a few European countries such as Denmark and the Netherlands far more respect is shown towards the human rights of homosexuals. But such, unfortunately, is not the case in Britain. There are numerous problems faced by gays and lesbians, due by and large to their unrecognized political and social status. Some of these problems have already been discussed elsewhere. The main problems focus on the lack of protection and rights; against violence, harassment and incitement to hatred in all shapes and forms. Differences in age-of-consent laws, family rights, custody rights, etc. compound the problems further. Same-sex partnerships are largely unrecognized in the majority of EC Member States, which exacerbates all the other problems.

In the UK there is no law against discrimination on the grounds of sexuality. Also, the law does not recognize same-sex partnerships. The laws relating to age of consent for sexual activity in the UK are discriminatory. The age of consent for heterosexual or lesbian activity is aged 16, and for male homosexual activity, 21.

All homosexual acts between men or women serving in the armed forces constitute an offence which is punishable by imprisonment. As a result of the exemption of the armed forces from the Sexual Offences Act 1967, which partially legalized homosexual acts between male adults, the armed forces have remained frozen in their attitude towards lesbians and gays. Apart from dismissing any homosexuals discovered, the armed forces retain the right, under the Army Act 1955, the Air Force Act 1955 and the Naval Discipline Act 1957, to court-martial and imprison them for up to two years and discharge them 'With Disgrace' for homosexual activity that would not be illegal under civil criminal law. Between January 1987 and November 1991, 329 people – 140 men and 189 women – had their careers brought to an abrupt end by this policy. Ironically, the Ministry of Defence claims to be an equal opportunities employer. A government policy of discrimination against lesbians and gay men in this area sets an appalling example to other employers.

On the educational front homosexuality is largely unmentioned in mainstream education, except (and I say this cynically) as a primary cause of AIDS. Little is taught on the subject of homosexual lifestyles as equal alternatives to the traditional family structure. In contrast, however, certain areas within the media rarely leave homosexuality unmentioned – the tabloid press is virulently anti-gay. Does this reflect the views of their readers, or a morality they are imposing on them? They are certainly succeeding in the latter: their readers are bombarded daily with anti-gay reporting and propaganda.

Discrimination against homosexuals in the field of employment highlights the need for an Act of Parliament (similar to the Sex Discrimination Act and the Race Relations Act) which would give individuals a right of direct access to the civil courts, and to industrial tribunals for legal remedies for unlawful discrimination.

Housing, goods and services which are all catered for under the auspices of the Acts governing sex discrimination and race discrimination have again been overlooked with regard to homosexuals. A gay couple therefore need to ensure that their home is protected in case, for instance, of the death of one member, as the usual legal arrangements for a deceased person's estate do not protect homosexual couples.

Combating any form of discrimination requires a firm resolve by government. The situation regarding homosexuality needs immediate government recognition within the context of the 1990s, in order to ensure that this minority group have equal opportunities to the same degree as other minority groups do.

Sexual Offences Act 1967

Perhaps the most concrete legislation that has been passed with regard to homosexuality is the Sexual Offences Act 1967. This Act covers areas as wide ranging as prostitution, soliciting, kerb crawling, bigamy, and sexual abuse of minors in addition to homosexuality. The Sexual Offences Act was passed as a result of the recommendations of the Committee on Homosexual Offences (often better known as the Wolfenden Report). It states that it is not an offence for a man to have sexual intercourse with another man provided that:

1 Both parties consent.
2 Both men have attained the age of 21.
3 The act was done in private.

Lesbianism, that is, sexual activity between two females, is not a criminal offence. Despite this being the case, it does not follow that a lesbian couple enjoy the same rights as a heterosexual couple. It is more a reflection of the fact that within the legal and political framework lesbians have been kept almost invisible.

Section 28 of the Local Government Act 1988

More recently, in 1988, UK MPs gave further voice to the prejudice against homosexuals by passing a special law – Section 28 of the Local Government Act, designed to prevent local authorities from taking positive action to counter hostility towards homosexuality. Development of equality work for gay people has undoubtedly been affected by Section 28. The main effects have been an undermining of civil liberties, and the reinforcement of discriminatory attitudes. However, it is significant that no court case opposing equality work on grounds of the legislation has taken place so far. But it is nevertheless a very dangerous piece of legislation, mainly because of the difficulties involved in its interpretation. As long as these difficulties of interpretation remain, there is the very real likelihood that, without cases ever coming to court, section 28 will be both misunderstood and misinterpreted, and used to justify decisions which result in discrimination.

Since the section came into force in 1988, there have been several examples of this:

- In January 1988 the director of the City of Leeds College of Music banned the students' Gay and Lesbian Society from meeting on college premises.
- In August 1988 Essex County Council issued a notice to all principals of further education colleges instructing them not to allow lesbian or gay groups to meet in colleges or in any other council-owned building.

'Section 28: A practical guide to the law and its implications' is a handbook published by Liberty. The authors point out that section 28 is a badly-drafted piece of legislation. The aim of the Liberty handbook is to provide a thorough legal interpretation of the section, and practical guidance to the understanding of it in terms of:

- What it does and does not prohibit.
- Who is affected, both directly and indirectly.

Before the 1992 general election, the Labour Party agreed to repeal section 28, and move towards an anti-discrimination bill for lesbians and gay men.

Sexuality: equal opportunities and trade unions

At the 1985 Trades Union Congress (TUC) conference a motion was passed which requires all affiliated unions to adhere to equal opportunities for lesbians and gay men. This motion was reinforced by resolutions at the 1988 TUC conference which condemned section 28 of the Local Government Act. The extent to which individual trade unions abide by and implement these overall policies varies greatly. Among the ones that have, many have complemented existing policy by developing their own specific policies of non-discrimination against lesbians and gay men. Lesbians and gay men can also use the Sex Discrimination Act and the Race Relations Act to protect themselves. Under these Acts you cannot bring a case to tribunal because of, for example, anti-lesbianism, as this is not against the law, but you could argue that as a woman you were less favourably treated than a man would have been. But even if the law as it stands is generously interpreted, it does not attempt to challenge the institutional racism, sexism or misogyny (see definitions in appendix 2) that occur.

Homosexual Equality Bill

Consultative process on a Homosexual Equality Bill was begun in 1990. The Bill was sponsored by the Campaign for Homosexual Equality, the National Council for Civil Liberties and the Stonewall Group. The Bill seeks to prevent gays and lesbians being continuously treated as second-class citizens. It seeks to change and improve a number of current practices, and includes abolition of the offences of gross indecency and anal intercourse; creation of a legal recognition of gay and lesbian partnerships and introduction of measures prohibiting discrimination on the grounds of sexuality. The latter would incorporate non-discrimination in the workplace as well as in the general provision of all goods and services. There has been no further progress on this bill since and it has not been enacted in law.

Sexuality: status without the law

Even if the law is not hostile towards minority groups, it does not necessarily follow that society will follow suit and wholeheartedly approve, or even that there will be an increase in tolerance and acceptance. In some countries, particularly in Eastern Europe, political and social attitudes towards homosexuality are markedly different than in Britain. In Poland, for example, the situation of gay people has been constrained more by social than legal prohibitions, though it remains to be seen what effect the religious revival which is sweeping across Poland will have. Legally, Poland has a very relaxed attitude to sexual matters; under communist rule the law was not hostile or anti-gay as such. Nobody was ever charged with criminal offences for having homosexual affairs. Neither did the law differentiate between when a man could go to bed with a woman, or when he could go to bed with a man. In Poland, 16 is the legal age for both homosexual and heterosexual sex. This situation is very different in Britain, where 16 is the age of consent for heterosexual sex and 21 the minimum age for homosexual sex. This five-year difference represents yet another area of discrimination. One school of thought popular in psychiatry and psychology states that a child's sexual orientation is already established by age five. If this is the case there is little justification for the age differential.

But while the law in parts of Eastern Europe is relatively open about, and relaxed towards, homosexuality, people are still afraid to be open about their homosexuality for fear of being socially victimized. The law, as has already been shown, can only go some way towards eliminating prejudice. Even when the wheels of the judicial system embrace an issue positively, social discrimination can and does still happen. It can mean that a person finds it difficult to find a job, or to find and keep suitable accommodation. Leisure time and socializing can be fraught with problems; at the very least, being unable to display affection through behaviour and rituals common in the heterosexual world.

Sexual harassment on the grounds of sexuality

Sexual harassment is often overlooked in respect of gays and lesbians. It is generally perceived to be a problem faced exclusively by women and created by men. However, while a homosexual man is unlikely to sexually harass a woman, he is more likely to be harassed because he is gay, and potentially to harass another man. Thus the definition of sexual harassment needs to be broadened to incorporate harassment on the basis of sexuality. It is worth noting that the Sex Discrimination Act forbids both indirect and direct discrimination against married persons in employment, but not against gay and lesbian partnerships. Since a far lower proportion of gays or lesbians are likely to be married than heterosexuals, the law clearly needs re-defining to endorse all partnerships equally. Furthermore, if the law were extended to forbid discrimination against single people alongside married people, then gays and lesbians should (in theory at least) be able to claim protection against discrimination under the terms and conditions of the Sex Discrimination Acts.

Homosexuals are perhaps the largest minority group in Britain, but at the same time one of the least visible. The law provides no special attention or protection against prejudice and discrimination on the grounds of sexual orientation. There is an urgent need for changes in the law to secure civil liberties for homosexuals and banish sex orientation as a ground for wrongful discrimination.

Offenders and Ex-Offenders

The Rehabilitation of Offenders Act 1975

The purpose of the Rehabilitation of Offenders Act (for a summary see appendix 1, table 6) is primarily to make life easier for people who have been convicted of a criminal offence in civilian life or in the services (Army, Navy and Air Force), and who have since lived on the 'right' side of the law.

The Act applies to anyone who has been convicted of a criminal offence and received a sentence of not more than two and a half years. Anyone, therefore, who has received a maximum sentence of two and a half years will benefit as a result of the Act, so long as he or she is not convicted again during a specified time (known as the 'rehabilitation period': see definition in appendix 2).

The main advantage of the Act is that once a convicted person's conviction becomes 'spent' he or she does not have to disclose it when, for example, applying for jobs or filling in forms for jobs or training. In fact, in most circumstances he does not have to admit its existence to anyone. The length of time it takes for some criminal convictions to become spent (or forgotten) after a rehabilitation period varies and depends on the original sentence.

Several organizations exist to help and support people with convictions. Advice, practical assistance and occasionally financial help is available to make the transition from prison to 'civvy street' smoother. The addresses of the main organizations (NACRO and the Apex Trust) are listed in appendix 3.

3

Equal Opportunities – Policy and Practice

The Background to Policy Development

An increasing number of organizations in the UK are calling themselves equal opportunities employers. What does this mean? In reality, it can mean anything from a scrap of paper pasted on the wall, full of words which no one has ever read, to a working policy where employers have put their equal opportunities policy into action and had not only the benefit of compliance with the law but a number of other advantages including:

- An improvement in motivation and morale which in turn can reduce turnover levels.
- An enhancement of outsiders' views of the organization so that like-minded and talented people committed to equal opportunities want to join.
- The good business sense of making full use of all the talents of everyone in the workforce. This helps to ensure the best return on what is often a costly investment in recruitment and training. This has particular benefits in the 1990s, in view of the reduction in the number of 18-year-olds in the population from around 900,000 in 1981 to approximately 600,000 in 1995. Similarly, the anticipated increase by 20 per cent in the number of people aged over 65 should encourage employers to provide training and career development opportunities for old as well as young staff.

It is partly correct to forecast that equal opportunities issues will be spearheaded by the impact of the Single European Market into receiving the same political and public attention that health and safety issues have been awarded. It became clear after the Sex Discrimination Act 1975 and the Race Relations Act 1976 had been in place for only a short time that in order for the legislation to work locally, employers would have to translate the law into a strategic and structured framework they themselves could operate within. Employers, much like individuals, are quite unique in their operations. In practice, therefore, equality proposals and conditions which might apply, for example, in the catering industry might be totally inappropriate in the construction industry. The principles of equality remain the same; only the activities undertaken to achieve full equality need differ.

Historically, there has been a tendency for many employers to ignore or overlook their obligations under the various Acts of Parliament governing equal opportunities. The very fact that so many organizations continue to contravene the legislation speaks volumes about its inadequacy, and invites the question, when is a law not quite a law? The fact that sex discrimination has been unlawful in employment in the UK for over 15 years yet still frequently occurs suggests that either the law itself is not stated clearly enough or it is not as enforceable as it ought to be.

The Seven-Stage Plan towards Implementing Equal Opportunities

There are seven fundamental steps involved in turning government policy into everyday practice (see figure 3.1). It should be noted, however, that the procedure is an ongoing developmental process, not a one-stop solution. The interplay between each stage is crucial in order that the process can be evaluated, re-evaluated and ultimately work towards full equality for all.

Let us look at each stage in turn.

Law What is the purpose of inventing a law? There are several reasons why laws have been drawn up, and in the context of equality one of the main reasons has been to provide a solution to an existing problem for a particular group of people. Laws are really little more or less than a set of guidelines for people to identify what their rights or obligations are. The extent to which people abide by the law depends on a number of factors: the extent to which it is enforced, the individual's character, the public or peer-group perception of how fair or necessary the law is, and the penalties attached for breaking the law. As we have already seen in previous chapters, many laws relating to equal opportunities (and indeed

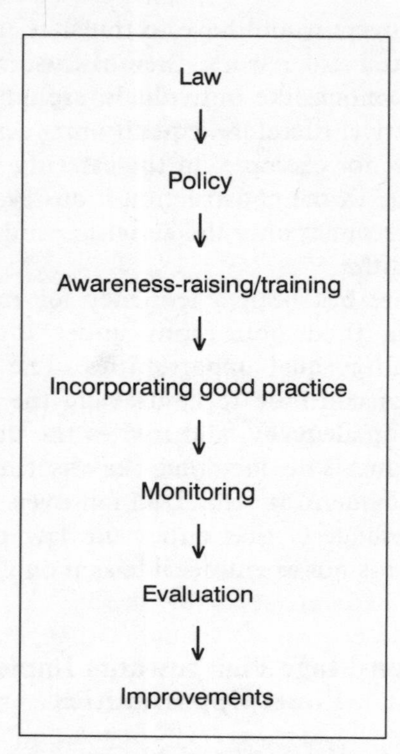

Figure 3.1 The seven-stage plan towards implementing equal opportunities

many revisions which have already been undertaken) need to be amended when they fall short of meeting the expectations of those people they are meant to serve. Flaws in the original Race Relations Act led to its revision and eventually to its replacement by not one, but two further Acts intended to respond more readily to the needs of its beneficiaries. Not all laws, of course, have been designed in the first place to promote equality; historically a number of laws have been developed to do just the opposite – take slavery laws, for example, which were not abolished until just over a century ago. Apartheid also has been supported by a legal system and extensive bureaucracy under South African law. However, the main laws in the UK and the EC governing the equal opportunities issues discussed in this book are generally aimed at combating discrimination and providing the groundwork for good equal opportunities practices.

In order for laws to operate effectively they have to be implemented and enforced. All EC member countries have various organizations whose specific remit is to apply the wide-ranging clauses of particular equality laws. Such organizations also serve to challenge institutions who are breaking the law and to investigate any other areas of existing discrimination. Equality laws should only be given the status of permanent fixtures when they are actually proven to be working as effectively as possible for as many citizens as possible. Until such time they should be continuously open to assessment, criticism and change.

Policy Laws in themselves are insufficient safeguards in promoting equality and challenging discrimination. National laws are of limited effect at local and regional levels if they are not complemented and supported by policy. In the past there has been a tendency for employers to limit their commitment to equal opportunities to a statement of intention; without the full-scale commitment and back-up of an equal opportunities policy. There are several possible reasons why this has happened. Developing an equal opportunities policy takes time and commitment which in a recession may not be very high up on an employer's agenda. In addition, from a manager's point of view a policy might pose itself as a threat to his or her control and staff relations. If people remain unaware of their rights, racism, sexism, homophobia, etc. can quite possibly be overlooked. Policy development goes far beyond and means far more than making a statement of good intention. Statements are vulnerable to all sorts of human weaknesses and are likely to be contravened, overlooked or forgotten about quite quickly. A policy is a means of addressing such issues as recruitment, selection, promotion and training in as fair and equal a manner as possible. It also makes sound economic sense, since improved staff relationships reduce staff turnover and lead to increased production capacity. Policies go beyond paying lip-service to equality and actually document working procedures for eliminating prejudice and developing human resources towards full equality.

Awareness-raising and training Once a policy is in place it is essential that each member of the organization is aware of both its existence and its specific implications. The most effective way to achieve this is via a structured training programme. Training can take many forms and can be developed from as many angles as an employer feels appropriate. Ideally, it should attempt to be as participative as possible and act as a forum for everyone's ideas and recommendations rather than merely an academic exercise. Equal opportunities training, from historical and legislative as well as confrontational angles, ensures that the issues are thoroughly explored.

Incorporating good practice When everyone within an organization becomes aware of their responsibilities under the equal opportunities policy, good practice becomes easy to identify and subsequently to implement. Effective equal opportunities practices vary enormously between employers. Some companies may discover that they were already applying the principles before the policy was introduced. On the other hand, evidence points to the inevitable difficulties of highlighting and eliminating inequalities without the framework and documented guidelines that a policy provides. Good practice may be achieved through a combination of positive-action programmes and re-evaluation procedures. Recruitment procedures, application forms and traditional career structures are commonly among the first systems in need of re-evaluation. Furthermore, adopting good practice enables the policy to be more effectively reviewed.

Monitoring Monitoring is the single most effective way in which the success of an equal opportunities policy can be measured. It is a means of stepping back and judging the entire situation with regard to all equality issues; and as such it is central to the achievement of equality. Monitoring relies on the usual methods of assessment, such as surveys, questionnaires, statistics, etc. Like policy development, monitoring requires both time and commitment in order to succeed. In the past some organizations have tended to develop an equal opportunities policy, and to rely on its existence alone as sufficient to guarantee equal opportunities. Unfortunately, this is an unreliable method which takes no account of personnel or structural changes within an organization. Monitoring is essential both as a means of assessment and as an instigator of change.

Evaluation Evaluation is action taken as a result of assessment and monitoring procedures. Incorporating equal opportunities into an organization overnight is unlikely ever to happen. Moreover, structured improvements implemented over time are likely to have a far greater and long-lasting impact than lightning changes. Evaluation helps readily to identify what improvements are necessary and enables a programme of short- and long-term changes to be developed. Evaluation is the ultimate means of turning policy into practice, and is therefore crucial to an organization's commitment to equal opportunities. The interrelationship between training and evaluation is crucial to achieving change effectively and smoothly. Traditionally many people resist the idea of change; if employees can appreciate the positive value of equality to the whole workforce they are more likely to cooperate than resist. An ongoing strategic training plan with maximum staff participation is an effective measure towards enabling everyone to cope with changes.

Improvements Ideally, each organization should strive to improve its equal opportunities 'ethos' all the time. It has already been shown that a single commitment is not sufficient to break down years of inequality. Equal opportunities has to be regarded in a much broader context than policy. Improvements are discussed here as an autonomous stage in their own right; but this does not imply that they should or can happen in isolation from the whole process. In fact, each stage is about improving the overall concept of equality. The main way to highlight flaws or loopholes in legislation is to actually 'test' the laws in practice. Improvements initiated at local level should really be incorporated into national policy, and in turn into European policy. No EC Member State is as far advanced in terms of social equality as it might be. How the legislation 'feels' in practice needs to be addressed as a serious issue with direct implications for government policymakers, since widespread improvements will not happen as a result of local achievements. Legislators have a duty to respond to the groups that their laws seek to protect – and if that means updating or improving the legislation then that should be an integral part of the process.

The interrelationship between the seven stages should now be clear. Each stage is a vital element in ensuring that maximum returns are gained from a policy. It is not enough to rely totally on the legislation (not least because it is inadequate) to provide all the answers to equality problems. More and more employers are deciding to provide equal opportunities, and are setting policies in motion to achieve that end. But there is also a trend towards increasingly restrictive laws which will ultimately have an effect on policy development (most notably, on homosexuality and sex orientation) and are subjecting people to more harassment and discrimination. These two trends are on a collision course. Lying beneath the surface is an overall wish for equality at societal level, which is not always answered by policymakers. In a democracy, the government is answerable to the people; if people want equality then it should be provided. However, to argue that vast improvements in current laws would be sufficient in themselves is too simplistic and naive. Promoting the principles of equality requires a commitment to each stage to ultimately influence attitudes and laws.

Vast differences in policy and what actually happens in practice exist everywhere, highlighting the essential nature of procedure as the primary catalyst for constructive change. Procedures serve many purposes. Firstly, they enable necessary action to be relatively straightforward to perform – and documentation, therefore, both consistent and easy to follow. They allow policies actually to perform the functions they were designed to. They force verbal commitments and promises into written guidelines which in turn alter the organizational structure for the better. In addition, they allow for progress to be assessed and followed more easily; which in turn helps to identify possible weaknesses. Finally, they also have a central role to play in planning new initiatives and developments, as well as encouraging more active participation in the policy processes.

Many organizations with excellent reputations on an equal opportunities front have found that the implementation of an equal opportunities policy stimulates a better and more productive atmosphere at work. In addition, management, trade union and employee relationships have improved.

In the past, some companies have been reluctant to get even remotely involved in equal opportunities as it has been seen as an expensive luxury. The thought of investing the time and money in such activities as equal opportunities training, fairer recruitment methods, monitoring, reviewing application forms, etc., has unfortunately resulted in many employers shying away from the subject.

I would argue that discrimination is very bad for business; while equal opportunities is cost effective and should therefore be incorporated into all management, personnel and employment policies and practices. Put very simply, discriminatory practices can often mean not recruiting the best person for the job.

The Equal Opportunities Commission recommends that the most effective way of becoming an equal opportunities employer is first of all to write an equal opportunities policy. This helps to focus everyone's attention on the subject and make public your intentions.

In the next few pages we will look at the formulation of an equal opportunities policy, and turning it into practice. Achieving an effective equal opportunities policy takes time and commitment; getting it right at the start is the best way to ensure that criticism cannot be levelled at it later.

What Should a Policy Include?

Most policies will include the following:

1. A definition of direct and indirect sex and racial discrimination, discrimination on the basis of marital status, age, sexual orientation or disability, victimization and sexual harassment and discrimination against ex-offenders. Simple definitions enable everyone to focus on the subject more easily.
2. A brief statement covering the organization's commitment to equal opportunities measures, so that everyone who isn't directly involved in producing the policy is aware of what is happening.
3. The names of the officer(s) responsible for the policy. It is quite common to meet hardly anyone within an organization who knows who their equal opportunities representative is! This highlights the low profile that equal opportunities unfortunately has within many organizations.
4. An obligation upon all employees, from the most senior manager to the newest junior recruit, to respect and act in accordance with the policy.
5. Procedures for dealing with complaints and cases of discrimination. This should include (perhaps in chart or diagram form) the route or procedure an individual should follow. It should highlight the names of all personnel who have a responsibility for equal opportunities.
6. Examples of bad practice: personnel and other staff involved in interviewing and recruitment can be helped by examples of discriminating questions and assumptions like

   Are you planning to get engaged or married?
   Do you have a boyfriend?
   Do you intend to become pregnant?
   Number/age of children?
   What are your childcare arrangements?
   When do you intend to retire?

How many years have you been in full-time employment?
What does your husband do for a living?
How many years did you spend at home looking after your family?

and assumptions/stereotypes like:

Black people are lazy.
Women with children are unreliable.
Married women and women of childbearing age are likely to have babies and leave.
Women are not mobile and may move because their husband's job takes priority.
Women will be unable to work away from home if the job requires spending time in other parts of the country.
Older people are not as productive as young people.
Older people are likely to have more sick leave.
Ex-offenders do not make reliable employees.
People with disabilities do not have the capacity to do the job.

There is no point in asking questions which suggest 'stereotyping' and cause suspicion of prejudice and discrimination.

7 Details of monitoring procedures. This intention should be made very clear as the successful implementation of a policy requires commitment from all staff. Monitoring depends heavily on cooperation from everyone, and can ensure that all staff feel involved in improving the status of equal opportunities within the organization.
8 A commitment to remove existing barriers to equal opportunities. In order to introduce an equal opportunities policy, existing barriers, such as outmoded policies and practices which have survived within the workplace, have to be considered and changed. Existing barriers can include a whole range of formal and informal, written and verbal arrangements within the company – which on close inspection have disadvantaged certain groups in the past.

Implementing the Policy

Perhaps the easiest job is the formulation and writing of an equal opportunities policy. To ensure that the policy is going to succeed a number of steps have to be taken. In logical order the following ten steps should be followed to ensure the full implementation of the policy:

1 Elect a person to be responsible for equal opportunities

This should ideally be someone from senior management, as that automatically gives equal opportunities a higher profile in the eyes of the workforce. If it is not a senior manager the person in charge should report regularly to the top. Obviously one person cannot carry out all the responsibilities so it is recommended that department supervisors, middle managers, and shop floor representatives are also elected for day-to-day responsibility.

At this stage it has to be stressed that making a policy a success requires the commitment and cooperation of *all* employees.

2 Ensure that all employees know about the policy

In the earliest possible stages of forming the policy its existence should be made known to everyone in the organization as well as to external groups that are associated with the organization. This includes managers, supervisors, employees and potential employees (via a copy of the policy being included with the application form). In addition, recruitment agencies, the careers service and job centres should all be notified.

3 Form an equal opportunities committee

Implementing the policy should be the responsibility of a particular individual or group, depending on the size of the organization. It is recommended that a joint working partnership between management, trade unions and employees should be considered. In some situations it is recommended that separate subcommittees be set up. Two areas which might benefit from the launch of independent campaigns are AIDS and HIV discrimination and age discrimination. In many circumstances a temporary subcommittee will suffice. Its primary task must be to tackle the broader questions about action to be taken against discrimination in the workplace affecting these groups. The main responsibility of all committees would be to review and adapt the policy with a view to increasing and maintaining good practice. Representatives on the equal opportunities committee should come from personnel, management, supervisors, trade unions and the shop floor. When the committee or working party has been established it is important that it should have clear terms of reference outlined, which will include the following duties:

- Analyzing the information provided by monitoring; that is, evaluating statistics to ascertain specific areas of weakness in equal opportunities practice.
- Acting as an arena for ideas and suggestions to develop equal opportunities further. Representatives can use this role as a way of involving staff in their departments by asking for their ideas.
- Assessing the success of suggestions which have been implemented. It is important to remember that even temporary or small measures can often be as effective as major developments in improving the equal opportunities profile of the workplace.
- Producing an equal opportunities bulletin which should be circulated around the entire organization and displayed prominently on notice-boards. This should include regularly updated news on all aspects of equal opportunities; for example, social events, educational and training events, and new legislation.
- Encouraging employees to contribute their ideas via questionnaires. This has the advantage of stimulating employee commitment to the objectives of the equal opportunities policy; the equal opportunities representatives can take action from their ideas to remedy any problems.

4 Train staff

Ideally all staff within an organization should be trained on what the policy means to the company and to them as individuals. If time and money are restricted, training should be targeted at all employees in personnel departments who come into contact with job applicants; for example, the office receptionist is often the first person with whom outsiders come into contact. Relevant parts of the policy should be highlighted that relate specifically to an employee's job description. Training should include:

- An explanation of the different types of discrimination and the usual forms in which it is manifested. For example, direct and indirect sex, racial and marital discrimination, victimization, sexual harassment.
- Guidance on the usual assumptions and prejudices – with ideas and explanations of how to handle them and avoid them.
- The need to assess people on their individual merits and ability to do a job – while at the same time avoiding misguided assumptions. This is essential if discrimination is to be avoided. For example, as a general rule age should not be used as a factor in recruitment and promotion decisions.
- Formal training sessions to complement written guidelines or codes of practice. As well as formal training on equal opportunities, there ought

to be an equal opportunities input into all other training courses. For example, interviewing skills, time management, management growth and business growth should all address equal opportunities as a serious issue, not just one to pay lip-service to.

5 *Examine existing policies and practices*

Past behaviour and lack of equal opportunities should not be ignored in the attempt to introduce an equal opportunities policy into an organization. The benefits of addressing current practices are twofold. First, one of the best ways to learn and improve is to make a mistake: far better for an individual or a group to learn and remember by having got it wrong the first time than to read up about good practice in a pile of papers. Second, adopting an equal opportunities policy will increase awareness of unintentional areas of discrimination in the past.

In order to identify factors which may be a barrier to equal opportunities, the status of all existing employees as well as practices, policies and procedures should be examined, and revised and updated where appropriate. Application forms, standard interview questions and job descriptions are just three of the current procedures which may need adapting to satisfy the equal opportunities policy. Some organizations may find it useful to carry out a full-scale monitoring procedure as a preliminary exercise prior to developing an equal opportunities policy. This would have at least two advantages. First, it would highlight weaknesses so that immediate improvements could be negotiated and introduced. Furthermore, it could assist in the formation of the policy with respect to drawing up a priority list for the various tasks which need to be undertaken.

6 *Make sure the equal opportunities policy is working*

In order to ensure that the policy is working it is necessary to gather information (see *monitoring* above) on the employment situation of women, married people, black people and other ethnic minorities, old people, homosexuals, disabled people and ex-offenders within the organization. Without this important information you can never be entirely certain that you are really providing equal opportunities.

The information gathered may well reveal, for example, that there are sections of the workforce where there are few, if any, women. It may discover that women and black people are concentrated in certain jobs or grades; or that gays who are open about their homosexuality are concentrated in the lowest grades and never offered promotion. Similarly, it may highlight the lack of training of older workers being undertaken. In each case the barriers to equal opportunities should be identified and methods of removing them examined. The analysis (see *evaluation* above) of information can be one of the best and most effective ways of introducing a programme of positive action.

7 *Allow time to monitor the equal opportunities policy*

No one would disagree that monitoring is a time-consuming and often frustrating task. The degree of monitoring obviously depends a great deal on the size of the enterprise. Each organization must decide what its own aims and objectives are with regard to monitoring and how it intends to carry them out. The aim of monitoring is to highlight areas where change is needed and to assess the progress made in achieving that change.

The equal opportunities working party should ideally do four things. First, it should decide priorities in conjunction with the workforce and agree on a programme of monitoring and how often monitoring is going to take place. Second it should agree to set aside time (both for the equal opportunities working party and the workforce) to carry out monitoring. This can involve compiling questionnaires and records as well as gathering information. Third, a reasonable time span is needed in order for the data to be analyzed. Finally, it will need to define a programme for future action to overcome current and future shortfalls in equal opportunities.

8 *Introduce positive measures*

Employers can (under section 48 of the Sex Discrimination Act and under the Race Relations Act) make allowances to take certain forms of remedial action to redress the effects of past discrimination. For example, if there have been few or no women or black people employed in particular departments for the past year, it is lawful to train members of that sex or ethnic group to help enable them to pursue that work. Training applies to existing employees only, not to potential recruits.

Positive measures should be included as part of an equal opportunities programme. Encourage minority groups in particular jobs to apply by staging special recruitment drives. This could include targeting advertising to appeal to minority groups. Recruitment literature could be prominently displayed at girls' schools, black youth centers and schools with a high percentage of children from ethnic minorities. Magazines and places popular among gays and lesbians should also be targeted.

Support should be made readily available for staff who move into jobs traditionally performed by members of the opposite sex. Career counselling and appraisal with special emphasis on career development is necessary for staff in a minority position within their departments. It is especially important not to ignore the career development of older staff, by falsely assuming that they are unlikely to be around for much longer. Career counselling is a very basic requirement to ensure that staff in a minority position receive help and encouragement in order to cope with the pressures they may face owing to their minority status.

Training is another positive measure which should be incorporated into the equal opportunities programme. Special training courses can be introduced for minority groups which aim to encourage people to assess their options in the workforce with a view to promotion or transfer into nontraditional areas; for example, offering women in the clerical department a chance to receive training in engineering skills.

Flexibility in working arrangements is a positive measure which would be welcomed by many people. Due to inadequate childcare services in this country, many women are faced with few options other than to resign from work to look after children. In order to enhance and increase the choices available, arrangements such as flexi-time, nursery facilities and extended maternity and paternity leave should be considered where possible as part of the equal opportunities programme.

Many employers have introduced quite attractive return-to-work schemes for parents after a spell of absence owing to child rearing. Some organizations offer guarantees of a job at the same level or grade for women who return after three years. In conjunction with this arrangement, updating sessions every three months are available to keep employees aware of progress within the workplace. To complement these sessions newsletters are sent to absent employees to ensure regular contact. Measures such as these should be increased and seen as an integral part of all equal opportunities programmes.

9 *Foster effective internal communications and external relations*

We have already seen the necessity of having a person in charge of equal opportunities, to coordinate all activities, policies, programmes and practices within an organization. In addition to this ongoing role, s/he should be able to offer appropriate advice and guidance on the handling of a complaint related to equal opportunities. The appointment of an equal opportunities 'manager', 'officer', 'liaison officer', or whatever his or her title is, can assist the implementation of an equal opportunities policy in several ways. Policy development has to continue, if the new equal opportunities policy is to avoid being just a one-day wonder. The officer can develop relationships with other equal opportunity employers, both on a local and national level, to build up links and even 'twin' with another group. Establishing such relationships can help towards the provision of role models; for example an organization which is largely science, engineering or technology based could twin with a hospital or art-orientated organization. Role models or mentors for one group could be used in training sessions with minority groups; supplying a female mentor from a traditional male job acts as encouragement to women who may be considering transfer to a nontraditional job or department.

I make no apology for repeating how critical training is towards the successful implementation of a policy. An equal opportunities officer can coordinate training activities within the organization as well as arranging for experts to come in and assist in training. Effective internal communication is bound to be enhanced if people are encouraged to be involved through participative training events.

Also crucial are effective external relations – that is, dealing with the Equal Opportunities Commission, the Commission for Racial Equality, the trade unions, media and press. An organization's equal opportunities policy has to be visible from the outside as well as internally. Any organization that calls itself an equal opportunities employer has a role in influencing opinion and helping to bring about change. This responsibility should be taken seriously in external platforms and meetings. Commitment to the full implementation of equal opportunities as a long-term issue and strategy should be in everyone's job description. However, the real catalyst for converting this commitment into action is the appointment and work of an equal opportunities officer.

10 Change attitudes

Changing attitudes is an aspect of the equality issue which needs institutional support. The formulation of a policy and changes in organizational structure are needed before this work can be undertaken effectively. Questionnaires can be very useful in opening discussions about attitude and influences. These can be completed anonymously, although an indication of the respondent's sex or ethnic group may be useful for subsequent analysis. Attitudes will never be changed immediately. A combination of equal opportunities awareness-raising, training, policy implementation, and cooperation of everyone at all levels can go some way towards focusing on the issue. Including all minority groups in a policy brings about awareness of the existence of these groups, an awareness which has possibly never been raised before. This may sound obvious, but prejudice can very often be avoided if people are regularly confronted with equal opportunities issues.

What Other Measures Can Be Taken?

One of the greatest obstacles to achieving equal opportunities and the greatest single cause of inaction is the common response 'We don't have a problem with equal opportunities.' Whatever role we are in – whether at school, college, university, in employment, training, retirement, or on the brink of something new like a job change, promotion, first job, or education course – it is important to become aware of our specific environment and to ascertain the 'ethos' of the organization with regard to equal opportunities. At first glance, many institutions seem not to have an equal opportunities philosophy built into their structure. It is important that all of us as individuals take some responsibility to ensure that discrimination becomes a thing of the past. In order to achieve this there are several activities that can help – examples are discussed below. These examples highlight positive measures that almost everyone can put into practice.

(1) Set up a discussion group to raise the subject of equal opportunities and gain support for other related activities. The benefits of a discussion group are very clear. The group can help focus everyone's attention on the issue of equal opportunities and

can act as a forum for ideas and activities to eliminate discrimination. Ideally the group should consist of a representative from all departments or subject groups. Feedback from the group should be given regularly to the rest of the organization. The recommendations of the group or working party should be communicated formally, via a newsletter or mail-shot, to everyone else.

(2) Undertake a statistical survey, such as a simple monitoring exercise to ascertain how the organization 'reflects' good equal opportunity practices. A statistical survey of your own school, youth group or workplace is a good place to begin when you are dealing with factual information. Statistical information is not an end in itself; however, it can provide a useful starting point to help devise an equal opportunities strategy.

(3) Devise an equal opportunities strategy. By gathering information and enlisting support it may be possible to introduce a formal strategy. This will immediately raise the profile of equal opportunities which is a positive step towards future action. An equal opportunities strategy is very similar to an equal opportunities policy. Inequality may have become so much the norm that discrimination and bad practice go unnoticed, and seem perfectly all right to everyone. However, change is possible and organizations all over the country are eliminating structural barriers to achievement and equality of opportunity. The objectives of the strategy need to be identified very clearly or the strategy will lose focus.

(4) Set up an equal opportunities working party – and if possible get support and representation from a wide cross-section of the organization. All organizations are different, so there is no blueprint for success. However, a working party can strive to achieve equality in the areas that are barriers to minority groups – without which such a group can often be overlooked.

(5) Become aware of advertisements and media influence. This is just one of the many issues that should be addressed by the working party. It can never be overemphasized how much effect the media has in influencing our beliefs and actions. The group should look at how both internal and external advertisements consider equal opportunities, and bring about changes were necessary. Job advertisements are found in both local and national newspapers as well as employment agencies. It is worth noting how many job

advertisements carry any reference to an equal opportunities policy, and how many of those endorse all aspects of the policy: sex discrimination, race discrimination, disability and age, homosexuality and ex-offenders, etc. Most policies or statements of intent supplied by an employer at the end of an advertisement omit homosexuality, older workers and ex-offenders.

Advertisement of products, such as household equipment, often reinforces stereotypes. Women advertising washing powder, washing-up liquid and household detergents reinforce the stereotype that women buy all of these products and women use them exclusively. Examine all of the advertisements that you see and gauge how realistic or unrealistic they are. Influence of the media can be fundamental in leading to discriminatory practices.

(6) Do not overlook terminology and language in reference to good equal opportunities practice. Sexist and racist language is unfortunately commonplace and embedded in the English language. An individual response is equally effective to a collective response in altering the trends within modern-day language. Everyone who believes in equal opportunities should question racist and sexist language and avoid using it. The question is often asked whether schools, education or training courses and employer-based equal opportunities awareness programmes can realistically expect to counteract the many influences which adversely affect the learning and acquisition of language skills and terminology. In order to modify environmental influences it is necessary to address the issue of negative and discriminatory terminology.

Negative terminology is very often used within the areas of racism and racial discrimination. Most people at some time or another have heard racist jokes. However, there is a more insidious aspect to racist terminology which many people who would perhaps claim they were non-racist help perpetuate. For example, terms such as 'blackmail' and 'black market' suggest a negative image of blackness; in contrast, 'whiter than white' suggests a positive or good image of whiteness, and is indicative of virtuous characteristics (see *negative terminology* in appendix 2 for a wider explanation). Words or phrases such as these can be used unintentionally, but it is important to understand their connotations. To describe a non-white person as coloured can be offensive; it is politically and socially more correct to use the term 'black'. If for a moment, you examined the actual colour of most people you would undoubtedly conclude that the majority are pink, grey, yellow, brown, black and white: and 'white' people are in fact more likely to change their colour more readily than any other group: blue when cold, red when angry and a pale shade of grey when ill.

Attention must be paid to terminology within all aspects of equal opportunities. Prejudices are formed very early and quite quickly but can take years to undo. An inaccurate or incorrect description of someone or something can lead to false assumptions being made, which in turn can lead to discrimination.

(7) It is worth considering the extent to which books and textbooks portray stereotyped images and whether they act as disincentives to learning for racial groups or for either sex. Books that incorporate the concept of equality are more conducive to good practice than those which reinforce traditional unequal beliefs. Individuals can enhance the profile and sales of the former by being selective in their reading. Examine books – both novels and textbooks – and draw your own conclusions about the degree of equality they display. Many books display quite brilliant illustrations but often these pictures only serve to reinforce an existing stereotype. Encouragement was discussed earlier as an aid towards positive measures in equal opportunities programmes. Imagine how discouraging it could be for a potential female joiner or plumber to see picture after picture of male plumbers, or for a black person interested in a job with an airline to be confronted with a book on civil aviation filled with pictures of white personnel. Yet images alone will not shape reality: a person with a physical disability might be portrayed in recruitment literature for a firm, only to face the fact that when a disabled person applies for a job the working environment doesn't seem especially helpful towards people with disabilities.

All organizations that are committed to providing equal opportunities should consider the type of literature (recruitment, novels, textbooks, introductory literature, literature on pension schemes, educational material) they stock. Literature can either be discouraging or encouraging; organizations should ensure that they provide only that literature which is the latter, and as such serves as a challenge to conventional racist or sexist beliefs. Fundamental areas of prejudice and discrimination could possibly be avoided if it were not for the bombardment of stereotyped images we encounter every day. But there are alternatives. Many publishers and bookshops have a whole range of books that portray positive images of minority groups.

(8) Remember that early learning and pre-school activities can play a major role in forming our images, ideals and prejudices. Even during the first five years of life stereotypes and prejudice can be formed. The open-minded parent and peer group which challenge stereotypes by their own actions, play a major part in influencing a child's subsequent behaviour. It is up to all of us to question traditional early experiences. Many children go through the first five years of their lives with very stereotyped images. Often mother is at home and spends her time cooking, washing, cleaning, ironing; while father is out at work earning money. Father is seen at the weekends washing the car, mowing the lawn or performing do-it-yourself jobs about the house. Perhaps in some cases the father is never seen doing any work in the house and is more often seen slouched in front of the television.

Even if both parents are engaged in paid employment, a child may encounter conflicting images in books. Most pre-school books available reinforce the traditional family image and stereotypes. Books, like advertisements, highlight traditional female and male roles. Children of single parents or of gay or lesbian parents are rarely catered for in the massive market of pre-school material. It is important to address the issue of pre-school stereotyping. The use of correct, non-racist and non-sexist terminology with children is important in forming their images of people and of the world of work.

(9) Women at work and within the world of work is another issue which can be examined within your own establishment. Unfortunately, despite being present in large numbers they are not awarded the high status or large salaries that many men receive. A combination of many of the activities discussed above can bring about change and improvements in the position of women both within and outside the workplace. It is a simple exercise to look at the number of women in the workforce and their position and grades in comparison to men's. If there are gross inequalities between the pay packets or grades of men and women, it is possible to set up an equal opportunities working party which can work towards removing these inequalities.

Checklist for Equal Opportunities Policy Implementation

The preceding pages have described the steps that ought to be taken to ensure that equal opportunities becomes an everyday part of your organization. A brief summary of the main procedures is outlined below. It is important to remember that each stage is not an isolated event but is an interrelated factor within the life cycle of business success.

From equal opportunities to practice – the seven-stage plan:

1 Law
2 Policy
3 Awareness-raising and training
4 Incorporating good practice
5 Monitoring
6 Evaluation
7 Improvements.

What should a policy include?

1 Definitions; for example, discrimination, victimization.
2 Statement of commitment to equal opportunities.
3 Names of personnel with direct responsibility for policy.
4 Obligation of all staff to adhere to the policy.
5 Procedures for handling complaints.
6 Examples of good and bad practice which might assist in, for example, recruitment and selection, training, induction, etc.
7 Details of monitoring procedures.
8 Commitment to remove existing barriers to equal opportunities.

Steps to ensure the successful implementation of an equal opportunities policy:

1 Elect a person to be responsible.
2 Ensure that all employees know about the policy.
3 Form an equal opportunities committee or working party.
4 Offer training.
5 Examine existing policies and practices.
6 Make sure you are an equal opportunities employer by actually providing equal opportunities.
7 Allow time to implement, monitor and review the policy.
8 Introduce positive measures and good practices.
9 Foster effective internal communication and external relations.
10 Work at changing attitudes.

4

AIDS and HIV: A New Area of Discrimination

Introduction

There are two main reasons why this subject warrants a separate chapter. First, AIDS has only been recognized as a disease for the last decade (it was first discovered in Britain in 1981) and as such is the most recent area in which discrimination can happen within employment. Second, as yet there is little or no legislation available to protect people suffering from prejudice and discrimination due to AIDS or its related illnesses. 'Employment' in this context refers to the workplace as a microcosm of society at large. It is widely acknowledged that people with AIDS (or even people suspected of having AIDS or being HIV-positive) are becoming the victims of discrimination in all aspects of everyday living.

Much has already been written about AIDS, from angles from medical to anthropological (not to mention the government's own leaflet – 'Don't Die of Ignorance'). I do not intend to write at length about the disease and its spread; the purpose of this chapter is to highlight the discrimination faced by its victims and recommend policy action to prevent this.

What is AIDS?

Acquired Immune Deficiency Syndrome (AIDS) is caused by the Human Immunodeficiency Virus (HIV). Unlike other parasites which often kill the host in a very short time, the AIDS virus attacks the immune system (the system in the human body which acts as a means of resisting all types of infection). It eventually kills as the person becomes weakened and susceptible to infections which previously could easily have been fought off.

There can be no doubt that AIDS has caused much anxiety and fear in society. Words like 'epidemic' serve only to frighten people and avoid the real issues at stake. To put AIDS in perspective, it should be remembered that the total number of deaths from AIDS in the whole of the last ten years is a very small percentage compared to the annual deaths from the real epidemics and killers like cancer and heart disease.

AIDS and the Gay Community

Originally AIDS was referred to as GRID – Gay Related-Immuno Deficiency. Inevitably this gave the tabloid press a field day: 'Gay Plague', 'Gay Epidemic', etc. were frequent headlines. Much of the propaganda that has been spread – for example, AIDS being God's 'judgement' upon homosexuals – would encourage us to believe that AIDS is exclusively a gay disease. This is not the case; as the government advertisements correctly point out, any man or woman can get the HIV virus.

AIDS has unleashed very powerful arguments in the eyes of many groups for a move back to chastity outside marriage, to the conservative values associated with the family, conformity and fidelity. Although these may be very good and praiseworthy 'moves' in their own right, they can only serve to increase the isolation in which many gay men live their lives. While the government, Church and the 'moral majority' extol the virtues of family life (by that is meant heterosexual family life) the enormous prejudice, discrimination and oppression endured by homosexuals will increase. The cry to return to the values of family life has intensified the oppression of the gay community.

The urgent need for government legislation which ends prejudice and discrimination against homosexuals has already been discussed (see chapter 2). If homophobia is in any way to be reduced, laws are necessary as the primary catalyst for change. Until homosexuals receive the same rights as heterosexuals, little can be achieved to undo the prejudice with which society views homosexuality and end the discrimination they endure.

Governments the world over are taking action to prevent the spread of AIDS. Different approaches have been taken by educational campaigns in different countries. The 'grim reaper of death' used in the Australian television campaign was widely criticized for using 'scare tactics'. In contrast, a Swedish cartoon character adopted a humorous approach, pointing out that safer sex can still be fun. The British government's first campaign was criticized by some viewers for being a little too obscure. In many countries AIDS has created a huge increase in social fear and in homophobia. Public homophobia has been exasperated by media coverage. Newspapers have given extensive and often 'sensationalist' coverage to the disease. The consequences in many countries have been a more unified and integrated approach to AIDS from within gay communities, with spasmodic efforts at education and prevention in the (more divided) wider society. The Netherlands is quite socially advanced in its attitudes to AIDS; neither has it indulged in as much scapegoating as is evident in many other EC Member States.

AIDS and HIV: Discrimination in the Workplace

Anxiety and misconceptions about AIDS, its causes, effects and modes of transmission, has resulted in widespread prejudice and discrimination against people with AIDS. In practice, this means that people with AIDS-related illnesses or the stress of knowing they are HIV-positive have found that their problems are compounded by negative social reactions towards their condition.

Widespread use of the term 'risk group' has led to stereotyping particular categories of people and assumptions being made about them. Gay men, intravenous drug users and people with haemophilia have been the main victims of misleading stereotypes. It is important to recognize that there is no such thing as a 'risk group' in relation to AIDS and HIV – only risk behaviour. Further, it is a common error to assume that even 'risk behaviour(s)' are somehow separable. A heterosexual man, for example, might also be an intravenous drug user; a heterosexual woman might have several sexual partners, therefore increasing her risk; non-drug users may have relationships with drug users. It is clear that there is an (inevitable) interaction which renders the term 'risk group' illogical anyway.

Reactions towards people with AIDS vary widely. Social ostracism, harassment, and verbal discrimination through to dismissal from a job are all, sadly, commonplace, and becoming increasingly familiar experiences for many people. Since the risks of infection through normal workplace contact are negligible, there is no justification for such discrimination.

A positive equal opportunities policy on AIDS is the most effective way of handling problems in employment. The AIDS policy needs to be complemented by an ongoing training and awareness-raising strategy in order for it to be successful. In addition, as is the case for any policy to work well, it must have the total support of management and of employees' representatives.[1]

AIDS and HIV: Policy Guidelines

Many organizations could adapt their existing policies on equal opportunities to include an AIDS policy. In addition to their current policy the following ten points should be carefully considered and agreed upon. (Points 1–3 relate to the Employer's Statement and points 4–10 to the day-to-day implementation of the policy.)

1 A statement should be prepared to the effect that the organization is committed to fighting HIV- and AIDS-related prejudice and discrimination in all its forms. The purpose of the statement is twofold; first, to make public your intention and commitment; second, to focus everyone's attention on the issue. An example of the sort of statement that could be used is:

> This organization is committed to ending HIV- and AIDS-related discrimination in all its forms. We will actively contest discrimination against people with AIDS, related illnesses, and people who are HIV-positive, as well as people often wrongly assumed to be.

2 A definition of discrimination (indirect, direct and victimization), and harassment is necessary in order to ensure that everyone is aware of what constitutes these types of behaviour.

3 Factual information and basic explanatory material is needed about AIDS and HIV, along with details about modes of transmission of the condition. More information and understanding on the part of employees ought to ensure greater compliance with the policy.

4 Appoint an individual with direct responsibility for the policy. This

[1] A charter banning discrimination against employees with AIDS or the HIV virus has been launched in July 1992 by the charity National AIDS Trust, with the support of 16 top British companies. National Westminster Bank, Body Shop, Rothschilds and Midland Bank are among those companies to have signed up to the *Companies Act! Business Charter*, pledging themselves to the 'principle of non-discrimination' when dealing with employees who have AIDS or HIV. The impetus for the Charter has come from cases brought to the attention of the Trust where people with AIDS or HIV have lost their jobs either through direct or indirect discrimination by their employers.

should ideally be someone with a thorough knowledge of equal opportunities policies and practice, and one who, of course, will totally respect confidentiality.

5 State that there will be no discrimination in recruitment, promotion, selection and training, against applicants externally or internally, on the grounds that an applicant is HIV-positive or has AIDS. Everyone, particularly staff who have a direct responsibility for such activities, has to be aware of this.

6 Enabling a person coping with AIDS to continue working is crucial. Many books have been written about the intrinsic value of work to an individual. Three very important issues relevant to people coping with the stresses of AIDS or HIV are:

(a) Work can help people maintain confidence in themselves.
(b) Work acts as a social forum for meeting other people. This is especially important for anyone who has little support outside of work, or indeed for anyone living alone.
(c) Work provides a social structure for day-to-day life for all of us, probably far more than most other activities can provide.

To ensure that an employee with AIDS would be suitably catered for in the workplace every effort should be made to adapt the employee's job description to this end. In addition, it should be made very clear in the policy that no one will be dismissed because of AIDS.

7 In a case where an employee is too unwell or debilitated to carry out all of the usual duties associated with his or her job, a job analysis should be carried out. Any changes which are necessary should be agreed by the employee, equal opportunities representative, management and the relevant trade union.

8 Any harassment or discrimination by an employer against a person with AIDS or HIV should be regarded as a disciplinary matter. Most organizations will already have existing measures for disciplinary action. Discrimination against employees with HIV or AIDS should be explicitly mentioned in the disciplinary procedure guidelines. In order to avoid such action, there is no better way to ensure against it then training. It is absolutely essential that ongoing training and up-to-date information is provided to all staff on issues relating to HIV and AIDS.

9 Normal company rules regarding sick leave should continue to apply for staff with AIDS or related illnesses. In addition, staff who have a responsibility for caring for people with AIDS have the right to special leave.

10 No organization can exist in complete isolation – each has customers, clients, users or buyers, etc. It is therefore important that no client dealing with the organization is denied the service of that organization because he or she has AIDS or is HIV-positive.

5

Opportunity 2000

Background

Against a background of equality legislation which has been in force for over two decades, widespread contraventions of the Sex Discrimination Act and Equal Pay Act still occur in the UK. The presence of such legislation has clearly had little real impact on the male-dominated structure of British industry and it has become evident that some men will resist any change in the reallocation of 'male' jobs and male control. Under such circumstances it is hardly surprising that women's role has been subordinated to the lowest ranks within employment; such ranks command lower pay, poor promotion prospects and little legal protection. In general, the laws have acted as little more than theoretical tools and failed miserably to achieve their intended results. While lawyers have got rich on the back of equality legislation, women's wealth and status has scarcely altered over the last 20 years.

The statistical facts about equality for women in the UK and, indeed, worldwide can be expressed simply:

- Women's average hourly earnings have remained around 74 per cent of men's for the last decade. In fact, the average weekly wage for women is £201.50 compared to £295.60 for men.
- Women occupy less than 2 per cent of all senior executive positions in the UK.
- Only 20 per cent of all managers in the UK are women.
- Globally, women receive only 10 per cent of the world's income.
- Women own less than 1 per cent of total world property.

The urgent need for increased attention to be paid to equal opportunities and the role of women in employment is clear. The quest for new horizons in the field of equal opportunities has often ended in disappointment. New programmes were announced but promises were not kept. The majority of organizations still consider, along neo-classical lines, that their future is in good hands. Yet equal opportunities problems cannot be solved in terms of equilibria, since successful equality implementation necessarily involves a dynamic process of change and re-evaluation. If equality theory and equality management are to be based on realistic assumptions, then a new and more pragmatic approach over and above legal measures is needed. Equality management has traditionally tended to be regarded as something which gives a boost to a company's external image though divorced from any internal activity. In a rapidly changing economy, equality issues cover the whole cycle of industrial life. Equality management is not just a matter of catering for the needs of previously oppressed groups: it can help solve complex problems associated with recruitment and selection, mobility, staff retention, productivity and quality, and can foster a good working environment, without which the scope for influence is otherwise limited.

Opportunity 2000

We know that in the near future our social and economic environment will be changing greatly; industry and education are directly influenced by this mutation. If equal opportunities are to be considered as an answer to the problems of everyday life and as a factor of an innovative process in the industrial European and international context, then we are faced with a need for a totally new approach and new curricula in equal opportunities. Demographic changes in the European labour market, influenced by increased longevity and a declining birth rate, are set to have a tremendous influence upon employers' recruitment and selection patterns. The participation of women in paid work is set to increase still further by the year 2000. Clearly the European labour market will have to be ready to redesign its patriarchal power-base in order realistically to reflect this changing structure. Opportunity 2000 is the first ever large-scale equality enterprise in the UK which reflects these changes and offers a new opportunity to redress the structures which have undermined the role of women.

Opportunity 2000 is about:

- Promoting awareness of equality for women.
- Demonstrating the potential of women.
- Training staff.
- Giving member firms an 'equality' back-up.

Opportunity 2000 is a self-financing campaign launched in the UK in the autumn of 1991, and supported by the Prime Minister, who announced his personal commitment to recruit more women into top-level government positions. It has been established as the result of work carried out by the Women's Economic Development Team, chaired by Lady Howe and set up by the charity Business in the Community (BITC). The campaign aims to encourage British industry to take full advantage of the economic potential of women. It emphasizes that equal opportunities at work constitutes good economic as well as common sense, without ignoring the humanitarian nature of good equality practice. It is a unique approach to improvements in equality of opportunities in the UK. Start-up members at the October launch included banks, building societies, major high-street retailers, government departments, the police, educational establishments, major engineering companies, most of the UK's recently privatized large employers, publishers and television companies – clearly, the complete range of British business is represented.

The Opportunity 2000 approach involves three key steps:

1. An active ongoing programme of organized reform to provide a full range of equal opportunities. Improvements which are introduced will be measured to enable effective evaluation of equal opportunity policy and practice.
2. The development of goals and targets based on a participating organization's existing situation and assessment of future needs. This will prevent the blanket approach common in the past which took little account of differences between organizations.
3. A public statement of commitment about a company's special goals in the context of Opportunity 2000, and regular reporting of progress in annual reports.

Opportunity 2000 recognizes that change of any nature is a long-term process. Any well-designed programme must therefore take into account existing barriers to equal opportunities and set achievable goals as well as complement all other organizational factors.

Thus, the planning of appropriate equality strategies is central to the chance of lasting success.

Practical steps which Opportunity 2000 members will incorporate include:

- Increasing maternity retention rates (the number of women returning to work after maternity leave).
- Increasing the number of women in key areas of business through a series of positive-action measures and statistical targets as a result of evaluation surveys.
- Building equal opportunities objectives into staff appraisal schemes at all levels: board-level, management, middle management, supervisory, clerical, shop floor, etc.
- Conducting attitude surveys among the workforce to assess the real rather than perceived or assumed needs of staff and to encourage greater organizational 'ownership' of equality measures.
- Undertaking regular monitoring and reporting of progress to highlight both the areas of success and areas of weakness in the equal opportunities policy and practice.

In the past most organizations have regarded equal opportunities as a marginal issue which can be largely ignored once a fine-looking policy is in place. However, for the dozens of UK companies already involved in Opportunity 2000, increased attention will be focused on equal opportunities as a central economic issue, as worthy of serious attention as any other business matter. Contrary to an idea which is far too widespread, equal opportunities is not the exclusive preserve of personnel departments. Implementing equality programmes forms the very basis of the success of some large organizations, e.g. Littlewoods, as a growing number of other companies are starting to discover. Certainly, the most high-powered companies in the UK owe their success to their human resource management practices which have enabled them to achieve and maintain leading positions in their sectors.

The environment for Opportunity 2000 exists already. The number of working women in the UK has been growing steadily since the 1960s. Where before, women have had to adapt to male-dominated structures, the reverse is soon likely to happen. Women now play a much fuller role in the economy and the pace of women's participation in all business sectors seems set to exceed that of men.

So far, Opportunity 2000 has the support of over 60 of the UK's top companies and major employers. Some participants have stated their intentions to implement ten-year target programmes on the numbers of women in management; while others are concentrating on making the workplace a more conducive place for women to combine effectively their roles as mothers and employees. Still more emphasis will be placed on the dual responsibility between the environment of employment and the home – with the role of men as parents likely to receive much long-overdue attention. Many other organizations which have joined Opportunity 2000 have already begun to introduce a range of positive-action measures designed to encourage more women to enter nontraditional female occupations, thus breaking down the traditional male strongholds which since the industrial revolution have sought to exclude women (most notably engineering and construction). Overall, Opportunity 2000 aims to support its members in a bid to increase both the number of women in employment and the quality of work they pursue. Inevitably, this will require a combination of initial equal opportunities training curricula and professional curricula – implying major changes from the present situation in the UK. Those changes are already underway in many organizations, but require greater impetus and greater participation by many more.

The Role of Equal Opportunities Training in Opportunity 2000

A one- or two-day workshop held outside the firm offers its board and management the opportunity to escape from everyday routine and to work efficiently under the guidance of an outside presenter on questions of specific relevance to the firm's equal opportunities strategy. Equal opportunities training programmes can show a clearer picture of the current equality ethos, and how with regard to an organization's strengths, weaknesses and strategic targets improvements can be obtained; and can demonstrate how, step-by-step, the objectives can be translated into action.

A workshop programme ought to be tailored to the requirements of each individual firm. The basis of the programme should be the knowledge of a company's equal opportunities planning strategy gained during an initial analytical interview in conjunction with the following four steps:

1 Analysis of a firm's current situation.
2 Analysis of potential.

3 Setting of realistic targets.
4 Proposals for immediate and long-term action.

(Ideally, the last two activities ought to be timetabled.)

The fundamental objective pursued in equal opportunities training is always to utilize to the full the creative in-house know-how and group dynamic processes available to encourage synergism between participants. An equal opportunities workshop thus represents an essential component of the strategic planning and implementation of equal opportunities practice. Trouble-free introduction of equal opportunities policies often fails because of opposition from a few staff, usually due to their inadequate level of knowledge of exactly what equal opportunities entails – possibly tinged with a hint of British reticence to accept change readily. Training in equal opportunities is therefore an essential prerequisite to the success or failure of policy and should be available for all staff at all levels within an organization.

The scheme aims to foster close partnerships between the firms involved. Such cooperative work undertaken now is also timely: by the time the Single European Market is firmly established and operational, firms in all Member States must be able to cooperate effectively; hence Opportunity 2000 is an expression of the UK's stance in this matter. Furthermore, Opportunity 2000 provides a chance for a greater number of British companies to benefit from EC equality measures, in particular, the EC Directives on Equal Treatment and Equal Pay for Men and Women, and the increased future emphasis and obligation upon national parliaments to ensure that 'equal pay for work of equal value' becomes a fact rather than merely a constitutional right.

The organizations which Opportunity 2000 already represents are significant because they are evidence of the thorough and painstaking study and experience which have led to the conclusion that equality, with its multiplicity of aspects, is a specialist field in its own right. Such companies are acutely aware of the crucial role women play in economic competition and success.

How Opportunity 2000 Can Help Your Organization

It is likely that far more organizations (not to mention far more women) could benefit from enrolment in the Opportunity 2000 campaign. Since equal opportunities provision makes sound economic sense, the practice ought to be pursued as a strategy for both survival and growth. The formulation of equal opportunities policy has often been found to be a common area of weakness. Companies need to undertake a thorough internal audit in order to assess what equality measures offer the best options, and to establish criteria for the subsequent selection and assessment of measures and goals. Monitoring and evaluation are very labour-intensive activities. However, numerous external sources of information and agencies exist to help (see addresses in appendix 3). Even with external assistance, if the right choices are to be made it is nevertheless crucial for an organization to involve itself fully in this effort and take full responsibility for the final decision.

Equality in employment will henceforth be an indispensable element of business development. If an equal opportunities programme is to be successful, not only must the necessary skills and training be available, but the project must also take into account the human resources available to the company and their various responses to such a programme. Participation in equal opportunities decision-making is vital to the success of the policy. Special emphasis is thus placed on the way companies cope with involving staff to ensure that equal opportunities becomes a part of the everyday life of an organization. Essentially, communication plays an important part in the management of equality programmes, particularly as the many disciplines involved in a successful programme give rise to a number of interfaces. Perhaps a major spin-off from involvement in the Opportunity 2000 campaign will be the chance for more companies and individuals to gain some hands-on experience of good equal opportunities in practice.

Whether or not an organization is already experienced in the area of equal opportunities, the benefits to be gained from participation in Opportunity 2000 include:

- Recognition as a good-practice employer in the field of equal opportunities for women; thus attracting the best recruits who share the commitment.
- The good economic sense of offering equal opportunities for women. Failing to provide such measures represents economic waste.
- Access through the Opportunity 2000 network to support, information and advice which will be specifically designed to meet the needs of member organizations.
- The opportunity to share and build on the experience and good practice of other member organizations.

At the heart of any measure which seeks to redress inequality in the workforce lie the formal and informal channels of communication. The increase in good practice likely to be brought about through Opportunity 2000 will be testimony to the value of communication. For too long now ideas about business success have been wrapped up in economic efficiency and productivity, which has given little consideration to the human potential which enabled such success in the first place. Business is all about interaction between people, which highlights the fact that the thriving enterprise of tomorrow will need to have two finely balanced and intercommunicating brains: a left hemisphere for management, profitability, productivity and finance, and a right hemisphere for sensitivity, intuition and equality. Hence the dependence of the present-day businessman or businesswoman, if he or she is to succeed, on his or her ability to communicate. Ultimately, business and communication constitute two links of a single chain and to break one is to break the whole.

Improved Internal and External Communications through Opportunity 2000

Here again, all the research being undertaken by Opportunity 2000 members and all the discoveries in the realm of equality are of vital importance, because the concept of communication embraces content, which is the basis of the left hemisphere, and the relational aspect, which is the basis of the right. As far as putting these discoveries into practice is concerned, Opportunity 2000 will be a focal point of future discussion. Opportunity 2000 consists in teaching or re-teaching us to utilize what is already available: women. The future success of firms will hinge upon the progressive utilization of their workers. Companies which have risen to the challenge of Opportunity 2000 will inevitably stand a greater chance of market success than those who ignore it.

Opportunity 2000 will assist employers in their recruitment and selection procedures. Selection itself is a creative act. In the past, there has been an abundance of non-creative decision-makers hidebound by white male tunnel vision, who based their appraisal of an individual on a set of criteria labelled objective but really the product of a sexist environment and acting as a guillotine to any originality. Opportunity 2000 will encourage managers and personnel to become increasingly objective in their recruitment and promotion processes.

In addition to all the communication skills which underlie an equal opportunities programme, applying it involves another simple factor which although universally recognized is seldom adhered to: namely, the involvement of all members of an organization at all stages of implementation and future development of the equality process. The earlier such participation is encouraged the more effective the equality measures will be; and this may well be the best way to avoid or reduce the negative effects of the notorious NIH (Not Invented Here) syndrome. Experience shows that even the most ridiculous or hackneyed idea may have a positive thread, however tenuous it may be, which in turn leads to a more positive commitment to the development of equality.

In conclusion, it should be remembered that everyone, and especially those within an organization who are directly responsible for the implementation of measures at the centre of Opportunity 2000, has a creative potential that is infinitely greater than the potential s/he actually uses. This potential can be released by encouraging as much participation as possible in the development of Opportunity 2000 in the workplace.

Part III

Equal Opportunities in the European Community

6
European Equality Initiatives

European Equality

What has the Single European Market got to do with equal opportunities? Quite a lot if you are a woman hoping for increased equality at work, or a disabled person hoping for better access to the labour market, or an older person concerned with age-related issues such as pensions and retirement. This is because Community action programmes have been developed for greater equality for women, the disabled and older people. These are some of the potential benefits of the process that began with the signing of the Treaty of Rome in 1957. The Treaty established a European Community in which there would be freedom of movement and equality of opportunity. The Treaty set up four institutions to implement its provisions throughout the European Community: the European Parliament, the Council of Ministers, the European Commission and the European Court of Justice.

One of the main objectives of the European Commission, which is charged with ensuring that the provisions of the Treaty of Rome are implemented, is to improve the living and working conditions of all the 340 million people who reside in the 12 member countries. The main problem facing minority groups in the European Community has been identified as that of equality: equality between men and women, between disabled and non-disabled, between older and younger people, etc. The European Community has quickly recognized that the success of its economic, social and structural policies will depend in no small way on its equal opportunities policy.

The headlines that swept across the newspapers of the European Community on 10 December 1991, after the Maastricht Summit, mainly referred to the grand designs for political, economic and monetary union that had been mapped out by the heads of state and government during the two days of negotiation. Much was made of the UK's opting out of the social protocol to the Treaty. The absence of unanimous support bodes ill for the success of some of the proposals. The 11 other Member States have agreed to be bound by its provisions, which include as general principles:

- The promotion of employment, improved living conditions and working conditions.
- Proper social protection.
- The development of human resources with a view to lasting employment.
- Equal treatment for men and women.

EC Directives on Equal Opportunities

The Community has so far adopted five Directives on equality of opportunity for men and women (for a summary, see appendix 1, table 1). Together, they have helped to promote statutory rights and obligations in the Member States – and have thus helped to reinforce individual rights and promote significant changes in procedures and terms relating to employment. As a result the Community has an advanced legal framework relating to equal opportunities.

The five Directives are:

1. The Equal Pay Directive: the obligation to apply the principle of 'Equal pay for work of equal value'.
2. The Equal Treatment Directive: prohibiting all sex-based discrimination in employment. By implication it guarantees equal treatment with regard to recruitment, vocational training and promotion.
3. The Social Security Directive: providing for equal treatment in social security schemes. If effectively applied and monitored this is encouraging news for older workers and people considering retirement.
4. The Occupational Social Security Schemes Directive: providing for equal treatment in occupational social security schemes (see discussion of the Barber case in chapter 2).
5. The Self-Employment Directive: providing for equal treatment in self-employment.

Besides the five Directives the Community has set up a series of 11 networks of equality with responsibilities in each Member State. They are called EC equality networks, and their creation forms a part of a series of practical measures designed to promote equality. The four main aims of the networks are:

1 The exchange of contacts.
2 The exchange of information.
3 The development of awareness initiatives.
4 The provision of financial support for positive action.

The Internal Market

As the completion of the internal market moves into its final stage, many adjustments will be needed – in the main, to improve the competitiveness of the Community's businesses and economy. In order to achieve this new competitiveness, Europe will need a qualified labour force, and the importance and contributions of minority groups cannot be overstated.

Women still tend to be concentrated mainly in low skilled and unstable employment. There is also a visible divergence in the unemployment rates of men and women within the community (7 per cent and 12 per cent respectively).

To achieve the fullest possible integration of disabled persons in the labour market measures must be taken in respect of vocational integration and rehabilitation. Numerous practical steps must likewise be taken, such as improving accessibility, transport and mobility.

In Europe more than 65 million people are over 60 years old. The European Community has recognized the importance of this group by adopting a Community Action Programme for Older People; and by a number of Community measures which, indirectly, have an impact on older people.

The Treaty of Rome that created the European Community is unique amongst international treaties because it grants rights from which Community nationals may directly benefit. These rights include the right not to be discriminated against on the basis of nationality, the right to work in another Member State of the community, whether you are unemployed or self-employed, and the right to provide services in another Member State. However, it is important to realize that these rights are granted only to EC nationals. There are about 13 million migrants living in the countries of the EC. The total population is 340 million. Among the migrant population about eight million are nationals of non-Member States (generally referred to as third-country nationals). The large majority of third-country nationals live in Germany, France and the UK.

The aims of the internal market are to remove the barriers to trade between countries, such as frontiers, bureaucracy, and different laws and standards. This is to ensure freedom of movement between member countries of people, goods, services and capital. To overcome the pitfalls of a deregulated Europe on minority ethnic lives, it is important to know what the pitfalls are:

- Legal protection from discrimination in the EC Member States is minimal. The UK is the only member country with a Race Relations Act.
- There is a Europe-wide strengthening of immigration control which has an adverse effect on many black and Asian lives.
- The goal of 1992 is to remove economic barriers and to create a more flexible economy. This will affect vulnerable workers unprotected by law who can be hired and fired easily. Black and ethnic minority workers feature prominently in this group.

In contrast to the EC action programmes on older people, on equal opportunities for women and on disability, there has been no equivalent action programme for gays and lesbians. Within the single market it is essential for the free movement of the labour force that homosexual and heterosexual citizens should enjoy the same legal status in all aspects.

Women in 1992

The main disadvantage for women in 1992 will be an increase in deregulated work – that is, part-time and contracted-out labour, which will directly affect the jobs where companies are tendering for contracts, like cleaning, childcare, catering and confectionery. It is in these traditional women's jobs that companies will be looking to cut hours, cut wages and employ part-time women workers on short-term contracts.

The impact of a single market on black and ethnic minority

women in the UK as in the rest of Europe is of particular concern. Legal protection from racial discrimination in the European Community is minimal. The UK is as yet the only member country to have a Race Relations Act. A major problem is passports – there are many people who have UK resident status but who do not have British passports. Particularly in Asian families it is often the women who are in this situation. These groups are going to find it much more difficult to move around as freely as other groups will be able to.

Britain's childcare provision is believed to be among the worst in Europe. In Denmark, Belgium and France, care for three- to five-year-olds is free. The government and the Confederation of British Industry (CBI) state that the cost of better childcare is too high. However, our strongest competitors, Germany, Italy, France and Belgium, all provide childcare, and better maternity provision, and it has not made them uneconomic. Moreover, it is an investment in both good labour relations and industry.

These are the issues that need to be addressed if women are to benefit from a single market. Some issues have been incorporated into the European Charter of Social Rights including: the rights of freedom of movement of workers, social benefits, fair wages, vocational training in the firm's time, and equal treatment for men and women. Britain is the only Member State to oppose the Social Charter. While adoption of the Social Charter by the UK would guarantee certain legal rights, it would still be only one way of tackling the structural problems that women face in the world of work.

The Third Equal Opportunities Programme for Men and Women, 1991–1995

The main areas within this programme are discussed below.

1 Development of the legal framework

The Commission is responsible for ensuring that the Member States incorporate the five Directives on equal treatment in their national laws. In addition to acting as the Community 'watchdog', the Commission will promote increased implementation of the laws on equal opportunities through the EC equality networks.

Several other proposals are in the process of being brought

forward. These include improving the current job classification schemes which are supposed to ensure that work of equal value undertaken by men and women is rewarded in the same way. In addition, improved parental leave (paternal as well as maternal) is likely to be introduced in the long term at least in some Member States. It was recognized at the time of the first Community programme on equal opportunities (1982–1985) that parental leave should be one component of such a programme. The modest aim was that either parent (but not both) should have a right to three months' leave to care for a new child, and that workers should have limited right to time off for urgent family reasons such as the illness of a child or the death of a near relative. However, Britain refused to agree to the proposal and it remains blocked.

2 *Promoting the occupational integration of women*

This second priority has particular relevance to most, if not all, organizations, as it is basically the incorporation of the principles of the NOW (New Opportunities for Women) programme. The NOW programme is a Community initiative which has been developed to promote vocational training and employment for women. The programme aims to ensure that women benefit from the economic growth which will follow the consolidation of the single market. To this end the Community will support moves to promote women in employment. These include moves:

- To enable more women to create their own businesses.
- To assist the re-integration of women into the labour market.
- To support measures for the provision of careers advice and guidance for long-term unemployed women, as well as for young unqualified women.
- To support a wide range of training courses for women.
- To assist in the provision of childcare facilities, which will allow more women to participate in training and employment while at the same time increasing the number of qualified workers.
- To undertake new initiatives to increase positive action ensuring equal opportunities for women within organizations – to ensure that they are represented in traditional male jobs as well as managerial positions.
- To support women's studies and related studies in Member States. In June 1989 a European Network of Women's Studies (ENWS) was approved by the Council of Europe and is represented in each Member State.

3 Improving the status of women

This final priority was introduced to counteract prejudice and discrimination against women outside employment. It has repeatedly been shown that women are as likely to suffer from the effects of discrimination in their free time as within the workplace. The Commission therefore intends to pursue steps through the Community media networks to improve the way in which the media portray women, and to promote training which challenges traditional female stereotypes. These and many other measures will be introduced at 'street level' via an increased number of equal opportunities courses supported by the Commission.

Organizational Involvement – The Possibilities Discussed

There are many ways in which all types of organizations (particularly those involved in training) could enhance their European 'profile'. Some suggestions are outlined below.

1 Providing information

In order for many of the steps mentioned above to become a reality at local level, information will have to be collected and disseminated to local areas. To this end, employers could build a comprehensive information network to enable staff to become experts. Through liaison with groups which deal with minorities (for example, the Placing Assessment and Counselling Teams, the Spastics Society, women's groups, etc.) a library may be developed. A library could serve two interrelated purposes:

- To collect information from local and regional employers – such as ideas and suggestions from equal opportunities policies and positive-action strategies – and use it to help other employers.
- To use all the information provided to give advice on training and employment to local groups who are underrepresented in particular areas of the labour market.

2 Training

- Run courses and workshops for disadvantaged groups such as people with disabilities, long-term unemployed women, ethnic minorities and ex-offenders.

- Provide training for women wishing to return to work after a long interruption due to family responsibilities.
- Conduct a training needs analysis of young unqualified women, and provide appropriate training, careers guidance and placements.
- Provide rehabilitation courses for newly disabled workers.
- Run access courses for people threatened with unemployment due to 'dying' industries, or in areas where employment prospects as a whole are in decline.
- Provide information and workshops for adults approaching retirement. Liaise with local employers to target individuals and groups who may benefit from advice and help on local opportunities.
- Provide information and training for people interested in starting their own businesses, and for businesses that have recently been established.
- Run workshops on 'alternatives' – for example, cooperatives, voluntary work, working from home.
- Provide information on grants and other types of financial assistance, as well as contacts for further help and advice.
- Run pre-retirement courses for workers aged over 55.
- Conduct research in liaison with 'age officers' into demographic conditions in an area, and apply initiatives to meet the needs of the older workforce.

3 *Education and industry links*

- Encourage companies to utilize women to the full and avoid sex-stereotyping occupational roles.
- Provide information to local industry on relevant positive-action measures they could introduce, to tackle the obstacles to equality created by past discrimination in the workforce.
- Encourage more companies to allow women to participate freely in the decision-making processes at all levels within the organization, including management, trade unions, employees' organizations and equal opportunities committees.
- Emphasize the economic advantages of training and promotion for the female workforce, and indeed for any minority group.
- Supply information and training for employers on the employment of workers with disabilities, including special schemes and grants which are available.
- Introduce a campaign for older workers and older people in the community. In order to prevent age-based discrimination, encourage local industry to recruit and train older people.

1992: A Checklist for Trainers and Personnel

By definition, a trainer is always at the leading edge of knowledge, information and skills. The leading edge in the future will be European, not, as in the past, national. The recently established Training and Enterprise Councils (TECs) in the UK have a special responsibility to equip local business communities with the necessary skills to succeed.

Some of the questions employers should address are:

- Do we need to understand the European market better? If so, how can we do so?
- What new skills are needed?
- Do we need to understand the concepts underlying the detail of the single-market legislative programme?
- What impact will the EC action programmes on the elderly, disability, and equal opportunities for men and women have on the organization?
- How may we implement the action programmes here?
- Are we truly reflecting the needs of our trainees?
- Are we a European business or a national one?
- What will the exact impact on our organization be?
- Will we need a different mix of skills?
- Will we need to recruit more broadly? Incorporate language skills?
- What are our competitors doing?
- How will free movement within the professions affect us?
- How should our training programmes change and adapt to Europe?
- How should we plan our training to meet the needs of the growing number of older people in society?
- Are we a good equal opportunities role model? Or are we not?

Equality Issues in the Single European Market

Sex discrimination and equal opportunities

If women are to benefit equally with men from the effects of the single market there are plenty of good role-models that can be extended to EC legislation and policy: for instance, the Italian law which states that the employees of a sub-contractor must receive wages as high as those of the primary employees; the German law which gives all home-workers the full status of employees; and the French statutory minimum-wage system. Without exception throughout the Member States more women than men are engaged in part-time work associated with low remuneration employments, so these incentives should be universally adopted if women are to receive equal benefits. Ireland has as recently as 1991 introduced legislation which enabled an extension to the existing benefits to regular part-time workers; the Worker Protection (Regular Part-Time Employees) Act was introduced into Irish law in 1991. In practice, this ensures that employees in continuous service of the same employer for 13 weeks or more may now enjoy the full benefits of various laws which previously only applied to full-time workers. At the moment these include the Unfair Dismissals Act, the Minimum Notice and Terms of Employment Acts and the Worker Participation Acts. However, in the near future it is intended to increase their benefits and rights under still more legislation including the Redundancy Payments Acts, Maternity Acts and the Protection of Employees Acts.

There has been a marked tendency in the past to regard unemployment and measures to reduce it as a genderless issue. Overall job creation has been regarded as more crucial than selective job creation targeted to specific socially disadvantaged groups. However, there is evidence which suggests that the characteristics of male and female unemployment vary enormously. Segregation by sex into traditional male or female occupational areas is still prevalent. For instance, occupational training fields such as engineering and construction are heavily male-dominated, whereas clerical jobs, nursing and the rag trade are female-dominated. Furthermore, similar differences also exist in the patterns of female and male unemployment. Throughout Europe, almost without exception, women represent the main victims of long-term unemployment. The rates are particularly high for young women and women approaching standard retirement ages. Unemployed men and women come from entirely different sectors of the labour market – with far more women than men coming from the service industries.

The problem of entry into employment or return to employment is a problem which again more women than men face. If women are not registered they are often not entitled to the usual services for the unemployed, such as job clubs. If the figures for female unemployment in the EC are to be reduced and the neglect of the workforce potential of women is not to be jeopardized, a uniform employment policy for both men and women is insufficient. Political strategies at all levels must at least in part be focused on the target groups of young women, older women, women returning to work and unemployed women. Increasingly, EC countries are providing special measures for groups of unemployed, with particular emphasis on unemployed women. In general, there have been two quite distinct approaches. One approach has been to implement policies aimed at vocational training and guidance with a view to increasing women's chances at job opportunities. The other has been to provide access courses and return-to-work programmes aimed at women who have spent time out of the labour market caring for their families. The UK has tried a combined approach, and both local and national initiatives have been developed towards increasing the opportunities available to a wide range of women with different needs. Fortunately, many such courses have gone some way towards breaking down oppressively traditional occupational barriers which have by their very nature kept women in low-status roles. Furthermore, much of the training has moved beyond the common stereotypes of what constitutes women's work and as such has incorporated engineering, motor mechanics, building work, etc.

The high rate of unemployment among women has led all Member States to deploy a variety of measures to stimulate employment and reduce unemployment. Some countries are far more advanced in their political approach and commitment than others. In the North of the Community employers have reacted favourably to introducing positive-action programmes to redress the imbalances of past discrimination. The major criticisms of such schemes throughout Europe have centred on the question of just how realistic the schemes actually are. Several of the schemes are particularly attractive to women as they have in-built creche and childcare services to enable more women to attend; however, the problems women have had in finding suitable employment at the end of such training schemes have been compounded by the overall lack of childcare facilities in the 'real world'. Although such attempts to target women and increase their participation in employment are laudable they do not necessary reflect the real situation in the wider labour market. This suggests that the political approach and options need to be expanded and diversified to tackle the root causes of female unemployment. By the end of the third equal opportunities programme the employment of women and employment policies for parents should be improved.

A lot may be achieved as part of a childcare programme within the context of the third equal opportunities programme. A European

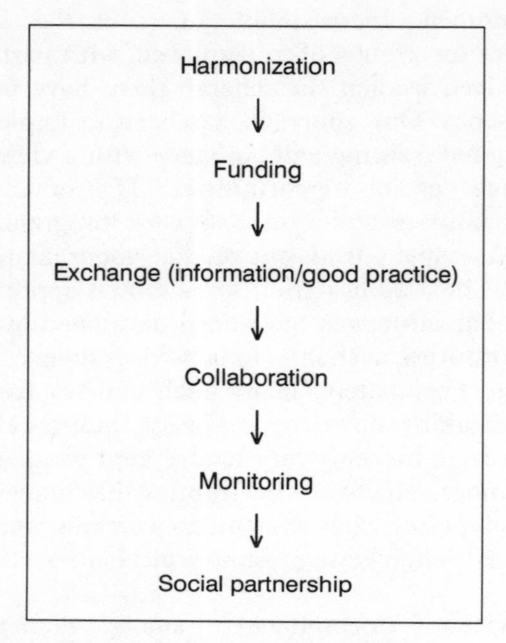

Figure 6.1 The six-stage childcare programme

dimension on the development of childcare policies requires work at local, national and European levels. The European level includes six main stages of work. The six stages are each part of a continuous interrelated process which allows for information to be collected and disseminated and improvements made. The six-stage childcare programme is outlined in figure 6.1. Let us take a look at each stage.

Harmonization This relates to unifying the objectives of the Commission's Directives on Parental Leave. The EC network believes that basic minimum standards should be established in each member country for each of the four main employment rights for parents. They are: maternity leave, paternity leave, parental leave and leave for family reasons. Harmonization should also be sought for the objectives of childcare programmes. Member States have developed different systems and there are wide variations both in the level of practical provision and in available funding. Whichever method a country adopts or develops, it should cover childcare issues from all angles including: the development of locally based high quality services for *all* children, regardless of their parents' income, their own age and the number of children in family; the expansion of publicly funded provision in equal measures in urban and rural communities; and not least, the assurance of equality of access for all children from all backgrounds to all services. In the past, there has been a tendency for tax incentives and high-cost childcare to act as disincentives for parents on lower incomes. Diversity in methods of service throughout member countries or throughout local and regional provision is not a problem as long as overall objectives are standarized and met.

Funding Structured funding can be used to support the development of childcare services. In the past evidence has pointed to the ineffectiveness of funds allocated to childcare in so far as the results achieved have fallen well short of the results intended. Obviously, it is important that funds which are earmarked for childcare services actually have a noticeable impact on the communities they are meant for. Central funds have to be allocated according to the proportion of children in each Member State's population. Likewise, local authorities ought to have equivalent amounts of cash in their childcare budgets. Geographical areas with a high proportion of lone parents and socially disadvantaged groups may require additional funding. National parliaments have a duty to set down minimum standards with regard to the level of service and budget control for local authorities. Above all, a measure of consistency is crucial to ensure that past discrepancies in funding between areas are avoided.

Exchange (information/good practice) Childcare provision in each Member State should not be regarded as simply a national issue with regional implications. Good practice and successful developments ought not be confined to a single country's policies and provision; not least because it is of enormous potential benefit to other member countries to learn from others and amend their existing methods. The dissemination and exchange of information and experience should be encouraged. Research projects, reports and their recommendations have an international relevance, and should be widely accessible to both employers and parents in the EC.

Collaboration Collaboration is very closely linked to exchange in so far as both processes may be achieved on a number of levels. Similarly, there are enormous potential benefits to be gained from cross-national or inter-regional collaborative work, including research, policy, action projects, lobbying, political campaigning, etc. Successful collaboration depends on the free exchange of information, experience, policy and the success or failure rate of recommendations as well as the national political will to learn from each other. The major potential benefit from collaborative work is the Europe-wide overall increase in good practice within the field of family and employment responsibilities.

Monitoring In order for any system to work effectively it has to be frequently reviewed and assessed. History has proven that laws and policies alone are not sufficient catalysts in initiating good practice. The Commission together with each member country has a vital role to play in monitoring childcare practices and services. In particular, special attention should be given to the employment rights of parents and employment policies which affect parental employment. Monitoring is the principal method whereby shortfalls in funding and provision can be highlighted and ultimately corrected. Surveys have an invaluable part to play in providing this sort of information. A Europe-wide survey of households with children would be the most accurate way of finding out about the real needs of working parents and their children, as well as about the methods/solutions that they feel are necessary to improve the overall situation. A survey of employers would reveal details about a whole range of issues, including not least attitudes to workers with children and workplace policies which affect parents' rights.

Social partnership Again this relates to collaboration and exchange of information and good practice. Social partners, geographical partners, and regional twinned partners should be encouraged to include childcare issues in the social dialogue and policy at a European level. A collective voice on childcare issues on a European scale ought to have a significant impact on future trends.

Race equality and racial discrimination

Despite the lack of a formal mandate, the European Community has taken a number of human rights initiatives since its inception, on the grounds that 'the construction of Europe is not only a matter of economics.' The Community institutions (the Parliament, Council and Commission) have signed two Joint Declarations: a very brief one in 1977, which requires them to respect human rights and fundamental freedoms; and a second in 1986, against racism and xenophobia. The Declaration against Racism and Xenophobia was adopted in 1986 by the European Parliament, the Council representatives and representatives of the Member States and the Commission. Later, in 1988, the European Commission went as far as to propose a formal but non-binding Resolution on Racism and Xenophobia, coupled with an action programme including educational measures to promote intercultural understanding. However, the Resolution which was finally passed by the Council in 1990 had been so watered down that Vasso Papandreou, the Commissioner responsible for proposing it, disassociated herself from the wording.

A report with over 70 recommendations has been drawn up by MEP Glyn Ford, called the Ford Report. It was drawn up on behalf of the Committee of Inquiry into Racism and Xenophobia in Europe and published in 1991. The report focuses on the general trend in national and international policies in both the Twelve Member States and non-EC European countries. The Ford Report concentrates on the need to promote anti-discriminatory behaviour in the European Community. It examines the portrayal of minority ethnic groups in education and within the media and recommends ways of harmonizing relations between all communities resident in Europe. By no means all of the recommendations have been acted upon by the European Parliament or its more powerful sister organizations, the Council of Ministers and the European Commission. In fact, very few of the recommendations have been paid the attention they deserve and few have been implemented. However, as a result of the report there have been some positive developments. A Migrants Forum and a Racism Working Group to monitor action throughout the Community have been established. The conclusions and recommendations of the Ford Report were formally voted upon and adopted by the Council of Inquiry in 1991. The report is intended to initiate real progress on the Joint Declaration against Racism signed in 1986.

The recommendations made to the Member States included:

- That an anti-discrimination law be drawn up condemning all racist acts.
- That member countries take measures to enable the immigrant population to gain legal status as residents and workers within a specified period of time.
- That Member States encourage rehabilitation programmes to improve the living conditions in metropolitan areas with large minority ethnic populations.

- That Member States step up the support that education can provide in the campaign against racism.
- That Member States set up systems responsible for monitoring the strict application of all legislation concerned with promoting racial harmony.
- That youth exchange programmes be promoted in the European Community to create an awareness among young people of past and present forms of racism, anti-Semitism and fascism.
- That Member States encourage full and active participation by immigrant workers in trade union activity.

There is a need for collaboration between organizations across Europe which are involved in promoting effective race relations and combating discrimination. There are huge potential benefits to be gained from exchange, including mutual support, shared experiences and action programmes. The message is clear: without extra help from central sources (the EC and national parliaments), already overstrained social, medical and housing services and underfunded educational and employment opportunities for all communities will soon be no longer able to cope, resulting in a real danger of an upswing in ethnic tensions and racism. Immigration issues have for too long now been regarded by policymakers as temporary problems which have thus merited little more than cursory attention. Ethnic minority groups are an established part of the EC Community who for far too long have suffered from inequality in education, employment and practically all social benefits enjoyed by the majority white population.

The benefits of affirmative action have traditionally been fairly narrowly interpreted as benefiting only the target groups; their benefits to society at large have been grossly overlooked. Positive-action programmes aimed at, for instance, reducing unemployment in ethnic minority communities have been regarded with cynicism in many quarters. They have been seen as favouritism, tokenism, unfair and unequal in practice. The central fact that these groups have experienced the worst kinds of social disadvantage has been overlooked in favour of using ethnic minorities as scapegoats for many of society's problems.

Disability

The situation with regard to European citizens with disabilities has moved a long way since the end of the World Wars. EC action for the disabled has been as significant as action on sex discrimination and the needs of older Europeans. Community initiatives for the disabled are relatively far advanced in comparison with those for other disadvantaged groups. Horizon, EUROFORM and NOW are three Community initiatives set up in connection with the reform of the Community Structural Funds (now called the European Social Fund or ESF for short). The Horizon programme aims to ease the way for 'handicapped and other disadvantaged people' to find a place in the labour market. Support from the European Regional Development Fund is assisting Horizon towards implementing its aims throughout the Member States.

The social and economic integration into society of disabled people is a vital component of the social dimension of the Single Market. It is not merely a question of social justice and human dignity; it is an economic issue in so far as their occupational integration represents an asset for the whole of society.

The first HELIOS (Handicapped People Living Independently in an Open Society) programme was adopted by the Council of Ministers in 1988 and represented a practical response to the needs of more than 30 million community citizens suffering from long-term physical and mental disabilities. The HELIOS programme established for the first time in the EC a framework for the development of an overall policy to promote the integration of disabled people. The first action programmes for people with disabilities were introduced in 1981, and have been greatly strengthened by the creation of the HELIOS programme in 1988.

Because of the essential need to continue to step up overall policy at European levels, a third Community action programme for disabled people has been developed and will span the period 1992–1996. The advent of this new EC action programme for disabled people (the third programme, but only the second HELIOS programme), from 1992 to 1996, provides the opportunity to reflect the interests of disabled people – within the framework of a major EC Social Affairs initiative. HELIOS II has prioritized two main activities:

- Vocational rehabilitation and economic integration; and
- Social integration and independent living (IL).

The HELIOS programme is designed to complement action taken at national levels. The EC is committed to full integration of disabled people into all aspects of life. Ultimately however, the main responsibilities for the social integration and independent way of living of disabled people lies with member countries. The cooperation and support they receive at EC level should assist the Twelve to improve and coordinate the measures they seek to implement.

Listed below are four of the measures which have been incorporated:

- Start-up assistance for services designed to help the disabled gain access to the labour market. In practice this can mean developing or adapting work transport, modifying premises, providing a reader service for a blind person, etc.
- Financial help towards adaptations of premises, and facilitating ease of circulation in buildings. For example, widening an entrance doorway to enable access by wheelchairs, or installing public toilets on the ground floor of an office block, etc.
- Further creation of vocational training centres.
- Dissemination and exchange of information and experience which relates to disability issues.

In addition to the provisions of HELIOS, early in 1991 a Directive on the mobility and transport to work of employees with reduced mobility was adopted by the Council of Ministers and called the Directive on Mobility. The legislation sets out minimum standards for public transport as well as transport which is arranged directly by employers and special transport for disabled workers. The latter might include transport, such as mini coaches and vans furnished with hoists, lifts and ramps for ease of access of employees with physical disabilities. A Council Directive has the effect, once adopted, of requiring Member States to enact legislation. The Directive therefore has a definite impact on UK legislators. It is certainly a welcome development for workers with reduced mobility and will at the very least bring increased public scrutiny to bear on government policies in this area. In addition, governments will be prevented from allowing provision to fall below the minimum requirements set out in the Directive. Supportive amendments to the Directive ought to include an extension in adaptations to cover all transport, not just certain categories of transport. Disabled people have social and personal lives as well as working lives and their transport needs should not be confined to provision for an average of eight hours a day. A second amendment ought to extend the groups able to oversee the implementation of the Directive, since problems have traditionally arisen when the legislation has been in place but has had a largely symbolic effect due to a lack of enforcement.

Handynet is an information system on medical and mobility aids for people with disabilities which was set up under the Horizon initiative as one of the many HELIOS activities. Handynet has made a significant contribution towards improving the integration of disabled people, since technical aids constitute an indispensable factor in the process both of training and employment. They also promote the autonomous living and mobility of members of this group.

The specific problems of disabled workers have long been recognized, if not vastly improved. However, the concept of the term 'worker' needs to be expanded. Many people with disabilities are *not* workers, solely because of society's prejudice, not because they are disabled. While an awareness of the needs of disabled people is brought about through their increased participation in the labour market, the needs of unemployed people with disabilities still need to be seriously addressed. All too often, potentially excellent workers are unemployed due to prejudice and fear of their disability. The Social Charter endorses the rights of all disabled people, so the needs of both employed and unemployed disabled people should be catered for.

Age discrimination

Throughout Europe, discrimination against people on the basis of age is equally prevalent in employment and in social benefits. The Social Charter includes the elderly in its remit and establishes a number of proposals for Member States to adopt. Eurolink Age is a Europe-wide network concerned with older people and the issues of ageing. It is involved in lobbying for improvements, disseminating information, and research projects, and is represented in all of the Member States.

The 'over 60s' account for an increasingly high percentage of the European population. In the past the vast majority of older citizens have been disadvantaged in a number of ways, and the attitude at government level has all too often been one of neglect.

In order for older people to gain maximum social and economic support an EC action programme has been adopted and was formally launched in mid 1991. The launch focused on a number of themes including the social integration of older people and the specific roles of government and non-governmental organizations. The programme has coincided with increased political activity at

EC level on age-related issues. To facilitate the implementation of the programme, 1993 has been designated as the European Year for Elderly People. In addition, the European Commission is building up a database of information on Europe-wide organizations and projects which are concerned with older people, with a view to a possible EC network of action projects.

One of the most welcome results of the Commission's commitment is a necessary increase in national levels of commitment. It has put pressure on Member States to take account of the needs of older people in existing and future social legislation, and emphasizes that a far greater effort should be made on the part of member governments to identify the needs of older people in society and make effective provision to cater for those needs.

The social dimensions of 1992, social integration, and further development of the structural funds are given quite extensive priority in the programme – all of which have a direct impact upon the lives of older people. It is evident that an ever-growing number of EC issues and legal proposals have a bearing on the lives and livelihood of older people. The need to act on the various EC initiatives in the interest of the 100 million older people in the EC is acute. Some of the steps being taken are discussed below.

Telecommunications and Information Technology for Elderly People (fortunately abbreviated to TIDE) is aimed at the socio-economic integration of disabled and elderly persons. Key priorities of the TIDE programme include developing appropriate technology for the working environment as well as rehabilitation technology. Ultimately it is intended that more older people will benefit from a much more widespread use of new technology.

The advent of the new HELIOS programme in 1992 provides an enormous opportunity for the EC to promote the interests of the almost 70 per cent of disabled people who are also elderly. HELIOS is expected to follow a similar pattern to its predecessor in that one of its main priorities will be proposals concerned with social integration and independent living. It is to be hoped that the policies within the HELIOS programme will reflect the specific needs of older disabled people. There is a risk that their needs will be submerged in a general grouping rather than receiving the independent, permanent representation which they require.

EURAGE and EURODEM are two research programmes on age-related issues which are currently underway. The former project relates to ageing and health, with a specific emphasis on age-related diseases. EURODEM is based on epidemiology and the prevention of dementia. It is also involved in researching the range of care systems available for elderly people.

The case for collaboration between such research projects on a European as well as a national level is strong, given the high incidence of diseases related to ageing and the demographic trend towards large numbers of older people. The social cooperation in these issues is important if medical developments are to ensure the wellbeing of older people.

Two other ESF initiatives will indirectly affect the lives of older people, particularly older workers. The New Opportunities for Women (NOW) programme concentrates on the development of vocational training and employment of women. The programme aims to improve equality and equal opportunities between men and women in employment, training and education as well as seeking to ensure that women benefit equally with men from the projected economic growth of the single market. EUROFORM aims to benefit the long-term unemployed throughout the Community and as such will have an impact on older female employees, who are a traditionally high-risk group in the labour market.

Sexuality

In contrast to the EC programmes on age, disability and equal opportunities for men and women, no such measure for gays and lesbians is included in the Social Charter. It has long been recognized that the EC is becoming an ever-increasing focus of political power, and that campaigns for equality have to move beyond national borders in that direction too. Acting without the relative empathy which other disadvantaged groups have received from society, the lesbian and gay movement on its own will have to persuade the EC that homosexuality is an issue it ought similarly to address.

The situation with regard to homosexual equality issues highlights very clearly just where the real power lies in the European spectrum. The European Parliament has repeatedly stated its commitment to homosexual equality, but it has very little political strength. In contrast, the European Commission and the Council of Ministers have much more power but lack the political will to direct it towards the promotion of lesbian and gay rights.

Problems facing homosexuals throughout the Member States are numerous. Lack of protection from violence and harassment is a European-wide problem. Differences in ages of consent and in family rights for homosexuals and heterosexuals perpetuate the discrimination. Lack of legal recognition of same-sex partnerships can restrict freedom of movement in addition to other social and economic disadvantages.

A central theme throughout the EC Charter of Fundamental Social Rights for Workers is the Equal Treatment Directive and the right to freedom of movement. Within the single market it is essential for the free movement of the labour force that all citizens regardless of their sexuality should have equal status in respect of migration, employment and social benefits. If this is not enforced, very many economically active gays and lesbians will be restricted in both their search for, and promotion in work. The following issues ought to be addressed:

- Rights of residence with partners. In practice, this means that domestic, housing, social security and immigration rights should be the same for gays and lesbians as for heterosexuals.
- Freedom of movement for partners. There is a tendency for far more problems to be faced by homosexual couples with regard to gaining citizenship and immigration rights; largely because they are not recognized by law in the same way as heterosexual couples are, by marriage, for instance. This should be agreed upon centrally to ensure that partnerships that are legal in one Member State retain their legal status in any other of the Twelve. A uniform approach is essential.
- The right of equal access to state social security funds including sickness, injury allowances and pensions.
- The right to non-discrimination on the grounds of sex orientation. This is currently under development in a small number of Member States but there needs to be a far more widespread commitment.

Most of these issues are interlinked; not least because they serve to highlight the traditional rights that heterosexual family relationships have enjoyed for a long time. In most laws and policies the concept of the family is referred to and catered for in terms of a traditional heterosexist concept. The concept and the context of 'family' ought to be extended to include all kinds of partnerships that make up units within society. In fact, since the family concept has been traditionally oppressive to women in general, and gays and lesbians in particular, the units ought to be re-defined to incorporate 'home' responsibilities, leave for home reasons, etc.; which reflects a broader range of lifestyles than the traditional 'family life'.

There is enormous potential for initiatives in this area to be developed by the EC. First of all, it is important actually to recognize legally the existence of gays and lesbians in society. That might sound very obvious, but few laws have succeeded in incorporating measures designed to protect the existence of the substantial minority in the Community who are gay and lesbian. Approximately one in ten people in the EC is gay or lesbian; such a large number of people should therefore be recognized alongside everyone else in the policies, laws and action programmes associated with the single market.

The EC has to establish a firm commitment to non-discrimination legislation for gays and lesbians. This should be supported by equality programmes on lesbian and gay rights and awareness-raising comparable to the firmly established equal opportunities programme for women (NOW). Furthermore, the EC ought to set itself up as a role model for homosexual equality, and to this end should include sexuality in its own employment and equal opportunities policies. This would put pressure on national parliaments to conform.

Sexual harassment and the dignity of men and women at work traditionally refers exclusively to women. Although the majority of sexual harassment is indeed suffered by women it is too generalized a concept as such. Protection from harassment on the grounds of sexuality is an equally valid entitlement which laws should endorse.

The EC is growing in power, status and influence. It is forecast that an increasing number of the laws which affect our lives will be decided at the European level rather than at national levels. Already almost 40 per cent of UK legislation originates from Brussels and that is likely to grow to a much higher figure by the end of this century. In view of this, all equality issues affecting all disadvantaged groups need lobbying at European levels as well as national.

Progress which should have been made in the field of homosexual equality has been hampered by lack of commitment from the major decision-makers. In 1984, the European Parliament agreed to the Squarcialupi Report. The report came about as a direct result of successful campaigning by lesbian and gay groups. Its main recommendations were that all the 12 states should establish common ages of consent for heterosexual and homosexual sex. In addition to this it recommended that the EC should prohibit workplace discrimination against lesbians and gay men. Seven years later, neither recommendation has been implemented.

In 1986, the European Parliament called on each national government within the EC to ban discrimination which is based on sex, marital status and (for the first time) sex orientation. Almost without exception in the Member States this has not got beyond the recommendation stage. Two EC countries (Denmark and France) have specific laws forbidding discrimination against lesbians and gay men, while the constitution of the Netherlands gives protection against any form of discrimination. Comprehensive legislation against such discrimination is being proposed in the Belgian and Dutch parliaments. Laws against public insults and incitement to hatred on the grounds of sexual orientation exist in Denmark and Ireland.

Yet more support from the European Parliament was implemented in 1989 through the Buron Report on the Social Charter. The report included the anti-discrimination proposal that all employees throughout the EC should be entitled to equal protection irrespective of their sexuality and sexual orientation.

All three of these recommendations in support of lesbian and gay equality have been largely ignored by the EC's main decision-making bodies; notably the European Commission and the Council of Ministers. Though the European Parliament is the single democratically elected EC institution, it is essentially little more than an advisory organization. In contrast, the European Commission is not democratically elected and consists of appointed representatives from each of the 12 countries. It has the power to initiate and enforce all EC legislation. However, the real power lies with the Council of Ministers: this group alone can override the wishes of both the European Parliament and the European Commission.

Positive developments have taken place in a number of EC countries, but on nowhere near the scale that is required. The EC representatives have been a little more encouraging in their support in the last few years. The usual tendency has been to 'group' people together on a general legal basis and to interpret narrowly the needs of specific minority groups. Certainly at the moment homosexual rights do not rate very highly on either the EC or national parliamentary agendas. Historically, however, most changes and improvements in the laws relating to sexuality have been initiated by the combined efforts of gays and lesbians themselves. On this basis, it seems that future prospects for change will have to be campaigned for by the gay community itself. Gay marches and the annual 'Pride' events focus public and media attention on the issues.

In theory these events ought to put pressure on parliaments to enact the changes in the law that are necessary. At all levels – international, national and local – there are hundreds of groups lobbying for equality and full gay rights.There is therefore a responsibility on elected governments to provide the impetus to improve.

The Three Major EC Human Resource Initiatives

Community Initiatives are one of the three instruments available to the Commission to influence the Member States' structural operations affecting employment. The new Initiatives came about as a result of reform of the structural funds; widening the range in this manner has enabled the Commission to put detail into the development of employment policy within the European Community.

Three structural funds finance projects in the Community; they are:

- The European Social Fund (ESF)
- The European Regional Development Fund (ERDF)
- The European Agricultural Guidance and Guarantee Fund (EAGGF).

On 18 July 1990, the Commission decided on the content of the three Community Initiatives in the field of human resources. The three programmes are discussed below.

EUROFORM

EUROFORM relates to the promotion of new occupational qualifications, new skills and the new employment opportunities which the Single European Market is expected to generate. Who benefits?

- The long-term unemployed and younger workers throughout the Community.
- The unemployed and those workers who are threatened by unemployment; perhaps, for instance, due to 'belonging' to a dying industry. This may, therefore, have specific relevance to older workers.
- Individuals under training, in apprenticeship schemes, for example.

The objectives of the EUROFORM programme are:

- To provide a European Community dimension for vocational training and employment development projects.
- To encourage the convergence of occupational skills, as well as the occupational and geographical mobility of workers.

EUROFORM is a transnational project: operators of the initiative may rely on regional or local technological consortia set up by all those who have responsibility in the fields of vocational training and employment policy. Therefore, the TECs have a major part to play in the dissemination of the programme at local level. Ultimately, all such operations and projects which are undertaken ought to be designed in such a way as to establish transnational partnerships and sharing of experience and expertise.

The Horizon programme

Horizon aims to improve the labour-market opportunities for marginalized sections of society and those that have suffered from the most disadvantage in their communities.

Who stands to benefit from the Horizon programme?

- People with disabilities; including workers with disabilities unemployed due to widespread myths within the workplace about the lack of ability of individuals who are subject to a handicap.
- Other disadvantaged groups. This may include the long-term unemployed, early school-leavers, and newcomers to the European labour market, such as newly arrived non-EC nationals.

The objectives of the Horizon programme are:

- To improve access for people with disabilities to the labour market, and to improve the equal opportunities 'ethos' of the workplace so as to enable more workers with disabilities to compete fairly for jobs and promotion.
- To help stimulate the integration of disadvantaged groups into the wider community and into all sectors of the labour market. The aim is also to encourage a rapid socioeconomic integration of all those individuals confronted with a socioeconomic context which is new to them.

The means for achieving the objectives of Horizon will be:

- For workers with disabilities: through the implementation of transnational projects which aim to improve access conditions to the labour market. Such projects will be operated by trainers and development agencies in order to relate to specific issues associated with the economic, social and occupational integration of this group.
- For other disadvantaged groups: through the setting up of pilot

schemes and projects within the framework of transnational partnerships. The Community aims to support the development of suitable methods; and, given the fact that the success of social policies in depressed areas depends largely on the ability to generate local participation, it will support these activities, and support the exchange of experience at the Community level.

Specific measures under the Horizon initiative will include:

- Training of trainers and other workers to assist in the transition of people with disabilities from a sheltered environment to the 'open' labour market.
- Assistance for the setting up of SMEs for workers with disabilities, and other forms of employment such as cooperatives. A fundamental part of the Horizon initiative is to ensure that all such projects are eventually capable of being fully integrated in the mainstream market economy.
- Accessibility and mobility assistance to ensure that an increased number of workers with disabilities gain access to transport facilities and building premises, thus automatically increasing their chances of success in the labour market.
- Promoting the exchange and dissemination of experience and technologies, such as rehabilitation technology, and any project which takes account of the problems of mobility in the workplace.
- The creation of vocational training centres.
- The creation and development of information systems and networks in respect to professional training and employment of workers with disabilities.

Activities for disadvantaged groups will include:

- Vocational training and counselling measures.
- Technical assistance.
- Measures to facilitate occupational integration, such as designing specific training courses or adapting existing qualifications or equivalents to the requirements of the labour market.
- Measures to be introduced or extended to improve the educational integration and settlement of children of newly arrived workers. Where applicable, language courses will be undertaken to preserve or improve mother-tongue language skills.

NOW – New Opportunities for Women

The major aim of the NOW programme is to raise issues about equal opportunities for women in employment and training.

Who will benefit from the NOW programme?

- Women who have been unemployed for more than 12 months, that is, long-term unemployed women. The NOW programme aims to address labour-market problems common to all women and emphasizes in its framework that age should be no barrier to assistance.
- Those women who are seeking to re-enter the paid labour market after a long-term absence. In practice, this includes all women who have been working in the home in childcare or other caring capacities.
- Women employed in SMEs, or in other businesses where they are threatened by unemployment. The latter could therefore apply to women in socially or economically deprived areas or to women in thriving economic areas who happen to be employed in 'dying' industries and thus need re-training to acquire new skills.
- In effect, the entire female working population will benefit directly or indirectly from the NOW programme. As women's employment issues are thrust onto political and economic agendas there is bound to be a positive spin-off at street level, and an increase in employers' commitment to equality for women in the workplace.

The main objectives of the NOW programme are:

- To assist in the upgrading and further development of women's qualifications, coupled with support towards changing the business environment to help more women set up their own businesses.
- To contribute to the re-entry of women into the paid labour market, in an effort to improve the stability and quality of work which women pursue.

How the programme will achieve the objectives:

- Through vocational training measures, including guidance and advisory and information services.
- Through assistance with the setting up of self-employed activities.
- Through other forms of assistance for related services which are designed to enable women to gain access to existing areas of employment.
- Through supplementary measures already established to enable more women to participate in the paid labour market: day nurseries, creches attached to vocational training centres, etc.
- Through technical assistance, planned to enable the support of existing measures and the transfer of experience and expertise on a cross-border scale.

The NOW programme has been set up to benefit as many women as possible. There is plenty of scope within the programme for a variety of operators to become involved with the projects. The public and private sectors should be equally encouraged through

NOW to participate, whether in training, practical measures or as information providers.

Transnational meaning of the Initiatives

All projects undertaken under the three Community Initiatives must be transnational. 'Transnational character' is reflected in the following:

- The exchange of trainers, training and those individuals involved in development work and research.
- A joint approach to each of the components of the Initiatives: projects, modules, teacher training, methodology.
- Any other activity which may beneficially 'overlap' on a cross-national basis: information, skills, successes, experience, rehabilitation technology.

Financing

The programme or grants available to each project should be the subject for joint financing by the EC and the Member State. Member States wishing to benefit from the Initiatives should present detailed proposals of programmes or grants. Further information about the kinds of local developments under the Initiatives in local areas may be obtained from certain government departments (particularly the Department of Trade and Industry's '1992 Helpline') or a local TEC.

7

Belgium

Belgium has a population of approximately ten million and is a parliamentary monarchy. All residents, whether foreign citizens or Belgian national citizens, are legally obliged to carry an identification card at all times. Belgium was a founder member of the EEC in 1957. The government is answerable to the people; democratic institutions and traditions as well as a free press ensure that human rights pledges are honoured. Ratified United Nations covenants on Civil and Political Rights and on Economic, Social and Cultural Rights have been in place for some time now and Belgium has one of the best records on human rights in the world.

The country is divided into two quite distinct groups which form two linguistic communities: the Flemish-speaking majority concentrated in the northern area of Flanders, and a substantial minority of French-speaking Walloons, based predominantly in the south. The latter group are concentrated in and around the heavily industrialized cities around Ardennes. While the majority of Belgians are Roman Catholic the church is not a strong political force.

The Position of Women

The capital city, Brussels, is also the headquarters of the European Community as well as over 800 European multinationals. How much women have benefited from the presence of so much commercial and diplomatic activity in Brussels is questionable. A large proportion of women still perform traditional female roles as secretaries, typists and general office workers. Many of the more highly sought-after jobs are dominated by men; banking in particular is male dominated. On the other hand, Belgium has signed the United Nations Convention on Equality for Women (though a signature is not legally binding; until a UN member country has ratified a Covenant it is under no legal obligation to abide by its Articles); and the Belgian Council of Women suggests that there has been a marked increase in awareness of the social and economic conditions of women's lives. The main advantage of the UN Convention on equality is that it provides a structural framework to act as a catalyst for change. The option of marriage for women in Belgium has more rights attached than marriage laws and conditions in most EC countries. A man and woman who intend to marry sign a legal agreement which states, among other things, what property each of them will bring to the marriage. Unlike in the UK, married women in Belgium retain their own family name legally; and few use their husband's name socially. Taxes are assessed independently.

The Belgian equivalent of the Sex Discrimination Act is known as 'Title V', which was introduced in 1978 into the Belgian Law of Economic Orientation. The law primarily deals with equality of treatment between men and women, specifically with regard to working conditions. However, it does not apply to statutory and extra-statutory social security schemes in respect of illness, unemployment benefits, retirement, family allowances, occupationally related diseases, or accidents at work – all of which are within the scope of the UK's Sex Discrimination Act. Under Title V, equal treatment is deemed to mean that there must be no direct or indirect discrimination on the grounds of sex or marital status. Unlike in the UK, the law in Belgium does not define what is meant by 'indirect discrimination'. It merely prohibits discrimination of an 'explicit' and 'non-explicit' nature, and the latter category seems wide enough to cover indirect discrimination.

Parental Rights and Childcare

In 1991 a number of new measures were adopted in the field of maternity leave and leave for either birth or adoption, in answer to a topical political concern for better attuning employment and family responsibilities. Pregnant women are now entitled to an extra week of maternity leave, 15 in total. The new laws also cover the eventuality of death or illness of the mother; in which case the maternity-leave provisions can be transferred to the father as paternity leave. In addition to this, paternity leave has recently been extended from two days to three days during the two weeks following the birth.

Belgium is one of the few European Commission countries which provides some tax relief for childcare costs – though it is the case in such arrangements that tax relief tends to benefit high-income families more than less well-off families. The only conditions attached are that parents have to provide some proof of payment, and use publicly funded or approved organizations. In general, creches and other public sector childcare arrangements are readily available in the cities; less so in smaller towns and rural areas.

Positive Action

Belgium has a recent history of project development and initiatives which aim to meet the specific training needs of employment 'high-risk' groups. Vulnerable categories of workers on whom the training is focused include ethnic minority groups, disabled workers, older workers and other groups who have traditionally been disadvantaged in the labour market. A wide range of activities including training, vocational guidance and preparation, job clubs and positive-action programmes has produced quite good results in regard to the employment prospects of disadvantaged groups. Most of the positive-action programmes have been conducted in the cities, with far fewer concentrating on the needs of workers in rural areas. Young women come from the provinces to live and try to find work in the cities; but the prevailing emphasis on family life and domesticity suggests that for many it is a stopgap until marriage.

Ethnic Divisions

Belgium is a country divided more by language than by any political or social division. French- and Dutch-based cultures overlap socially, economically and politically; though both cultures retain their ethnic and national distinctiveness to some extent. In the 1920s class tension in Flanders (in the north) was entirely to do with a heated struggle over language use. After much debate, different languages still exist, although successive governments have attempted to reduce or eliminate conflicts and tensions, particularly in areas of language use between the two communities. However, the creation of two separate Ministries of Culture in 1968 has emphasized a long-standing tendency for the two linguistic groups to go their separate ways. In 1945, after the end of the Second World War, Flanders grew relatively faster economically than Walloonia. Flanders is now rapidly industrializing, while the older Walloon industries are in difficulty; so that the two halves of the country tend to rival more than complement each other. Governmental and constitutional changes have provided Flanders and Walloonia with independent regional executives. This is even enforced at a national level; central government has to include a fixed proportion of Ministers from each community. The main advantage of this method of proportional representation is probably that it maintains a political equilibrium, which other political systems would be more likely to unbalance. On the other hand, it could be construed as perpetuating ethnic divisiveness simply by trapping citizens within such a formalized structure.

Disability

Belgium has one of the most advanced rehabilitation technology programmes in the European Community. Advanced technology enables severely disabled people to control their environment. The rehabilitation technology which has been developed in Belgium has enabled a large number of disabled students to gain access to higher education institutions and a wider range of job opportunities. The reason for this is twofold. A seminar in 1990 at the University of Mons in Belgium held a conference entitled 'A European University for students with special needs'. The main purpose of the event was to stimulate debate on the entitlement of people with disabilities to high quality training. As a result the number of disabled students in universities is rising progressively. Secondly, the HELIOS programme of activities in Belgium has encouraged employers and educational institutions to adapt their premises to meet the needs of disabled people.

Throughout Belgium many sports centres and exhibition centres have been adapted so that disabled people may participate in the activities. Many employers have also implemented special aids for their disabled employees; for example, special switches and eye interfaces which allow the person to use a telephone or typewriter.

Age Issues

In 1990 a new organization called Entr-ages was introduced into Belgium. Initially the stated aim of the network was twofold. The first was to break down the psychological and social isolation of many elderly people in residential care; in order to achieve this, residential homes have been opened up to local people of all ages to encourage a social and inter-generational mix. Its second aim was to increase awareness among the younger generation about age-related issues. Ultimately, this 'exchange' of knowledge and customs between age groups should go some way towards eliminating prejudice and stereotypes about and towards older people. On a practical level Entr-ages organizes and conducts regional social events at residential homes which aim to encourage as wide participation of as many people of different ages as possible and to provide a complete neighbourhood service which does not depend on age limits in its criteria. As such Entr-ages provides for a far broader community relationship which goes beyond the usual parameters of youth groups and pensioners' groups. In comparison to most of Europe, this represents a major step towards challenging age discrimination. A new quarterly magazine called *Aktief* has been launched in Belgium by the Flemish League of Large Families and Young Homes. It is aimed at grandparents, and is intended to be enjoyable for older readers. *Aktief* covers topics such as grandparents' visiting rights, housing issues, health and diet and financial matters.

In the 1980s a law was introduced which brought early retirement payments into line with state pension payments. Socially, the consequence of this move was that the system of authorized working activities for retired people was in effect extended to include those workers who had retired early. Clearly, this acts as an incentive for individuals to leave paid employment earlier than they would previously have considered. In addition, there have been several recent examples of retired workers being re-employed in order to participate in the training of younger workers. In general Belgium has made relatively substantive headway in its identification of the potential and value of older people to the workforce, even after they have formally retired.

Sexuality

Homosexuality in Belgium is viewed with somewhat less harshness than it is in the UK but there is as yet little room for complacency. Belgian citizens have a personal right to homosexuality between consenting adults from age 16. It is worth noting that Belgian law does not differentiate between the homosexual and heterosexual ages of consent. The law does not recognize same-sex partnerships, nor are there any laws or anti-discriminatory measures on the grounds of sexuality or against incitement to hatred. In practice, this means that lesbians and gay men have almost no protection from violence or harassment inside or outside the workplace. However, the government at least is currently considering proposals for such anti-discriminatory legislation. In practice, if such laws are introduced they will provide homosexuals with some of the employment rights which are already well established for heterosexuals. Homosexuality is no bar to serving in the armed forces. The Military Penal Code contains no specific provision concerning homosexuality. During recruitment of forces personnel, no distinction is made between candidates on grounds of sexuality.

8

Denmark

Denmark has a population of just over five million and is a parliamentary monarchy. Neutral in the First World War, Denmark was occupied by Germany in the Second World War. After the war it helped to set up the Nordic Council. It joined the EEC in 1973. An identification card is legally required at all times. Denmark has ratified the United Nations Covenants: the International Covenant on Civil and Political Rights and the International Covenant on Economic, Social and Cultural Rights. It has also ratified the Convention on Equality for Women. The predominant religion is Lutheran Protestant; 90 per cent of the Danish population belong to the National church and its affairs are regulated by royal decree. In contrast to the predominant religions in most other European countries, there are a number of women priests. Although the church is patronized by the majority of the population it does not interfere with or have an overt influence on national or local social and political affairs.

The Position of Women

Danish women gained the right to vote in 1908, which was a number of years earlier than many of their sisters in the rest of Europe did. While in many ways the social structure in Denmark is quite similar to Britain's, one overriding contrast which falls within the realm of sex equality is the higher status of women in most aspects of Danish life. This is particularly reflected in the Danish Parliament, known as the Folketing, which boasts over one-quarter female membership, a completely different picture to the UK Parliament which is almost exclusively male. A significant development in

Denmark over the last decade is the growth of women's studies; courses on all aspects of women's lives and herstory have now taken their place alongside the more traditional male-based history. As well as the proliferation of such courses in further and higher education, they also have an increasingly important role within the field of secondary education.

Although nuclear-family groups and traditional sex-roles are the enduring prototypes, most women work in some form of paid employment outside the home. Since the mid 1970s there has been free abortion on demand and all methods of contraception are readily available. Traditional inequalities in marriage and divorce to women's disadvantage are not nearly as prevalent in Denmark as they are elsewhere.

The Equal Treatment principle in Denmark is overseen by the Consolidation Act on Equal Treatment for Men and Women as Regards Access to Employment, which was introduced in 1987. The Act requires employers to apply the Equal Treatment principle in respect of all the following areas: recruitment and selection (including advertisements for employment), promotion, vocational training and careers guidance, and working conditions (including dismissal). The Danish equivalent of the Sex Discrimination Act is broader in its conception than the UK law. The most significant clause which it contains is its coverage of anti-discrimination measures against someone who is not married; whereas the SDA only caters for married persons. This is a clause which should gain top priority for amendment in the UK and other member countries legislation. In theory, at least, a lesbian or gay in Denmark could therefore receive equal protection to that offered a married or unmarried heterosexual person.

Parental Rights and Childcare

Paid maternity leave is guaranteed under the law of maternity leave of 4 June 1980. There is no continuous employment requirement. Women are entitled to 28 weeks maternity leave; four weeks before the birth and 24 weeks after. The last 10 weeks of these may be taken by either the father or mother or shared between them.

By 1988 Denmark had the highest level of women (with a child under ten) employed in the European Community. A year later, in 1989, there were childcare places for nearly half of all children under three years old – again the highest level in the Community. Denmark also has by far the most extensive entitlements to paternity leave. Paid paternity leave is guaranteed under the law of maternity leave. There are no length of service or other requirements for eligibility. A father is entitled to two weeks leave after the birth or the arrival at home of the child. There has been growing public interest and political debate about the economic and social position of children and their parents which reflects Denmark's commitment to progress in this area. Danish policies have been among the first to endorse the important role that fathers play in the care and development of their children. In other countries, legislators have been remiss in this respect and paternal needs have not been seriously addressed.

Positive Action

A national action plan for equal opportunities was introduced in 1987. Above all, it set out to deliver and implement ongoing programmes towards improved positive-action strategies. Their aim is to ensure that women receive appropriate vocational training with realistic employment prospects at the end of training courses. The Danish so-called P47 programme launched in 1988 by the Danish labour market authority to train unskilled women for male-dominated jobs has been declared a success. An evaluation in 1992 of this nationwide scheme showed that most of the women found jobs within six months of completing their training.

A total of 22 projects were set up throughout the country training women in electronics, metal and iron work, storage and transportation, the processing industry and in some cases tourism. As a result of the evaluation, P47 will now become a permanent part of the Danish vocational training system. It will be extended to other sectors and will include both women-only and mixed training.

Disability

In Denmark, social policy and the basis for funding services for people with special learning needs has been successfully decentralized. The switch from large, usually isolated, institutions to smaller community-based units is taking place smoothly. This success is partly because Denmark has a policy of local self-government, which has resulted in an increasing number of functions being delegated to local and regional levels. A wide range of activities have sprung up as a result of this de-centralization. In Denmark new policies for Independent Living, actively encouraged by the HELIOS programme, are leading to real improvements. These are incorporated within the 'Live and Neighbourhood' schemes in many areas. Through these schemes normal family housing within the local community is being provided to people with special needs. This is very different to an institutional philosophy, and as a result many disabled people are spending most of their time in small, friendly community-based units.

In December 1991, the Danish Parliament adopted a law under which a personal assistant may be provided to disabled workers to enable them to have the same chance of performing a job as non-disabled people. The new legislation is based on findings of a pilot project which included personal assistants for disabled workers. This has become a statutory and permanent scheme as of 1 January 1992 and is administered by the Public Employment Service. The new facility of personal assistants is available not only to employees, but also to self-employed people who need special assistance to perform their work due to blindness, diminished sight, deafness, impaired hearing or other serious handicaps. The subsidy is granted to enterprises who employ people with disabilities, or to disabled people themselves.

Age Issues

Denmark has also been in the vanguard in respect of its provision of sheltered services to all age groups, through a system it calls 'Collective Housing'. In practice, a Collective House provides facilities such as restaurants, domestic cleaning, child-minding and laundry. The impact of such services on the lives of older people is particularly remarkable. The multiple benefits gained from such accommodation include a decline in isolation and loneliness and a uniform and customized approach to care. In addition to this, inter-age contacts reduce prejudice and discrimination in the wider society's perceptions about older people. Another positive development for older people in Denmark was outlined in 1990. The Danish Council Branch of Eurolink Age proposed to undertake a four-year study on the lives of older people and the economic and social issues facing them. Its target group is citizens who will be aged over 60 at the start of the 21st century. In the past there has been a tendency for research of this nature to be directed almost exclusively at the real and perceived health problems of older people; whereas this study has been much more broadly defined. Health issues are examined but share an equal status with other issues including housing, family, relationships, work, money, leisure and political participation.

Sexuality

Denmark also takes an impressive stance in the treatment of gay men and lesbians. Consenting adults are free to practice homosexuality. The laws relating to age of consent for sexual activity are equal for homosexuals and heterosexuals. The consensual ages have been set at 15/18: the higher age applies if authority is exerted or undue influence is used. In 1984 the Danish Parliament passed a resolution to establish a commission to study ways of eliminating discrimination against homosexuals. Following this, in 1987 a law was passed which seeks to protect lesbians and gays from discrimination in the provision of public services and in access to and use of public facilities. Two years later, in 1989, the Minister of Justice confirmed that this also applies to discrimination in employment. In fact, the picture provides a complete contrast to the UK, and also a disparity with most other European Member States. There is also a law against incitement to hatred in Denmark which incorporates protection for lesbian and gay men. In addition, since 1989 same-sex couples have been able to register their relationship; by April 1990 over 1,500 gay people in Denmark had taken advantage of the new law allowing them to marry. There are many advantages to this, all of which at least in theory bring gay and lesbian rights into line with the rights of heterosexuals; in particular, rights and responsibilities in respect of taxation, residency and inheritance. Unfortunately, homosexual and heterosexual rights have not been entirely equalized and a few outstanding exceptions defy the principles of equality. The most significant exception is the fact that gay and lesbian couples may not jointly adopt or have custody of children, even their own children. It is, however, anticipated that pension and adoption rights for homosexuals will be pushed through in the Danish Parliament in the near future.

9

France

France has a population of approximately 54 million and is a Democratic Republic. The country has a reputation of good democratic traditions and a commitment to the rights of the individual. However, a large influx of people from the ex-French colonies has caused a great deal of social tension and calls by fascist groups and extremists for a return to 'France for the French'. There are no compulsory documents which are legally required at all times for citizens, but an identification card is nevertheless a social necessity. France has ratified the United Nations Covenants: the International Covenant on Civil and Political Rights (ICCPR) and the International Covenant on Economic, Social and Cultural Rights (ICESCR).

France has a wide range of manufacturing industries. Paris is known especially for its luxury and fashion products; Lyons is known for textiles; Marseilles and Bordeaux are major industrial ports; and Lille, on the north-western coalfield, is centre of a large industrial region. France was a founder member of the EEC in 1957. The main religion is Roman Catholicism.

The Position of Women

It was not until 1944 that French women got the right to vote. Two decades later, divorce and marriage laws changed and contraception became legal. Ten years after that in 1974, abortion became legal. Today there are still economic and social inequalities working to women's disadvantage in both marriage and divorce proceedings.

France has signed the United Nations Convention on Equality for Women. In law, education and employment the sexes are equal; but although women's rights may have been institutionalized, in practice they have hardly scratched the surface of machismo. The growth of a women's movement in France has been characterized by division during the last couple of decades. In 1971 the group 'Feministes Revolutionaires' was active in campaigning for women's rights to abortion and had the full support of left-wing feminists. Around the same time another group became active with the title 'Psychoanalyse et Politique', abbreviated and referred to as 'Psyche et Po'. In contrast to the revolutionary and left-wing feminists, Psyche et Po concentrated on a Female/Feminine yet anti-feminist revolution. The two groups worked in opposition throughout the 1960s and 1970s; with most of the progressive improvements made during that period attributable to the campaigning of Feministes Revolutionaires.

The Equal Treatment Directive has been incorporated into the French labour code. Under the labour code the concept of direct discrimination has been incorporated into French legislation; although it has not specifically developed the concept of indirect discrimination, the law is written in terms wide enough to be interpreted as prohibiting it.

French law permits employers to discriminate in favour of one sex where the needs of the job demand. The categories in France are not as broad as in the UK, and are limited to actors specifically playing male or female roles and models.

In contrast to the UK, in France violations of the Equal Treatment principle can carry with them criminal sanctions. Within the French criminal code it is a criminal offence for any person to discriminate on the grounds of sex. Individuals who consider that they have been unfairly discriminated against on the grounds of sex can sue their employer for damages in the French civil courts. Alternatively they can refer to the court to enact an order that they be reinstated or promoted. It is worth comparing this to the situation in the UK where only industrial tribunals have the power to recommend such remedies.

Parental Rights and Childcare

France is about midway in the EC on a scale of the generosity of commitments to statutory maternity and paternity provision. Paid maternity leave for 16 weeks at 84 per cent of earnings is guaranteed under the terms and conditions of the labour code. Paid paternity leave is guaranteed under the same code for three days within a period of two weeks of the date of birth. France is in line with most other Member States in the position on leave for family reasons, in that it does provide some form of statutory right to time off for weddings or bereavements.

In the latter half of the last decade there have been several developments in equality issues relating to childcare. The objective of government policy has been to increase publicly funded provision for childcare while at the same time increasing the emphasis on high-quality service. These objectives contributed to the current trends towards far greater diversity in childcare services.

Positive Action

During the mid to late 1980s a number of positive steps were undertaken to ensure an increase in female participation in the labour market. Retraining courses and localized occupational vocational training programmes were among the measures put in place which aimed at finding suitable occupations with appropriate training for women who were underrepresented in, or disadvantaged by being out of, particular areas of employment. The courses were administered by the French National Employment Fund. Subsidized training schemes, apprenticeships and alternating periods of school and training are three of the strategies recently launched by the French government in an attempt to curb rising unemployment. An agreement signed in January 1992 by employers and trade unions on training and apprenticeships is expected significantly to increase company involvement in training. The measures aim to increase the number of apprenticeships from 230,000 to 400,000 by 1997.

Race Relations

Race relations in France have historically been far from smooth. Most immigrants arrived in the 1960s and 1970s in response to widely advertised job opportunities. Many came from the ex-French colonies of Martinique, Guadeloupe and French Guiana. In addition, there are a quarter of a million Africans in Paris and three million Muslims settled throughout France. The majority of the Muslim population have come from Algeria, Tunisia and Morocco. Many immigrants found jobs in the public sector – the civil service, police, hospitals and public transport.

During the last decade there has been a marked resurgence of racism in France. The racism that already existed has been strengthened by the growth of 'Le Front Nationale' (FN) which became a significant political force in the 1980s. This should be compared to the position in Britain, where the identically named organization, the National Front, achieved its political and social prominence during the 1970s, and has been much quieter on the political front since. In response to the spread of racial discrimination a group called 'SOS Racism' has formed and grown over the last five years. SOS Racism seeks to challenge institutionalized racism through musical and educational channels. SOS Racism does not confront the Nazis directly. Instead it organizes carnivals and debates about the need to improve people's living conditions in order to root out racism and improve race relations.

Racism is entrenched in the French language. Ethnic minorities are referred to as *immigré* or *étrange*; or more often still in cities like Marseilles as 'les Arabs'. This is predominantly a manifestation of French racism. With such negative separatist terminology racism is unlikely to subside, and any attempt at assimilation to be impossible to achieve. The prevailing living conditions of ethnic minorities in France include squalid housing, frequent harassment and high levels of unemployment; and each factor is made worse by constant police checks. Moreover, the overriding difficulties of getting a work permit in the first place are compounded by the multiple problems associated with keeping hold of the permit for any length of time. It is clear that these problems are unlikely to disappear without the presence of firm legislation and measures to ensure non-discrimination on racial grounds.

Disability

Accessibility for people with disabilities as well as older citizens with mobility problems is better in France than in the majority of EC countries. A 'Law of Orientation of Handicapped Persons' implemented in 1975 gave the government the power to regulate the development of vehicle construction as well as modes of access.

Following this, in 1977, a programme was introduced to oversee the coordination of a framework for action on mobility, transport and accessibility. As a result of this programme several modifications have been made to all types of public transport. Outstanding improvements and developments have been made to the French railway system (SNCF). SNCF have been actively involved in researching and improving overall access facilities to trains throughout the last couple of decades. The principal aim behind the French railways plan is to create a completely non-segregated service.

Age Issues

The basic French national insurance pension is in the top half of the 12 Member States. The British situation is generally mirrored throughout Europe where there is an overall lack of evidence of any major government policy changes to encourage older workers to stay in employment, but France is at least in theory an exception to the rule. It is at present the only Member State with legislation against age discrimination. It has enacted measures prohibiting discrimination in both recruitment and selection processes, and in redundancy procedures for older workers. Recent legislation in France sets a European precedent which could well provide for future EC legislation. Since 1986 French laws have guarded against age discrimination in job advertisements by banning upper age limits, but it is understood that in practice this is not really enforced in any significant manner.

Since 1987, employers are no longer permitted by law to make older workers redundant solely on the grounds of age. In 1989, further legal measures were adopted which actively discourage employers from making older workers redundant; these include:

- Increased employer costs for redundancies of workers aged over 55 by placing an obligation on the employer to contribute the equivalent of three months' salary to *L'Undeic* (the French unemployment fund).
- The right to priority for re-employment for workers made redundant for up to one year after the original date upon which they were made redundant.
- An increase in state contributions to ongoing vocational training for workers aged over 45 years.
- An employer exemption from social security contributions for all employees recruited aged over 50 who were previously unemployed.

On a practical level an entrepreneurial form of positive action has been quite widely introduced by some French municipalities. Throughout the country such enterprises have decided to subsidize neighbourhood general shops in an attempt to encourage and enable local people to use local shops as opposed to visiting hypermarkets at greater distance. This proposal has clearly recognized the important role such local shops have in maintaining the social fabric of neighbourhood life, and acknowledged that many people, especially as they become older, either do not or cannot travel great distances in order to purchase basic requirements. Local services work to increase interpersonal contact for people who may be otherwise socially isolated, in a manner which the more impersonal atmosphere of a huge hypermarket does not. British planning laws ought to be encouraged by such developments, and consider safeguarding such neighbourhood shopping districts in the UK.

Yet another French initiative with respect to older citizens is 'La Flamboyance', launched in September 1989 in Paris. It is a new movement in France which aims primarily at celebrating longevity and dispelling the prejudices associated with the ageing process.

Sexuality

Homosexuals in France have a slightly higher status than in many other EC countries in several ways. First, the age of consent for gay or lesbian as well as heterosexual sex is 15, so there is no discriminatory age gap as such as there is in the UK. However, if authority is exerted or undue influence is used 18 is the minimum age below which it is an offence. In addition, the law prohibits discrimination on the grounds of 'sex', 'family situation' and 'moeurs' (the latter meaning morals or lifestyle – which includes sexuality) within employment and in access to all goods and services. Furthermore, discrimination in the terms and conditions of employment, including financial benefits for employees and their partners, is forbidden under the Code of Labour Law. In contrast to the situation in many other member countries, homosexuality is no bar to serving in the armed forces. As in most EC states, however, the law in France does not recognize same-sex partnerships. However, in 1992, as the French National Assembly debates reforms to its law book, the Napoleonic Code, a bill granting partnership rights to lesbian and gay couples has been prepared by two socialist deputies. It aims to 'unify and classify the situation nationally for all sexual partnerships'. The measure would give lesbian and gay couples the same rights as heterosexual married people in the areas of residence, property ownership and inheritance. The French Prime Minister, Edith Cresson, is expected to support the bill because her Socialist Party manifesto, adopted in 1991, promised a reform of the cohabitation laws.

10 Germany

In 1949 West Germany became a Federal Republic and East Germany a People's Democracy. A treaty between the two Germanies in 1972 reduced tension and paved the way for their entry into the United Nations. In the west, a prosperous economy, a free press and a thriving parliamentary democracy have long been established for its 60 million inhabitants. In contrast, citizens in East Germany have lived as subordinates to the ideals, aims and powers of the ruling Communist Party. Both Germanies have ratified the United Nations covenants on Civil and Political Rights, and on Economic, Social and Cultural Rights; and both have signed the Convention on Equality for Women. The extent to which these rights have been met in East Germany has up until very recently been very poor.

By far the greatest single achievement since the end of the Second World War has been the reunification in 1990 of the two German states: the German Democratic Republic (GDR), or East Germany, and the Democratic Federal Republic (FDR), West Germany. For over 40 years the two had lived independent existences with two very different economic, social and cultural systems. With rare exceptions, not even relatives could move from East to West Germany. (It is worth noting, however, that only older people were allowed the freedom to travel in both directions; although particularly in the East, many could not afford to. The thinking behind that is likely based on ageist assumptions that older people haven't the capacity or desire to start a revolution.) Full political and economic unification is now underway, but with far more problems than had been anticipated. All this could change in time and the systems equalized. Before 1989, the 16-million-strong population of East Germany enjoyed far fewer rights than westerners. In fact, 40 years of a single-party communist state created major violations of human rights pledges.

The Position of Women

The women's movement in West Germany had its roots in the student activities and campaigns of the late 1960s. Many groups were established with the aim of liberating women from their traditional roles as a first step towards their freedom. At the beginning of the 1970s there was a split in the movement: one part took Marxist social ideas for its strategic base, while other groups put the opposition of the sexes before the class struggle. The latter were heavily influenced by American feminist ideology. Later, the two sides were drawn together by the campaign for abortion which successfully gained much public and political attention. Many women's centres sprang up in the mid 1970s, from which evolved a large feminist sub-culture. Today, the women's movement is a mixture of independent groups which maintain loose connections through publications and conferences, as well as action on national and international issues. The basic aim, of course, of all the groups remains the same – to shift the gross imbalances of the economic, social and sexual oppression of women. The movement is not alone in Europe in sharing different opinions as to how best to do this and achieve full sex equality: whether from a separatist feminist or a socialist feminist stance.

In East Germany women have a relatively high status and are represented at most levels in the workforce – far more so, in fact, than in other Eastern bloc countries. Women have entered the professions in large numbers and the public status of women is far higher than in other EC Member States. This can be partly explained by the fact that so many men were killed or went missing during the World Wars that the country was almost exclusively rebuilt by women. Their role in the rebuilding seems to have been both recognized and valued. Feminist activity is widespread and women's trade unions, community groups, creche facilities and action groups all co-exist, though without an organized feminist movement as such. It is worth remembering, though, that while other countries were organizing themselves into feminist movements in the late 1960s, East German women were wallowing in a system which had state control of all academic, intellectual and censorship rights. Today, probably largely due to its post-war history, it is one of the most radically feminist countries in Europe.

The West German Parliament introduced the Equal Treatment Directive into its legislative structure via the 'Labour Law EC Amendment Act' of 1980, the contents of which are bound in the West German Civil Code. The law does not make the distinction between direct and indirect discrimination, though it agrees that both forms exist and thereby are liable to contravene the Directive. West German law does permit sex discrimination to be lawful in limited circumstances. Examples of this might include actors, models or supervising staff in prisons which are exclusively male or exclusively female. However, unlike in the UK, the legislation does not seek to define these types of permitted discrimination in such detailed terms.

Increasing and improving the opportunities for women at work remains a priority of the labour-market policy as well as the social policy of the federal government; and their aims have been reiterated through the Employment Promotion Law. Furthermore, the federal government has taken practical steps to enhance the promotion of women at work. In addition to this, measures designed to encourage more women to participate in vocational programmes have become more commonplace.

Parental Rights and Childcare

Paid maternity leave has been guaranteed in West Germany under the 1968 'Maternity Protection Law', and the provisions were improved upon by an amendment in 1979. In contrast to the UK there are no continuous employment requirements necessary to ensure eligibility. A woman receives 100 per cent of her normal pay for 14 weeks. The parental leave system was introduced in 1986, and either parent may now take 18 months' leave. Up until 1990 leave was only granted for 10 months. Although there is no statutory provision for paternity leave as such, the civil code does allow special paid leave for personal reasons, which is usually taken to incorporate a short spell of paternity leave. Two days' paid leave for the father at the time of the birth is generally permitted through collective agreements.

Singularly in the Twelve, West Germany has introduced major changes since 1986 in the field of childcare provision. Childcare allowances and leave were introduced as a general right for all parents; up until then the rights had been restricted to civil servants alone. Under the same law, parental leave is also guaranteed. In addition, leave for family reasons is guaranteed under the Civil Code as it is in, e.g., France and the Netherlands. In Spain, leave for family reasons is guaranteed under Article 37(3) of the 1980 Workers' Statute. In Denmark, although there are no statutory rights to leave for family reasons, a number of collective agreements do provide for leave. A unique example of such eligibility in West Germany is wedding anniversaries, for which leave is granted. In practice, therefore, married persons get an extra day's holiday over single people and over gays and lesbians.

Germany has a federal constitution, and chief responsibility for policy on services lies with individual state governments. The predominant type of publicly funded service for children from three years of age to primary school is kindergarten, most of which are provided by national private organizations. In practice this means that public services are available for at least three years for each child as children do not start school until they are aged between six and seven; on a European scale this represents very generous provision.

In the last few years employers have paid increasing attention to the context of family responsibilities in their employment policies. However, their commitment has been far more to do with the anticipated shortage of skilled workers in the nineties than out of any love for the principles of equality. The effects of labour-market trends together with the impact of 'Women's Equality Officers' created throughout Germany in recent years have all contributed to putting public pressure on the government. In addition, families who have moved over from East Germany and had been used to a much higher level of service in the past have exerted their pressure and influence. Provision in East Germany was very generous in so far as it included 12 months' parental leave with full earnings for the first four months, and 80 per cent earnings for the remainder of the year; either parent could take the leave but, needless to say, it was used almost exclusively by women. The economic need to return to work is of course more prominent in a less well-off country than in a prosperous one. Wages in East Germany have traditionally been very low. As a consequence employment rates among women with children in East Germany in 1989 were around 90 per cent, and as such were among the highest in the world.

Race Relations

In 1991 it was agreed that the federal labour minister should provide financial support for the integration of ethnic minority groups into the labour market. The new fund is to be directed at vocational and language training programmes, as well as towards subsidies to independent charitable groups for the care of ethnic minority workers. Although the emphasis is on the integration into the labour market of all ethnic minorities, there is a particular accent on women who have suffered additional disadvantage.

Germany has a history of quite generous immigration laws. These laws have meant that thousands of refugees have arrived in Germany. As the numbers have grown, so have the numbers of special camps which they have been confined to. In 1991, Germany had over 250,000 asylum applications, the highest number of applications in Europe.

The arrival of immigrants has fuelled racial discrimination. The resurgence of Nazism throughout Europe is evidenced by the increasing votes Nazi groups are gaining for their ideas. The Germany REP, which is equivalent to the French FN, has members in the European Parliament.

Age and Disability Issues

A number of trends are apparent in West Germany which could have a potential impact on all equality issues, particularly on disability and age. The availability of 'mixed age' services is increasing in several areas, with specific emphasis in some on offering more flexible services which remain open for more hours than in the past. Much more attention is also being paid nowadays to the relationship between services and the local community they are designed to serve. Consequently, there is a trend in many areas towards wholly neighbourhood organizations.

The Quota system, which in the UK places an obligation (which is very rarely enforced) on employers over a particular size to recruit registered disabled people, is far more strictly applied in Germany. Fines are issued to organizations if they fail to comply, and the funds collected are transferred towards training costs for people with disabilities. To apply Quota as strictly in the UK would be a very welcome and long overdue move.

In line with the majority of EC member countries, Germany has no legislation on anti-age discrimination, though the social rights relevant to the aged are very advanced. In East Germany medical and social rights in no way equalled provision in West Germany. Pensions in what was the GDR were raised on 1 January 1991 by 15 per cent, and a further increase of 15 per cent is predicted within the near future. If the second increase goes beyond a promise it will bring pensions to around 70 per cent of the level in West Germany. Across the whole of Germany older people represent an ever-increasing figure within the population.

'Grey power', or the pensioner movement, is only very gradually growing in the UK. In Germany, it represents a new political party, the Greys, which fought in the parliamentary elections in 1990. Not surprisingly, main issues were pensions, ageism, employment and social benefits as well as health provision. Furthermore, there are several practical measures contained in Germany's approach to its older citizens. Several cities mail out information about services for the elderly as soon as they reach pensionable age. Every residential service is obliged by law to have a residents' committee; committee members decide for themselves what the important issues are, rather than being confined to those issues which some institutional regime considers to be important. In West Germany retirement ages are more flexible than in most other Member States and priority is given to the individual's wishes at the discretion of the organization. It is to be hoped that the EC measures for the elderly will benefit older people throughout the whole of Germany.

Sexuality

The law has not yet been unified between the old GDR and the FDR in respect to ages of consent for sexual activity. Proposals for a single age of consent of either 14 or 16 were presented to the Bundestag in 1991. It is possible that the process of reunification could adversely affect the legal status of gay male sex. The penal code of the Federal Republic includes a paragraph which sets the age of consent for homosexual sex at 18; this could be applied to the whole country. East Germany repealed the law over 20 years ago when it adopted 14 as the age of consent for all sexual activity. The only exception was when an abuse of authority had occurred, for which the consensual age of 16 was applied. At the moment the standing East German consensual laws do not discriminate between heterosexuals and homosexuals. In Germany, like most Member States, there is no law protecting gays and lesbians from discrimination. A contradiction exists in the situation regarding the recruitment of homosexuals into the armed forces. Gays and lesbians are eligible to serve in the military if they so wish, but they are not allowed to become officers or enter the highest ranks. This represents yet another example of the widely held misconceptions about sexuality, inherent in the belief that in positions of authority homosexuals are likely to exercise a corrupting influence on the lower ranks.

11

Greece

Greece has a population of just less than ten million and is a parliamentary democracy governed from its capital city, Athens. Since gaining membership of the EEC in 1981 Greece has become more closely linked with Western Europe. The government is answerable to the people and many democratic governmental as well as non-governmental institutions exist. An improved standard of living as well as a free and cultured press continue to contribute to the consolidation of a parliamentary system since the overthrow of military dictatorship in 1974. Greece has ratified two UN Covenants – the Convention on Equality for Women; and the Covenant on Economic, Social and Cultural Rights. Citizens are legally obliged to carry an identification card with them at all times.

In 1984, a law ended the requirement of religious marriages and introduced civil marriages for the first time. This relatively recent liberalization of laws relating to marriage and divorce is slowly transforming a complacently male-dominated society where, like Italy, machismo has for centuries been the established and accepted pattern of behaviour. The large majority of Greeks belong nominally to the Christian Eastern Orthodox faith.

The Position of Women

Legislative reforms have gone some way towards consolidating the otherwise highly polarized attitudes towards women. The Family Law introduced in 1983 contained three new concepts. First, and perhaps of most significance, it prohibited dowry, and by doing so abolished all the gross injustices which had for centuries prevailed around that practice. Second, it stipulated that there was to be complete equality in status between men and women. Unfortunately, it omitted to implement immediately measures to assure full equality; so for a time it remained as a mere constitutional symbol. Furthermore, it introduced for the first time shared property rights in marriage for men and women. In many areas the laws have been lent support with considerable success; in others, the opposition of men to what they perceive as the undesirable 'politicization' of women remains a seemingly impenetrable barrier. The Family Law has had a tremendous impact in urban areas, but much less so in the rural areas where women's roles as mothers and homemakers are deeply ingrained, to the exclusion of any other role that a woman may wish to pursue. Most women also work outside the home, and have to combine this with running a house and catering for the needs of its occupants. Men, for the most part, consider themselves exempt from domestic tasks and home responsibilities. The latter is a fairly typical result of the full weight of machismo in practice. While these attitudes persist, the legislation enacted to reform many of the more traditional areas of inequality is unlikely to bring much relief.

The women's movement has emerged in force during the last two decades. The Women's Union of Greece (WUG) was set up in 1976 and represents by far the largest organization which draws public attention to many aspects of women's lives, such as employment, contraception, sexuality, home responsibility, and in the beginning, the oppressive implications of dowry. While it is an autonomous voice, it has traditionally been closely linked to the socialist party. Similar to other Mediterranean countries within the EC, most of its related groups and activities are socialist-feminist in outlook, based on the belief that a large number of Greek women are doubly oppressed, primarily because they are women, and secondly as members of the lower economic classes. Partly because of the physical nature of Greece and its islands, a number of independent feminist groups have been established and campaign locally for equality.

The Equal Treatment Directive was implemented by Greece through a law enacted in 1984. The same law, called Law 1414, also implemented the Equal Pay Directive. Sex discrimination is prohibited in respect of working conditions, promotion or career development and progression. Greek law on positive action is more generous in practice than UK law. It is incorporated into Article 10 of Law 1414, which states that it does not constitute unlawful sex discrimination for an employer to take measures in favour of one sex – providing that such steps contribute to breaking down existing discriminatory barriers and establishing good equality practices. Damages suffered by an individual as a result of unlawful discrimination may also include 'moral damages', since sex discrimination in Greek law is an actual offence against a person (not merely a contravention of an Act as it is almost everywhere else). Both of these measures – positive action, and sex discrimination treated as an offence – highlight the political commitment towards full sexual equality and should be adopted by all national parliaments.

Without doubt, the most significant clause within Greek law is its prohibition of all acts of discrimination on the grounds of sex or marital status in respect of *any* programme which contributes towards an individual's cultural, economic and social development or promotion. In theory, therefore, this could be interpreted far more widely than equivalent laws in other Member States.

Parental Rights and Childcare

Since 1982, paid maternity leave is guaranteed for a period of 15 weeks at 100 per cent of normal earnings. Although there are no continuous employment requirements as there are in the UK, it is necessary to have 200 days of contributions paid during the two years preceding the entitlement to benefits. The right to parental leave, previously restricted to the private sector, was extended to the public sector in 1988 by force of a Presidential Decree. Parental leave was originally implemented and guaranteed to the private sector under a law enacted in 1984 about the protection of workers with family responsibilities. In the EC, the period within which any system of parental leave must be taken varies from country to country; in Greece, entitlement expires after the child is 30 months old, which is more generous than many other systems.

In the mid 1980s the Greek government introduced for the first time services for children aged under 30 months, and the number of publicly funded places for this group has increased steadily since. As elsewhere, there have been a number of financial and planning constraints on the future expansion of such services. Athens has been very densely overdeveloped: half the population of Greece live in and around the capital, so housing alone is a major cause of land development. Most of the services are, however, available almost exclusively in Athens; childcare services in rural areas lag well behind. There have also been severe constraints on public expenditure, which have led to new services being provided but not being able to operate and take children. For example, 155 nurseries (to take children under 2½) were added to existing kindergartens in 1989, but only 45 have been in operation since. There has been little growth in services for children over 2½.

Disability

Participation without full integration has been the usual experience of disabled people in most social, educational and sporting events in Greece. Financial constraints have meant that integration programmes have been formed, but unable to operate fully. Also, due to the geographical nature of Greece and its islands, services to the disabled are not evenly distributed. In general, the suburban areas are better provided for than rural districts.

In 1990 Greece won three significant HELIOS Independent Living Awards. The Spastics Society of Northern Greece, based in Thessaloniki, won an award under the Access to Public Building and Facilities category. The project enabled disabled children and adults to take part in cultural and leisure activities with the support of volunteers. As a result, they are now fully involved in summer camps and outings to cultural and recreational facilities both in Greece and abroad. Another HELIOS award was presented to the Spastics Society in Athens. In 1990, the Society undertook the first comprehensive survey into accessibility in Athens by disabled people. It examined all aspects of the city and their suitability for disabled people. A third HELIOS award was made to the Rhodes Municipal Welfare Association. The award was presented to the municipality on the basis of its comprehensive policy for services for disabled and elderly people. In a historic site such as Rhodes they have managed to provide facilities for all the citizens, without damaging the intrinsic features of the town.

Age Issues

Greece has a higher percentage of older workers than most other Member States, most notably Ireland, which has the youngest population. In recent years Greece has built up a state deficit of over £3 billion for pensions and health care. In view of this, in October 1990 measures were introduced to reform social security legislation. Key changes anticipated will have implications as much for the private sector as for the status of public servants. Many of the issues are bound to provoke a degree of controversy. Rationalization and restrictions on the qualifying conditions for pensions (including the universally unpopular length-of-service condition) and health care provision are both due to be changed in the not too distant future. Clearly, this could dramatically effect the financial security of many older workers and retired people. Since women are likely to have served fewer years in the paid workforce than men, and to have had more family-related disruptions in their careers, this ruling will no doubt adversely affect more women than men.

In 1990, it was proposed (and immediately implemented) to raise the age of retirement. It is now set at 55 for men and 52 for women – and as from 1997, it will rise still further to age 60 for men and 58 for women. Furthermore, a levelling out of the pension income an individual may receive is under review. Coinciding with measures to reduce expenditure a number of incentives aimed at prolonging working life are to be introduced along with disincentives for early retirement. The rights of individuals to flexibility, autonomy and right of say in retirement issues are clearly being increasingly undermined. The implementation of the EC Action Programme for Older People is well represented through its various initiatives in Greece, but organized pensioner/grey movements are not as well established as in other Member States. National commitment to anti-age-discrimination measures, as well as steps to ensure independent living, are crucial if the action programme is to have the desired effect in Greece.

Sexuality

Homosexuals in Greece, as in most Member States, are not protected under the law against discrimination on the grounds of their sexuality. This is despite the fact that homosexuality has actually been legal in Greece since 1931. The age of consent is set at 15 for gay, lesbian and heterosexual sex, so there is no discrimination between the age at which each type of behaviour becomes legal. However, in all three categories prosecutions are possible if authority is exerted upon a partner. Like almost all other Member States Greece does not recognize same-sex partnerships, so the established rights of immigration and social benefits taken for granted by heterosexuals are denied to the gay and lesbian community.

12

Ireland

The Irish Republic has a population of just over three million and is a Democratic Republic governed from its capital city, Dublin. The Republic of Ireland occupies 80 per cent of the island of Ireland and contains 26 counties, divided into three provinces: Connacht, Leinster, and Munster. The six north-eastern counties of the fourth province, Ulster, constitute Northern Ireland, which is part of the United Kingdom. In 1919–1921 the Irish fought for independence, finally achieving dominion status as the Irish Free State. It became a republic in 1949 and joined the EEC in 1973. The unification of Ireland remains a central political issue. The orthodox Roman Catholic Church is followed by the vast majority of the population in the Republic; more so than in other EC countries the church is a central factor in peoples' lives. It is the single most formidable obstacle to the progress of the Irish women's movement. Crucial areas of equality such as birth control, divorce and abortion are in direct conflict with the Catholic Church's stance. However, despite religious resistance there has been a significant growth in feminism within Ireland since the 1970s. This may partly be due to the Ireland's predominantly young population. Ireland has signed two United Nations Covenants: the International Covenant on Civil and Political Rights, and on Economic, Social and Cultural Rights.

The Position of Women

The Equal Treatment principle in the Irish Republic is incorporated in the Employment Equality Act introduced in 1977. Outwardly, the law is broadly similar to the equivalent in the UK, although its implications are very different. The 1977 Act makes it unlawful for employers to directly or indirectly discriminate on the grounds of sex or marital status in recruitment, promotion, training and other conditions of employment. The Irish definition of indirect discrimination is clearly different from the UK in that it avoids the loophole of 'justification' inherent in the Sex Discrimination Act, and states that a condition or rule must be 'essential' to the job in question. Since justifying anything is so often open to individual subjective interpretation, the UK should amend its act to exclude the justification clause. Ireland has a governing organization similar to the UK's Equal Opportunities Commission (EOC) which is called the Employment Equality Agency (EEA). Like the EOC it is empowered to carry out formal investigations into discriminatory practices, issue non-discriminatory notices to non-compliants and generally promote effective equal opportunities policies and practices. The Irish government is nowadays setting itself up as a role model of good equal opportunities practices. As an employer it is quite progressive in equality issues, and many public-sector employees have more equality rights than their peers in the private sector.

In 1990 Ireland introduced a new programme, the 'Programme for Economic and Social Progress', as a direct result of the success of the 'Programme for National Recovery' which created both economic and employment growth. The Programme for Economic and Social progress provides a structured framework for the nineties, with specific proposals including the development and improvement of worker participation and women's rights.

Parental Rights and Childcare

In 1988, 23 per cent of women with a child under ten years old were employed – the lowest level in the Community. Paid maternity leave for a total of 14 weeks is guaranteed under the Maternity Protection of Employees Act 1981 and the Social Welfare (Amendment) Act 1981. There is no continuous employment requirement. The woman receives 70 per cent of gross pay from the Department of Social Welfare. At the moment there is no statutory paternity leave, parental leave or eligibility to leave to care for sick children. In practice, however, many employers allow two days' discretionary leave to fathers around the birth of their child. In 1989 there were three significant developments which directly affected childcare in

Ireland. The first nationally agreed wage scale for childcare workers was debated; the negotiations coincided with the first training course for family daycarers which began in Dublin. In addition to this, an association of managers, owners and employees involved in childcare provision was established. These projects were a major factor in increased social and political interest in childcare issues; and were complemented by increased media coverage. In 1990, the Minister for Labour set up a working group to examine how the public and private sectors within industry might take initiatives to provide childcare services for all parents in employment. The government recommended that childcare services be provided for employees in the public sector. Furthermore, they stated their willingness to provide many of these services themselves. Around the same time, a second commission on the economic and social status of women was established. Clearly, the Irish government is increasing its commitment to family and employment related issues, and recognizing the inseparable impact that one role has upon the other.

Disability

There have been several success stories throughout the disability movement in Ireland since the mid 1980s. Rosslare harbour is a major rail, road and sea crossroads for travellers in Ireland. The overall design from conception through to completion has the disabled person in mind with the aim of promoting integrated and independent travel.

A range of centres for the therapeutic, recreational, educational and physical advancement of disabled adults has been developed. Their aims include provision, in a home environment, of social training and learning facilities, and the preparation and education of trainees for job opportunities in the community. Some of the centres are independently run, while others are attached to educational institutions. The centres also act as reference centres for further information and assistance with communication techniques, rehabilitation technology and the adaptation of premises and use of special equipment.

Age Issues

Ireland is one Member State within the EC where the overall population is not ageing – mainly as Ireland does not have the declining birthrate common in most other member countries. Undoubtedly, this is partly to do with the difficulties Irish women in particular face in securing adequate birth control. Only as recently as 1985 was a Bill passed which permitted sales of condoms and spermicides to over-18s; and still the availability of birth control is quite restricted in comparison with other EC countries.

The number of people aged above 60 is expected to decline by the year 2,000. Nevertheless, Ireland is faced, like all Member States, by the many challenges involved in ensuring good provision and care for its older population. In order to cater for this a series of new initiatives are being developed. National policy on provision for the elderly is governed on the whole by the clauses and recommendations of a report produced by a working party on services for older people published in 1988 ('The Years Ahead: A Policy for the Elderly 1988'). The group chiefly responsible for compiling the report was the National Council for the Elderly. The report was welcomed by the government. It highlighted several objectives of public and social policy in respect to people over the age of 65. Emphasis was placed on the need to maintain older people in their own home and to encourage and support the care of the elderly in their own local communities by family, neighbours and voluntary organizations in as many ways as possible. In addition, the provision of good-quality hospitals and residential care was proposed for elderly people when they can no longer be maintained independently and with dignity at home. In pursuit of these objectives far more emphasis is now placed on the coordination and regulation of provision of services at national, district and local levels.

The Irish EC council member of Eurolink Age is the National Council for the Elderly. The role of the National Council for the Elderly, the membership of which is drawn from relevant government departments, the area health boards, the medical and nursing professions, the trades unions and voluntary bodies of all kinds, is to advise the Minister for Health on all aspects of ageing and the welfare of the elderly.

It does this by maintaining a dual focus, advising on matters pertaining to the welfare of the elderly population generally and on matters specific to vulnerable groups within the elderly population. It has been instrumental in the establishment of an ongoing national promotion of positive attitudes to older people, age and opportunity. It has also initiated and set up a national organization, the Irish Association of Older People.

The Association of Older People has coordinated a public educational positive-action programme directed at challenging the common negative stereotypes about ageing. This is to be achieved through a dual approach: by encouraging increased understanding and empathy between the generations and as such making progress towards tackling prejudice and discrimination; and by highlighting the potential and the untapped skills and experience of older people. Its second role is crucial if older people are going to be considered as 'useful' and active members of the community. Interestingly, in 1991 central government added weight to its policy by prohibiting the upper age-limits for entry and recruitment into the Irish civil service. In theory this means that older people can apply on an equal basis with younger people for posts throughout all civil service departments – which constitutes a major public-sector employer in Ireland. Eventually it should also mean that older people get more say in the decisions of policymakers as they become more actively involved in policy formation.

Sexuality

The situation regarding homosexuality in Ireland is similarly achieving a new political and social openness. In theory, practicing homosexual sex between consenting adults has carried a threat of ten-year to life imprisonment; in practice, though, the law has rarely been enforced. Sexual activity between gay men is still illegal in Ireland, but following a judgement against it in the European Court of Human Rights the Irish Government agreed to reform the law in 1991. The new president of Ireland, Mary Robinson, is already being credited with altering the mood of her country. Almost straightaway after her inauguration in 1990 both the Prime Minister and the Justice Minister announced their intention to proceed with new laws towards decriminalizing homosexuality. Unfortunately, however, the Irish presidency is only about as powerful as, for instance, the European Parliament – which as an elected organization actually has far less real political power than the Council of Ministers or the European Commission.

The Law Reform Committee has recommended a single age of consent of 15 for lesbian, gay and heterosexual sex. The only exceptions to their recommendation are that age 17 should be the minimum age for both heterosexual and homosexual anal intercourse, and age 17 if undue influence or authority is used. These changes will bring Ireland into line with the rest of Europe, since out of the 12 member countries it was alone in proclaiming homosexual sex between men as illegal. The discrimination has been particularly aimed at homosexual sex between men, since lesbian activity is legal from the age of 17.

In other areas relating to homosexuality the Irish stance has been broadly similar to that of other Member States. The law does not recognize same-sex partnerships. In addition to this, there is no law against discrimination on the grounds of sexuality; although guidelines issued by the Minister of Finance do make it illegal in the civil service. Lesbian and gay men are not allowed to serve in the armed forces; it is claimed that this would have a negative effect on standards of discipline and order. Any individual serving in the forces and subsequently discovered to be lesbian or gay is discharged. To conclude on a positive note, however, the Prohibition of Incitement to Hatred Act introduced in 1989 makes it a criminal offence to incite hatred against any individual(s) on the grounds of sexuality.

13

Italy

Italy is a republic in southern Europe. It has a population of just over 58 million. The main industrial region is the triangular area formed by Turin, Milan and Genoa. Italy was a founder member of NATO in 1949 and of the EEC in 1957. It is a constitutional democracy, with an elected Chamber of Deputies and a Senate elected on a regional basis. Members of both houses serve five-year terms. As in France, an identification card is more of a social than a legal necessity. Probably the two most prevalent characteristics of Italian society are the Catholic Church and the traditional family grouping. Although most Italians are members of the Roman Catholic Church, following a revised concordat it is no longer the state religion. The Church does, however, play an important but no longer central role in peoples' lives in Italy. Italy has ratified two United Nations covenants: the International Covenant on Civil and Political Rights; and on Economic, Social and Cultural Rights. It has signed the Convention of Equality for Women.

The Position of Women

Today every major Italian city has a number of feminist organizations. The roots of the Italian women's movement go back to the late 1960s, and founders are commonly referred to as 'the '68ers'. Feminism and Communism have been more closely tied in Italy than elsewhere; many of the former political activists of the '68ers still belong to the large Italian Communist Party. Italy is a country which has wide regional variations and presents two quite distinct pictures, from the prosperous and more liberal north to the poorer and more traditional south. Traditional marriage-roles persist, particularly in the south; in fact, the degree of independence and freedom a woman is likely to enjoy can to a certain extent be geographically predicted. A woman born, educated and employed in Florence, for example, is more likely to have greater equality than a Neopolitan.

Italian law relating to the Equal Treatment principle was enshrined in law number 903 in 1977, and on several counts it is more generous in its provision than equivalent laws in other EC member countries. The law prohibits all types of discrimination based on a person's sex, marital status and, in the case of women, pregnancy, with respect to appointments, transfers, promotion, dismissal or any unfavourable treatment in any other area. The latter clause provides for tremendous leeway in its interpretation. The same law extends to cover non-discrimination in retirement ages, which means that sudden and unprotected dismissal for workers, particularly women, over arbitrarily set retirement ages, common in many of the Twelve, is prohibited.

A law introduced in 1991 signals the introduction of far more positive steps towards increased sexual equality. The measures included in the law aim to foster employment among the female population. In addition, they aim to achieve real equality between men and women in all employment-related matters including vocational training and career prospects. The law also provides for the possibility of financial incentives for those employers or cooperatives which undertake positive action to redress the imbalances of past discrimination. The most significant step in the consultation process about the law was the establishment of a National Committee to implement the principles of equal treatment and equal opportunities. Other functions it sets out to perform include the removal of economic and institutionalized barriers to sex equality and monitoring of employers' recruitment policies, in addition to the standard equal opportunities policies. It intends to promote the more widespread development of positive-action programmes. It is interesting to note that the primary function of the committee is to develop and improve upon the legislation that has already been in place for some time now. Italian policymakers have been the first to accept that equality laws demand continuous reappraisal and assessment, and cannot be expected to work adequately if they are regarded by central government as one-day wonders. The latter move would be a welcome measure for all other Member States to follow.

Parental Rights and Childcare

Italy is among the most generous of EC countries in terms of duration of time off for maternity leave: a woman may take up to 44 weeks off work and receive 80 per cent of her normal earnings for the entire period. The earnings are paid by the social insurance fund. A further six months' leave is optional during the child's first year, payable at a 30 per cent rate of normal earnings. An added benefit of the Italian law is the availability of two hours per day paid time off until the child's first birthday. Widely implemented on a European scale, this entitlement would ensure far higher participation of mothers in the labour market. The right to daily time off was introduced in Italy as far back as 1971. There is no continuous employment requirement for maternity provision under Italian law; the law merely states that a woman must be employed and insured at the beginning of her pregnancy. A 1987 court case gave fathers the right to the maternity-leave period and to the daily rest periods at work before a child's first birthday in the case of the mother's death or severe disability.

There have been several positive developments in the period 1985–1990; though their potential effects have been hindered by inadequate funding and underdevelopment. There has been little growth in publicly funded services during this time and publicly funded nurseries have faced cuts by central government. The needs of parents for longer opening hours in childcare provision, and the opposing call for a reduction in the hours of workers in childcare services, have created many problems and little common ground on which to set up an agenda for change. The fundamental problem is that longer opening hours require more workers – and this is obviously not compatible with a policy of reducing public spending.

Positive initiative enacted during the same period include a report commissioned by the government on pre-primary educational provision. This went far beyond what can standardly be expected of such reports, and was much more than an academic exercise in so far as it paid special attention to the objectives and methods of pre-school education – and sought input from the public in order fully to reflect needs. The final result was a report which took into account the recommendations not only of politicians and educationalists, but, for the first time, of trade unions, employers and parents too. The educational function and style of nurseries has been developed and improved in many areas, and several moves towards greater flexibility in both the provision and delivery of services are apparent.

A number of bills have been presented to Parliament by members of the Communist Party as well as women's groups which have jointly proposal paid parental leave in response to the right of adequate 'care' provision for all citizens. The proposals emphasize that unemployed citizens are deprived of adequate care, and also emphasize the right to 'care' for all citizens, not just those who are employed. Political rhetoric aside, there has also been an increased amount of grassroots debate about such issues as childcare, equal opportunities and the importance of the right to choose alternative lifestyles. These debates continue into the 1990s and serve to challenge the more traditionally held beliefs of Italy's past; and may ultimately serve to force political consideration of the redistribution of paid work and the provision of care.

The 1977 law gave both men and women the right to time off from work when their children under three years old are sick. This is in stark contrast to the situation in the UK where no such eligibility exists and time taken to care for a sick child has consequently to be taken from annual holiday entitlements.

Race Relations

Italy has traditionally been regarded as more typically a nation of emigrants than of immigrants. In the past it has usually had a relaxed attitude to multi-culturalism and migration. Historically, there have been pockets of migration of Italian workers to more prosperous areas in northern Europe. Guestworkers arrived in the UK, for example, and the majority settled in the Midlands and the north and found work in the motor industry. The very term 'guestworker' suggests that they were regarded as temporary, and therefore not eligible for all the usual rights associated with having a permanent status. As Italy's economy prospered, however, many guestworkers returned to the more thriving cities of northern Italy, while others remained in northern Europe and have readily assimilated.

Nowadays, however, the situation is entirely changed. Italian immigration policies, like those in the rest of Europe, are at the top of the political agenda, and Italy has prepared in much the same way as other countries in the EC for demographic conditions in the Single European Market by getting ready to protect its borders from non-EC nationals.

Historically, immigration into Italy began later than in the rest of the EC, and therefore the growth of a multi-ethnic community is a more recent occurrence. Italy was to colonize parts of Africa and the West Indies later than other EC countries, whose colonization was quite well established by the time Italy took her 'turn' to become colonial presence in Africa. The end of the Second World War saw the end of the Italian presence in Africa, but it hailed the beginning of an African presence in Italy. One million migrants have arrived in Italy in the last 15 years; most have come from the ex-colonies, parts of north Africa, the Philippines, the Middle East, Cape Verde, Guyana, Senegal and Somalia. The majority arrived in two separate stages – the mid 1970s and a decade later in the mid 1980s.

Starvation, poor sanitary conditions, few chances of work and poor future prospects at home have led many migrants from the ex-colonies to be lured by the prospect of jobs and a better future in Italy. In a similar way to all other EC countries and their past colonies, as the Italian labour force got used to the post-war economic boom, the more traditional industries like manufacturing and agriculture were deserted. Clearly, in Italy as elsewhere, if governments are advertising for migrant workers they ought also to implement economic and social policy to cope with the needs of minority groups, as well as to clarify their position on immigration.

The Italian public, like the British public, have shown a tendency to grossly overestimate the scale of immigration, and frequently refer to the minority population as if it were present on a scale of billions. In fact, in Italy, out of a total population of 56 million, there are one million who have come directly from third-world countries.

Many immigrants have tended to concentrate in southern Italy, where the Mafia has provided (albeit illegal) employment opportunities. Living conditions for migrants are typically poor and an individual's attempt to improve his or her circumstances is fraught with the problems associated with not enjoying a legal status. Due to the difficulty in the past (and current impossibility) of gaining legal status, there are consequently more illegal than legal immigrants in the south of Italy. The Italian government held an amnesty in 1990 for immigrants to register by the 1st June of that year or not at all; anyone who did not register or who has arrived since may no longer do so. For the illegal immigrant, access to education, formal employment, hospitals, basic medical care and all other basic rights is denied; therefore merely surviving is a problem in itself. Most illegal immigrants work as street traders, car windscreen washers, cigarette 'lighters', or within the sex industry and agriculture. Agriculture is a major employer, with over half of the tomato crops being harvested by African workers, typically working 14 hours per day at very low rates of pay. Illegal workers, simply by virtue of their status under the law, have little right of appeal against bad working conditions or low pay.

A number of divergent approaches have grown up in response to immigration in Italy. Lega-Centro, a political party prevalent in the north, have two seats in the European Parliament and are more interested in stricter immigration control than in fostering good race-relations. They rely heavily on a white racist vote for election. The 'Martelli Law' has, in theory, unified policy on immigration and introduced a quota system of specific numbers it intends to permit access to. The current quota figure is set at 0 per cent. The Martelli Law's measures include a requirement to integrate all legal immigrant workers who comply with the laws of Italy. Needless to say, for immigrants who cannot even attain legal status this is an impossible requirement. One school of thought believes that it is generally better to remain illegal anyway. Informal employment is easier to get and informal welfare systems are more readily accessible. The Italian Catholic Church has done more for the welfare of minority communities than the government has. In Rome, it has set up a 'Centre for Immigrants' which aims to provide shelter, welfare, food and basic health care for illegal immigrants who cannot attain those services elsewhere. They also have a network of welfare groups called 'caritas' across the whole of Italy.

Italy is the most recent member of 'the Schengen Countries', along with France, Germany, Belgium, Italy, the Netherlands and Luxembourg. The Schengen Agreement, which each of these member countries signed, concerns the joint demography and immigration conditions of the member countries, and goes some way towards coordinating policy on immigration between neighbouring states. Implicit in 'Schengen' is the requirement to 'share' information between members about asylum applications, visa applications, immigration and identity details. Ultimately, it is likely that the effect of the Schengen Agreement will be to help identify a stockpile of workers to be sent from country to country as and when the demand arises, and readily disposed of after the demand has been met. Clearly, it will not enhance race relations and anti-discrimination measures when the emphasis is so overwhelmingly on immigration control.

Disability

The full integration of disabled people into all aspects of social and economic life in Italy has been a major theme since the early 1980s. The significance of the Italian Integrated Cooperatives for the employment of people with special needs provides a good practice role model which other Member States could adopt. One of the main characteristics of the Integrated Cooperative is that disabled people work alongside non-disabled people as equal partners in a real production team. Although there is financial support for the cooperatives, they represent more than simply a sheltered workshop environment. It is an expression of the whole social-cultural context of Italian society where solidarity and equal rights are very important.

Italy has also won a number of awards under the HELIOS Independent Living Awards Programme. In Torino a project entitled 'Apriti Sesamo' won a HELIOS award in 1990. The project provides equipment which allows a severely disabled person to completely control his or her environment. The system is controlled by a voice recognition system and allows for normal computer operation plus control of doors, windows, telephones, radios, lights, etc.

Age Issues

The Italian Communist Party addresses the needs of older citizens and extends the term 'care' to include the care of all people, whether young or old, economically active or unemployed. In many countries the system of financial care networks has depended heavily on an individual's income and status; as a consequence good quality care has benefited high-income households far more than it has benefited the less well-off. The Catholic Church has done more through its well-developed welfare system for the less well-off than the policymakers have. The growth of the Independent Communist Party is also making much progress in its policy and activities with disadvantaged groups such as the elderly.

Throughout Italy there are hospices for the old, called 'Houses of Rest'. However, these vary greatly in number and quality depending on the town they are in. In many northern towns there are well-developed services for older people. For example, in Trieste there are discounts for old people on buses and at cinemas, and cheap lunches are provided. The municipality also organizes holidays to the sea or the mountains and free laundry for those in need. The further south, the weaker the central organization and the more the family takes its place, particularly as far as looking after older people is concerned.

One interesting development for older people is The University of the Third Age. The idea for this originated in France and has now spread to about 50 cities in Italy. An additional service has also been set up, called 'Tribunal of the Third Age', which consists of three retired magistrates and four members of a university course. The Tribunal meets once a month on Saturdays and deals with complaints from older people about transport, water supply and administrative services, and gives advice where necessary.

Sexuality

The legal age of consent for gay, lesbian or heterosexual sex in Italy is 14 and as such does not differentiate between one form over another. A minimum age of 16 applies if the older person is a guardian or teacher, or any other person in a position of responsibility over the younger partner. There is no law in Italy against discrimination on the grounds of sexuality, which means that a gay or lesbian can be freely discriminated against simply by being open about his or her sexuality. As in several Member States, homosexuality is considered justifiable grounds for unfitness for military service. In addition, Italy does not recognize same-sex partnerships, which in practice means that gay and lesbian couples are denied many of the basic social and economic rights available to heterosexuals.

14
Luxembourg

Luxembourg has a population of less than half a million and as such is the smallest member of the European Community. It is a Grand Duchy located between Belgium, France and Germany. Germany occupied the country during the First and Second World Wars and left its mark for several years after. In 1944 Belgium, the Netherlands and Luxembourg formed the Benelux Customs Union. Luxembourg was a founder member of NATO in 1949 and of the EEC in 1957. It is governed by a constitutional monarchy with an elected Chamber of Deputies, and it has a tradition for respecting human rights treaties. Luxembourg has ratified the United Nations covenants: the International Covenant on Economic, Social and Cultural Rights and the International Covenant on Civil and Political Rights. It has also ratified the Convention on Equality for Women. Most of the population throughout the entire country can speak and write several languages. In everyday conversation, the Luxembourg dialect (with its limited vocabulary) is generally used to begin with, with the discussion moving rapidly into French or German when dialect becomes insufficient. Luxembourg is a prosperous country and its citizens enjoy many of the benefits which are not available to others in less well-off Member States.

Luxembourg has developed a successful economy even though it has few of the more common heavy manufacturing industries built into its economic base. There is a strong dependence on foreign trade and an extensive recruitment of foreign workers; in fact the number of foreign residents is generally about 25 per cent of the population at any given time, the highest in the Community. Because of its reliance on and familiarity with foreign workers there is a much less noticeable level of institutionalized racism or ethnocentrism. Cosmopolitanism has created a fairly relaxed attitude to alternative lifestyles, different cultures and minority groups in the community.

Its economic, social and geographical structure have necessarily led Luxembourg into a close cooperation with other countries. In addition, it is playing an increasing role as an international finance centre. In such an economically lively country it is not surprising that business has thrived and benefited the population. Women, however, are concentrated in the lower status and lower-paid jobs, and for many the traditional role of fulfilling family responsibilities remains the norm. Luxembourg has a wealthy tradition, reflected in its position almost at the top of Member States in GDP per capita. The economic necessity to work is perhaps not as much of a priority in Luxembourg as it is in poorer member countries, and consequently part-time work is far more common than in other states.

The Position of Women

There is no formally organized or central women's movement as such and the feminist sub-cultures that have grown up have been heavily influenced by 'imported' feminist activity and theory from neighbouring countries. Due to the high number of foreign male workers a sophisticated network of fairly traditional businessmen's clubs has grown up. For women, who are not nearly as economically active as men, the British Ladies Club and the American Women's Club provide the social and cultural base – clearly more from a traditionally feminine than feminist standpoint.

Luxembourg provides a fine example of the opposing forces of the nature of oppression which leads to the growth or decline of organized women's movements. Prosperity in the general standards of living has a tendency to hide much of the oppression which is lurking beneath the surface, and the need to react against such oppression is not as prominent as when poverty serves more blatantly to reveal oppressive structures. Interestingly, today it is the poorer countries in the world which are providing much of the impetus of the late twentieth century women's movement; unlike in the past when it grew out of an almost exclusively white middle-class perspective. There is evidence which suggests that the richer a country becomes, the more overwhelmingly entrenched are the disparities that exist between men and women in terms of pay, conditions and indeed all types of social and economic benefits – a system which benefits men far more than it benefits women, and only serves to perpetuate women's conditioning as wives and mothers when the economic need to 'be' anything else is reduced.

Parental Rights and Childcare

There is in Luxembourg no continuous employment requirement for women to be eligible for maternity leave. Social security coverage for a minimum of six months during the year immediately preceding the year of confinement is sufficient. Paid maternity leave is guaranteed by law since 1975. The entitlement lasts for up to 16 weeks and the woman receives 100 per cent of her normal earnings. In contrast to Spain, but in line with most of Europe, there is no statutory paternity leave; though a bill on parental leave in the private sector was given its first reading in 1983, it has made little progress since. There are differences in Luxembourg law between the rights and entitlements of public and private sector workers, with the latter faring slightly better.

In a similar fashion to Belgium, France, Greece, Portugal and Spain, Luxembourg has specific laws for leave for family reasons. Statutory rights to leave for family reasons was guaranteed under Article 16 of the law introduced in 1966. Whether because theirs is one of the longest-standing laws of this nature or because Luxembourg is a wealthy country, entitlements are a little more generous than in other member countries. Bereavement and illness are the standard reasons respected throughout most of Europe, and are incorporated alongside the wedding of a child, one's own wedding and moving house. The entitlements for each may be improved either by collective agreement or by an individual employer's custom and practice. Whichever arrangement is made, full pay is guaranteed under the law.

Since 1979, there has been continuous government support for the development of childcare services. The main priority has been to increase the number of services provided by non-profit-making private organizations, and subsidized by public funds from the Ministry of the Family. The number of such places funded by the government grew by nearly 50 per cent in the five years between 1985 and 1990. Another positive development is the attention that is being given to providing more flexible opening hours in childcare centres, which enables parents to be more flexible in their working arrangements.

Disability

Luxembourg has developed several successful Local Model Activities (LMA) under the HELIOS programme for the integration of people with special learning needs. The theme of de-institutionalization has been the subject of much research in Luxembourg since the early 1980s. The research points out that people with special learning needs who have experienced institutional life very often need practical help if they are to be equal members of society and be integrated successfully. The LMAs' task has been primarily to diminish the dependency that is fostered by institutional life. This is an important stage to work through to prepare for an independent life. The activities administered under HELIOS in Luxembourg have focused mainly on the 'exit' aspect of the institutionalization-to-integration process.

Age Issues

Luxembourg has one of the highest rates of pension expenditure as a percentage of GDP in the Community. Clearly this is of great importance to the relatively high number of older people in Luxembourg in comparison to most other Member States. In fact, by the year 2,025 Luxembourg, along with Denmark, will have the highest percentage of older people in its population. The key implications of the EC action programme for the elderly are therefore of special relevance to Luxembourg. The Luxembourg representative on the Eurolink Age Consultative Committee is the Minister of the Family, which at least would seem to guarantee age-related issues a place on the domestic political agenda.

Sexuality

Similar to UK legislation, Luxembourg law discriminates between homosexuals and heterosexuals in that it differentiates between the ages of consent for the two forms of sexual activity. For a gay man or lesbian the minimum age is 18, four years above the minimum age limit for heterosexuals, which is set at 14. It is worth noting that the consensual age for gay male sex is the second highest in the EC, lower only than the UK. In addition, there is no law against discrimination on the grounds of sexuality; therefore gays and lesbians are unprotected against all forms of harassment and victimization. The same legal situation prevails in Luxembourg as in almost all EC countries in that same-sex partnerships are not recognized, so that the standard problems of immigration and social security rights prevail.

15 The Netherlands

The Netherlands is a prosperous parliamentary monarchy in the north of the European plain. It has a population of just less than 15 million. The Netherlands joined NATO in 1949 and was a founder member of the EEC in 1957. Its last two monarchs, Queen Wilhelmina and Queen Juliana, both abdicated in favour of their daughters. Queen Beatrix became head of state in 1980. The parliament consists of an upper chamber with 75 members elected by the provincial legislators, and a second chamber of 150 directly elected deputies. Equality is regarded as an important and real issue by government, and the Netherlands is renowned for having one of the highest human rights ratings in the world. The Netherlands has ratified two United Nations covenants: the International Covenant on Civil and Political Rights, and on Economic, Social and Cultural Rights. It has signed the Convention on Equality for Women. There are no compulsory documents such as an identification card which are legally required at all times.

There are essentially two Hollands: Amsterdam, and the rest. Amsterdam is very liberal in contrast to the entrenched conservatism of the rural provinces. Outside the capital life can seem parochial and restricted; and behaviour readily accepted in the capital would be frowned upon in the provinces, especially in the Catholic areas of the south. The main religions are Roman Catholicism and Protestantism.

The Position of Women

The large diverse women's movement had its origins in the radical movements of the 1960s. The movement spearheaded numerous important campaigns, particularly the move in the 1970s to legalize abortion. Women are more politically active and centrally involved in domestic politics in the Netherlands than in most Member States. Their high profile in mainstream politics is reflected in the hundreds of women's groups associated with the labour party alone. In contrast to the UK, the Netherlands have established a registered trade union called the 'Women's Union'. The principal aim of the union is to raise the level of public awareness about the social conditions of the women doing unpaid work – notably, housewives. It has a long-standing tradition of active campaigns aimed at improving their economic and social status.

Equality of the sexes during marriage and divorce proceedings is more of a reality than in the rest of Europe. Property and financial rights are fairly evenly balanced between the sexes. In addition to this, contraceptive pills and condoms are freely available and there are no restrictions on their sales. Although women have access to most areas of employment, representation at the very highest levels is still quite poor and white male dominance the prevailing pattern.

The Netherlands have implemented the Equal Treatment Directive under the 'Act On Equal Treatment of Men And Women' which was introduced in 1980. Immediately following the Act, the Dutch Civil Code was amended to incorporate a new provision forbidding any direct or indirect discrimination between men and women. The Act has very wide-ranging provision and applies to all forms of inequality, including unequal pay arising from indirect discrimination, direct discrimination, marital status and family life. Discrimination in recruitment, advertising, training, employment conditions, promotion, termination of employment and vocational guidance are all prohibited by the Act. However, similar to the position in the UK, discriminatory retirement ages for men and women contravene the Equal Treatment principle.

Any dispute or grievance arising from differences in the legislation and contracts of employment are submitted to the Cantonal Court. Where a claim is brought by an employee or when an employer wishes to check whether legislation is being breached, reference can be made to the Committee on Equal Treatment for Men and Women at Work. The Committee has an equivalent remit to the Equal Opportunities Commission in the UK in that it is empowered to conduct investigatory work into problems and draft a report on its findings. If a dispute still exists the matter can be brought to the Cantonal Court who have ultimate power to decide upon appropriate action. It seems, therefore, that contravention of laws is penalized more strictly than in most other Member States.

Parental Rights and Childcare

In the Netherlands paid maternity leave at 100 per cent of normal earnings is guaranteed under the 'Sickness Law' implemented in 1967. It is worth noting that such a law represents one of the first of its kind in Europe, although its incorporation under a 'sickness' law suggests a rather negative perception of pregnancy. It was originally intended to provide for 12 weeks' cover only, but it was extended in 1990 up to 16 weeks. The payments are administered in much the same way as all other sickness payments are. The Netherlands has no continuous employment requirement clause.

A number of fairly recent proposals suggest that an overall improvement in parental rights may come about in the near future. One such proposal is to extend the eligible time-period for leave after the birth. Although officially there is no paternity leave as such, the birth of a child is considered to merit leave for 'personal reasons'. In addition, there are currently no statutory rights to parental leave, but it is under proposal and has been approved by the parliament. Recent positive developments in childcare within the Netherlands include a substantial increase in employer-provided childcare services. Childcare has gained a place on the political agenda and is widely debated, although the discussions tend to be focused rather too narrowly on the concept of childcare. As in several other EC countries, the debate centres on the economic reasons for improvements in the system, rather than on the broader equal responsibility issues between mothers and fathers, and between parents, employers and, indeed, society as a whole.

There have been important changes in the funding of services, and since 1987 all policy and expenditure on childcare provision has been de-centralized. Regional provision differs widely as local authorities are entirely in charge of deciding how much to spend and what sorts of provision to offer. Tax relief on parental childcare costs was introduced in 1984 and was ended in 1989. The substantial revenue saved was diverted to the Department of Welfare for providing more childcare services for as many working parents as possible. Presumably, the second method has benefited more lower-income families than the original tax-relief plan.

It seems that although there is much political rhetoric and activity both at a national and local level being centred on childcare issues, the political approaches are not altogether united. In the late 1980s, developments have unfortunately been hampered by the closure of the 'National Childcare Organization', abolished as part of a massive reform of all private organizations. Now, its various roles have been split between many other organizations, with a consequent loss of direction and the power of a central voice on the issues.

Positive Action

Positive-action programmes have been implemented to improve the position of women in the labour market. Several of the strategies which have been launched have received government funding and support towards encouraging much wider support and participation by women in such programmes. The broad aims of the projects have been about easing the access and return of women to the world of paid work. The specific objectives have included positive action on a dual basis; both the training of women for traditional male jobs which they have previously been excluded from, and eliminating occupational sex-stereotyping through increased awareness-raising. Emphasis has been placed on the benefits to women in employment of acquiring new technological skills. Further, emphasis on encouraging women to set up their own businesses as a way of entering the labour market has grown in the past few years.

Furthermore, in 1989 another programme was launched which was far broader in conception than its predecessors. In addition to focusing on the special employment needs of women in general, it was extended to include both women from ethnic minority groups and other groups of women traditionally affected by long-term unemployment. As such it targeted older women and women with disabilities, as well as women facing discrimination due to past offences. The types of training offered have been tailored to meet the needs of the employment market.

Race Relations

Despite the Netherlands having built up a reputation of liberalism and tolerance, it has one of the highest unemployment rates in

Europe for ethnic minority groups. Currently the level of unemployment among ethnic minorities is four times higher than among the white Dutch population. The majority of minority groups in the Netherlands are from Surinam, Morocco and Turkey. The largest numbers arrived in 1975; as Surinam, the Netherlands' former colony on the coast of South America, became independent, 150,000 of its former population of 400,000 had left for the Netherlands because of the threat of civil war between the creoles and the Hindus – a war which did not materialize.

Since 1975, restrictions have been imposed on the entry of minorities. Immigration controls and restrictions are a fairly typical response of the majority of EC countries to ethnic minority migration. Disillusionment and alienation coupled with pressure to assimilate and conform characterizes race relations in Holland. White European attempts at forcing minorities to assimilate and integrate are, moreover, far more to do with loss of ethnic identity than genuine commitment to racial equality from the policy-makers.

The Employment Board considers the improvements to ethnic minority job expectations to be essential. Their new aim is to provide job placements for the same percentage of job seekers from ethnic minority groups as their share in the unemployment figures. The agreement aims to create 60,000 new jobs in industry for minority groups by 1996. It is proposed (though not likely to be enforceable) that employers set their own targets in form of work plans and measures. Although the Employment Board and the Labour Foundation both consider training of minority groups to be extremely important, they are not willing to go so far as to impose sanctions or to penalize an employer who does not comply. The history of equality issues has shown that without, for example, a Quota system whereby percentages are enforced and regularly monitored, the proposals may have little effect.

How far ethnic minority communities will benefit from such proposals in the Netherlands remains a subject of much speculation and debate. In 1991 the Central Employment Board and the Labour Foundation reached a consensus about the implementation of an agreement on ethnic minorities. In order to fulfil the agreement effectively the Employment Service have appointed 50 extra staff to assist in its implementation. The Employment Board has also stated its intention to pay extra attention to the training needs of job seekers from ethnic minority groups.

Disability

The concept of Independent Living (IL) originated on the campus of the University of California at Berkeley, in the US. In order to enjoy a full social life, the disabled students joined forces to pay for the services of assistants. This student movement grew into a political movement which culminated in the passing of an anti-discrimination law (The Americans with Disabilities Act, ADA, 1990). Individuals suffering with a disability can now appeal to this law to demand equal rights and facilities. In the meantime, the concept of Independent Living has continued to gain ground in Europe, and disabled people are now demanding the right to assume responsibility for their own lives.

In the Netherlands, Independent Living has become a reality for many hundreds of disabled people. An organization called Independent Living Netherlands has been set up to monitor Independent Living projects at local and regional level. Four working parties have also been established. These include a public relations working party to promote the idea of Independent Living and organize pilot projects; a procedural working party which seeks to guarantee the principle of Equal Treatment for participants; a counselling working party which constitutes a network of experts from health and welfare fields; and, last but not least, a 'personally-oriented budgetary system' which works towards 'personally-oriented' budgets so that disabled people can provide for their own assistance services. The development of a personal assistance model is vital within the Independent Living movement.

Age Issues

The Netherlands has one of the highest rates in pension expenditure as a percentage of GDP in the EC. By the year 2,025 it will also have one of the highest population percentages of older workers in the Community. Unfortunately, however, it does not have any legislation against age discrimination. On the other hand the Netherlands has in the past responded quite well to the special needs of older people. Concern over what was considered to be a high rate of institutionalization resulted in the setting-up of a central referral system, whereby every potential applicant for institutional care undergoes a diagnostic assessment in order to determine the most appropriate kind of care. The Netherlands, like Sweden, has placed special emphasis on 'adapted housing' and on a type of accommodation they call 'pensioners' hotels'. In both pensioners' hotels and adapted housing, older people live independently in self-contained apartments, with complete access to communal facilities such as dining, recreational and medical services.

Sexuality

In line with the Dutch reputation for acceptance, no other European city accepts homosexuality as readily as does Amsterdam. It says a lot about the strength of the Amsterdam community that the arrival of AIDS was not accompanied by the marked increase in homophobia witnessed in many other places. In 1991 the Dutch government approved a law which sets the age of consent for both homosexual and heterosexual activity at 12. The change is part of a clarification of the 150-year-old Morality Act. At first, the Justice Minister who put forward the new law, proposed decriminalizing only consensual activity for heterosexual people between 12 and 16; while retaining penalties for gay sex under age 16, consensual or not. Needless to say, this met with scorn from a number of organizations and was withdrawn in favour of the non-discriminatory proposal which was passed. Similar to most other European countries the higher age-of-consent limit of 16 holds if a younger partner files a complaint.

Gays and lesbians in the Netherlands have more protection against discrimination than in most other EC countries, with the notable exception of Denmark. Article 1 of the Dutch Constitution provides that there should be equal treatment on all grounds; this was later interpreted and translated as also prohibiting discrimination on the basis of sexuality. Civil law grants equal status to homosexuality and heterosexuality. Furthermore, the Dutch government is considering proposals for introducing comprehensive anti-discrimination laws which explicitly protect lesbians and gay men. Unlike in the UK, homosexuality is no bar to serving in the armed forces. The situation regarding same-sex partnerships is also more progressive in the Netherlands than in most other Member States. Same-sex partners or unmarried couples (whether heterosexual or homosexual) can enter into a cohabitation contract. The contract assists towards the practical organization of relationships in areas such as property rights, taxation, next-of-kin visiting rights in hospitals and prisons, etc. – but it does not give unmarried couples entirely equal rights to married couples. Its main shortfall is that is has no effect on third parties; so, for instance, it cannot be used to require a pension fund to provide spousal benefits to a same-sex partner. In conclusion, 1990 saw the beginning of legal proposals towards the equal recognition of all partnerships whether gay, lesbian or heterosexual. The proposals were favoured by most political parties in the Dutch government. Such partnerships would ultimately have similar legal social and economic benefits (and constraints) as marriage contracts.

16

Portugal

Portugal is a republic in the Iberian peninsula; much of the land is an extension of the Spanish meseta. It has a population of around ten million, several million of whom are employed in the thriving tourist industry. Between the 1930s and the early 1970s Portugal had an autocratic government; since then democracy has returned in two stages. A coup in 1974 led to the restoration of democracy and to independence for Angola, Cape Verde, Guinea-Bissau and Mozambique in Africa. The ousting of the 1974 dictatorship was followed by the dissolution of the Council of the Revolution in 1982, which finally ended the participation of the military in government. Today Portugal is a parliamentary democracy. The main religion is Roman Catholicism. Portugal has ratified the Covenant on Economic, Social and Cultural Rights and the Covenant on Civil and Political Rights, and has ratified the Convention on Equality for Women. Portugal is one of the most recent members of the European Community. The north–south divide within the EC is inescapably apparent in Portugal. Wages are among the lowest, if not the lowest, in Europe. Citizens are legally obliged to carry an identification card with them at all times.

The Position of Women

In addition to providing a sudden independence for the colonies, the 1974 revolution led to enormous changes inside Portugal. Women campaigned and organized alongside men for alterations in family laws and the assertion of workers' rights. Constitutional equality of the sexes in marriage and divorce proceedings had been prevented by traditional religious factors working to women's disadvantage; these are gradually being overcome by the overall social progress and a general consolidation of democracy and human rights. Positive legal reforms were welcomed, a woman Prime Minister was briefly in office, and there has been a higher profile and participation of women in further and higher education. However, given the persistent strength of tradition, the Portuguese women's movement has had tremendous problems organizing on the large scale evident in other member countries, even though their demands have been relatively modest. Compared with other Mediterranean countries the movement today is small, but is well organized centrally from Lisbon. Also, in contrast to other Latin countries, machismo is far less rampant in Portugal. However, Portuguese society is still heavily male-dominated and in many of the rural areas women are still primarily recognized within the context of their family relationships: somebody's wife, daughter, aunt, sister, etc.

While women achieved equality on paper within half a decade of the revolution, feminism has had little institutional or social support within the corridors of the white male socialist government. More worryingly, equality principles have not been enshrined in autonomous laws as they have elsewhere, and have been merely 'tagged on' to existing laws and amendments.

Parental Rights and Childcare

Portugal is among the most generous in the EC in respect of maternity pay rates. Paid maternity leave is guaranteed through social security, and 100 per cent of normal salary is provided. It was originally guaranteed under the Maternity and Paternity Protection Law which was introduced in 1984, and further improved amendments were enacted by Decree Law in 1985, and by Regulatory Decree in 1987. In addition, there is no continuous employment requirement. Paid paternity leave is guaranteed under the same law which governs maternity provisions. In Portugal, fathers are able to take the last 30 or 60 days of the mother's maternity leave in the event of her sickness, or all the outstanding leave in the event of her death. The mother or father may take unpaid leave of between six months and two years to look after a child until it reaches the age of three. These rights, which apply to both private and public sectors, apply also to adoptive parents. Employees have the right to return to their old job on the expiry of their leave entitlement. Portugal is in a similar position to most other EC countries in that it provides some form of statutory right to time off for family reasons such as ill health, bereavement or weddings.

In the late 1980s, well over half of Portuguese women with a child under ten were employed, representing one of the highest levels in the Community. Significant developments in the late 1980s included tax-relief measures towards a proportion of childcare costs, and a firmer commitment to parents' rights on the political agenda. A new Education Law has made the state responsible for developing a system of pre-primary schooling for all children from age three upwards. The official objective is to ensure provision for 90 per cent of five-year-olds and 50 per cent of three-year-olds to be in place by 1983, either in pre-primary schools or in kindergartens. The same law also proposes that traditional schooling should be complemented by other activities to stimulate the all-round development of children.

Positive Action

In the recent past Portugal has implemented positive-action programmes aimed at securing work for young unemployed women in traditional male occupations, which due to institutional and cultural traditions and prejudices they have been excluded from in the past. The first such projects were involved in joinery, painting, plumbing and electricity, and guaranteed the participants practical assistance in securing a contract of employment. The additional benefit of a childcare allowance was included to secure a realistic 'take up' by mothers. Later projects have been supplemented by management training which focused on the setting-up of small businesses and cooperatives, thus enabling women to enter the labour market through self-employment.

Positive-action measures in Portugal have been established with far broader aims than many equivalents in other Member States. A Ministerial Decree in 1988 laid down vocational training subsidies for the activities of the government's own employment and social security departments. Women were targeted among the priority groups alongside people with disabilities, ethnic minority groups, migrant workers and the long-term unemployed. Practical-skill training tailored to the needs of the employment market aims at providing the participants with the necessary skills to compete fairly.

Race Relations

At present, the population of African origin living in Portugal is quite small, numbering about 50,000. The majority of them (about 30,000) are from Cape Verde and the rest are from Angola and Mozambique. In Portugal, there is no legal statute covering immigrants, which makes the administrative process for legalization (work and residence permits) difficult and lengthy. This leaves many immigrants in an irregular situation, which can have serious consequences – lack of social security, housing, trade union rights and schooling. Many Portuguese residents of African descent have been the target of racist propaganda from a number of fringe political groups. One group, CEDADE-Portugal, European Circle Of Friends Of Europe, was formed in 1980 as an affiliate of the Spanish Nazi group CEDADE. It espouses traditional Nazi beliefs and is believed to have only a small membership.

Disability

Many of the services to Portugal's disabled population are concentrated in Lisbon. A committee is responsible for many of the services for disabled people in the Lisbon region. The services include a fleet of 12 adapted vehicles for people with physical disabilities and a sign-language interpreter service. The interpreter service aims to support the deaf population of Lisbon in a number of situations: going to the doctor, taking a driving test, attending meetings and conferences, etc. It also offers sign-language interpreter training.

Portugal has won an award under the HELIOS Independent Living Awards scheme. The Cerebral Palsy Society, based in Lisbon, won the award for the accessibility of its buildings. The society also provides a total training and preparation-for-work programme for young people with cerebral palsy.

Age Issues

Portugal is in a similar demographic position to Ireland in so far as the average age of the workforce is substantially younger than in most EC states. For both older workers and retired people, the rate of unemployment benefits and state pensions is relatively poor. Government expenditure on pensions as a percentage of GDP is among the lowest in Europe. The implementation of the EC Action Programme for older people in 1991 should in theory go some way towards decreasing the disadvantages of older citizens in Portugal.

Sexuality

Portugal has the same age-of-consent laws as Spain; the law does not discriminate against the age at which an individual may practice gay, lesbian or heterosexual sex. The age scale rises from 12 to 16 or 18; the higher age applying respectively if deceit or pressure is used, or undue influence is exerted. As in almost all countries in the EC, there is no law against discrimination on the grounds of sexuality, which in practice means that there is no protection from prejudice, discrimination or harassment for gay men and lesbians. The law does not recognize same-sex partnerships. Article 22 of the law on Military Service excludes from the armed forces those who have been involved in 'offensive acts'.

17

Spain

Spain was declared a republic in 1931 but a civil war between 1936 and 1939 ended in defeat for the republicans. General Francisco Franco became dictator and head of state, although Spain was, in fact, technically a monarchy. After nearly 40 years under fascist rule which ended in 1975 when Franco died, Spain successfully returned to democratic rule. Prince Don Juan Carlos became King and a new constitution was promulgated in 1978 which stated among numerous other clauses that there should be no formal state religion. An unsuccessful army coup took place in February 1981, and peaceful conditions have prevailed since.

Spain has a population of just over 38 million. The official Spanish language is Castilian. However, Basque is spoken in the north in the provinces bordering the Bay of Biscay; Catalan is spoken in the north-east and Galician in the north-west. Separatist movements have developed in these regions and, in 1980, regional governments were established for the Basques and Catalans. In 1981 a similar government was set up in Galicia.

Citizens are legally obliged to carry an identification card at all times. Spain joined the EEC in 1982. Spain has ratified two United Nations Covenants: the International Covenant on Civil and Political Rights and the International Covenant on Economic, Social and Cultural Rights. It has signed the Convention on Equality for Women.

The Position of Women

The new liberalization which swept across Spain after Franco's death was accompanied by a tremendous upsurge in the Spanish women's movement. Organizations sprang up everywhere, eager to reform the oppressive patriarchal structures which had influenced women's lives for so long. Campaigning, lobbying, demonstration and protest were the characteristic activities at the start of the movement. Feminists won the right to contraception and increased emphasis was given to independence and choice; although there is a tradition of constraints on production and sales of contraceptives even to adults due to widespread Church opposition.

The Socialist government, despite constitutional provision for equality, has not made women's emancipation a priority in its programmes for social, political and economic change. Traditions and cultural and religious factors have combined to prevent women's equality issues from moving beyond the stage of formal promises and equality on paper. The strong presence of the Catholic Church is still a major factor influencing the lives of many people. The same factors also work to women's disadvantage in marriage and divorce proceedings.

The main activities of the women's movement are nowadays undertaken by the Feminist Party, which is a registered political organization. Issues as wide-ranging as pornography, disarmament, herstory, sexuality and employment were all subjects debated in the 1980s. The new wave of liberalism has brought about many changes in Spain, but not all the changes benefit women. One of the immediate side-effects of increased freedom and non-censorship is the proliferation of pornography. Before the new constitution was in place women could be prosecuted for any sexual activity outside marriage, and serve time in jail for the 'crime'. Length of sentence was quite arbitrarily assessed and women were often left to stagnate in jail for indefinite periods until such time as their husbands were so kind as to forgive them. Needless to say, no such law was ever enacted to cover male indiscretions – which is probably just as well since not even the most sophisticated and widespread prison system could be expected to cope with the demand. Similarly, before 1978, women involved in the sex industry were discriminated against in the labour market by having to spend periods of time in 'correction houses', in an attempt to indoctrinate them with established moral beliefs. Sex has always had its workers, and will continue to do so; so it is equally valid that non-discrimination occurs in that industry as in every other. As is common in other EC countries, attitudes remain polarized in Spain with religion and conservative values much more prevalent in the rural districts than in the more cosmopolitan areas and large cities.

Spain's Equal Treatment obligation is established in its constitution. The obligation is expressed in Article 17 of the 'Workers' Statute' and is expressed in quite wide terms, so it was not considered necessary to amend the statute to comply with the EC's Equal Treatment Directive. Spanish law does not make a specific distinction between direct and indirect discrimination, but simply prohibits all forms of discrimination. Indirect and direct discrimination are, however, very different and both merit independent coverage; in this regard the Spanish system falls short of the provisions of, for example, the UK's Sex Discrimination Act, which prohibits both types. Where the Equal Treatment principle has been infringed the aggrieved employee can file a claim with the labour magistrate. The court has power to award compensation in regard of the breach; and in contrast to the UK there is no statutory maximum on the amount of damages that can be awarded. The fact that non-compliance could potentially be a very expensive business ought to be sufficient incentive for employers to comply, regardless of their personal feelings about equality issues. The principle of Equal Pay did not become law in Spain until 1988. It was introduced in order to comply with the EC's Equal Pay Directive.

Parental Rights and Childcare

Paid maternity leave is guaranteed under the 1980 Workers' Statute, which was amended as recently as 1989 though with few significant improvements. Paid leave for a total of 16 weeks to be taken before and after the birth is guaranteed and is remunerated by 75 per cent of the basic salary. There is no continuous employment obligation.

Significant improvements in the form of legal measures on paternity leave have occurred in Spain since 1986. Both Spanish parents may now reduce their working day up until their child reaches the age of five. Additionally, either the mother or the father may take up to three years' unpaid leave to look after a child; with a guarantee at the end of the leave period of a job of equal status to the previous one. Furthermore, since 1989, if both parents are in paid employment the father is entitled to take the last four weeks of the statutory maternity leave in place of the mother. The only clause attached to the latter agreement is that a return to work does not entail any risk to the new mother's health. In the event of the mother's death, the father is entitled to the entire period of maternity leave which is outstanding. The new laws are a direct measure of Spain's commitment to both actively encourage wider participation in childcare responsibilities among fathers, whilst simultaneously releasing women to return more readily to the workforce.

A major reform of the whole educational system was proposed by the central government in 1987. The legislation which has been implemented makes the age group 0–5 the first stage of the educational process and it allows for much diversity in provision. In addition, the government has set up as a priority the provision of school places for all three-year-olds to be achieved by 1992. Its aim is to provide pre-primary schooling to all children whose parents wish them to attend. The aim has been achieved in the larger cities, but not to the same degree in towns and rural areas.

Positive Action

In line with most other EC states, Spain has introduced a programme of positive-action measures for women. In 1988, the new ministerial decree governing initiatives in employment and occupational integration covered a plan for more affirmative action to redress the effects of past discrimination. This decree superseded the previous one of 1987 and agreed to the setting-up of a specific vocational training programme for women in areas of the labour market in which they were poorly represented. This coincided with the broader plan for full equal opportunities for women, which itself had a number of far-reaching and positive measures. The most significant development was the nationwide promotion of careers guidance services to women, who previously had typically received far less than men. A further progressive step has been the adoption of a research programme on the specific needs of defined categories of female workers. The categories which were identified included women living in rural areas, women working in domestic service and home-workers. It went further than a standard research exercise in that it also incorporated a retraining plan for women returners.

Throughout the last few years it has become overwhelmingly clear that women in rural and agricultural sectors have been facing higher than average levels of discrimination; so they have been targeted through almost all the programmes which have been implemented. Another development since 1989 has been the growth of a new programme for women whose economic status is vulnerable, or women who have little educational or formal qualifications. A short time afterwards, the plan was extended to include women from ethnic minorities and women serving prison sentences. The most recent equal opportunities programme provides for measures to be undertaken to prevent discrimination from occurring in the first place; and as such is placing a renewed emphasis on the legislation and policies that are already in place. Furthermore, the government is actively encouraging an overall improvement in the status of equality issues within all areas of employment, in order to achieve greater non-discrimination within the workforce.

Since the beginning of 1991, there has been a more significant balance between the practices of the labour force and the economic decisions that are made by government. Representation from outside government is drawn from within a cross-section of the trade unions, employers' organizations and equality officers. This has developed as a direct result of a law adopted on the rights of workers' representatives to information in respect of employment contracts. Monitoring Commissions have been set up to achieve a more readily accessible method of disseminating specific information about the labour market – and ultimately to redress any imbalances in the position of the workforce. In addition to this, the Commissions are empowered to evaluate the results of all equality programmes, and to make recommendations as to what still needs to be improved. The involvement of employer representatives with policymakers signifies a progressive step towards creating realistic and informed policy; which is, moreover, likely to be more relevant to the real needs of the labour market than government-controlled policy has generally been in the past.

Disability

Within the disability movement in Spain, particular emphasis has been placed on integrated training and specialized courses for deaf people. The aim of the campaign has been to increase awareness among employers that vocational training and employment of deaf people is beneficial to everyone. The organization which has monitored the campaign is the Audiofonology Institute of Valencia, who point out that the under-employment of deaf people represents an enormous waste of talent. The central aim has been and continues to be the full integration of the Spanish deaf community into all aspects of social and economic life. At a 1990 seminar organized by the Audiofonology Institute of Valencia and various rehabilitation professionals, a number of conclusions were drawn and recommendations made. These included:

- The level of qualification of teachers of deaf people must be improved.
- A university education/training for sign interpreters should be set up.
- There is a lack of awareness about the abilities of deaf people, in particular among trade unions and employers.
- There is a lack of collaboration between institutions working for/with deaf people.
- There is a need for increased research into the application of employment programmes for deaf people.
- Developments in new technology for deaf people should be examined and its use increased.
- Adequate legislation for the vocational integration of deaf people must be implemented Community-wide to ensure that their basic rights are respected.

In 1992 most of these conclusions and recommendations are at various stages of being implemented or improved. Several projects to assist families with disabled young people have been introduced as a result of the Institute's recommendations.

In other parts of Spain, the HELIOS programme has been put into action through a series of Independent Living projects. Accessibility and mobility programmes are underway in many of the larger cities and towns. Since 1981 Bilboa has been improving upon one of its most innovative projects. The outcome has been the introduction of a fully accessible bus and underground scheme in Bilboa which incorporates Braille timetables, cues on hand-rails combined with audible information, as well as safety colour-coding. It is hoped that similar projects will be implemented through the HELIOS programme in many other Spanish cities.

Age Issues

Pension expenditure as a percentage of GDP almost doubled in Spain between 1975 and 1983. However, even with that impressive leap Spain still falls within the bottom half of the Twelve in terms of its expenditure on pension funds. As is the case in most Member States (France being the outstanding exception), Spain has no legal commitment to non-discrimination on the grounds of age. A recent blatant example of age discrimination in Spain lies in the terms of a proposal forbidding anyone over the age of 70 to possess a driving licence. Placing upper age-limits on an individual's rights to participate in any activity fundamentally contravenes all principles of equality.

Sexuality

In Spain, unlike in many other EC member countries, homosexuality is no bar to serving in the armed forces. In other countries victimization, harassment and dismissal are common experiences for gays and lesbians engaged in military service. However, there is no law against discrimination on the grounds of sexuality, which means that homosexuals have no protection. In common with most of the Twelve, Spanish law does not recognize same-sex partnerships. The age-of-consent laws, however, comply more with equal opportunities than other Member States, most notably the UK, in that they do not discriminate between different lifestyles. The consensual ages for all forms of sexual activity have been set at 12/16/18: 16 if deceit or pressure is used; 18 if undue influence is used.

Part IV
A Way Forward

18

Conclusions and Recommendations

Sex Discrimination and Equal Opportunities for Women and Men

All European countries have come a long way since women got the right to vote, but there is little room for complacency as yet. Since the women's movement began in the late 1960s commitment has both grown and diversified. As well as sexism, issues central to the movement like education, sexual harassment, employment, racism, peace and disarmament have been joined by a growing commitment to women's studies, lesbian studies and herstory courses. European women have had a strong voice within the peace movement, and are using it to widely publicize the overwhelming contradictions between feminist values and the world's ever-increasing militarism. Nowadays, the concerns of women's organizations throughout Europe range from the already well-established consciousness-raising and protest to positive-action programmes geared towards teaching women traditional 'male' skills which in the past have excluded women from the ranks of professions such as construction and engineering. In practice, this has meant that more women than ever before are participating in the labour market, and many are attaining the high status that has previously been restricted to men.

All in all, in spite of the lack of force behind the equality laws, the women's movement is very much alive in Europe in the 1990s. The increasing number of young women who are beginning to challenge the traditional male institutional framework is an encouraging development. In addition to this, such young women are starting to take a firm stance on their role in traditional family responsibilities, and are rejecting the man-made female role of wife and mother, or caregiver and provider, in favour of other options. Marriage is being regarded much more than in the past as a largely token gesture which is not an overriding necessity.

Increasingly, in response to the growing social discontent with marriage, governments (most notably in the US) are introducing cohabitation laws. In theory, these laws are designed to protect the individual's rights in much the same way as marriage laws are intended to. However, it could be argued that they are an alternative method in maintaining women's position as second-class citizens since they are designed from a male perspective. As long as cohabitation laws actually provide equal rights and equal benefits to women and men they are an important contribution to lifestyle options; if they perpetuate inequality then they are not.

So, what is the way forward? What more has to be achieved? The Sex Discrimination Act and the Equal Pay Act, with equivalent laws in place in the rest of the EC, are the legal framework in the UK on which to focus. The effects of the Acts on the employment of women have barely scratched the surface of inequality in most respects. Laws should not be one-off documents: they should be open to regular public assessment and scrutiny. In the past there has been an inclination for society to claim itself as taking a liberationist stance; while any subsequent autonomous feminist activity has been regarded as subversive. That in itself is a ludicrous concept since the sexual reforms that have taken place appear somewhat tenuous in the face of what are still, especially in the government of the UK, deeply entrenched male conservative values. There is a pressing need for governments to re-address their equality laws and not isolate them still further from the groups they are meant to serve. In Italy, a National Committee has recently been set up to promote the development and improvement of equality legislation that has actually been in place for some time now. A similar committee established in the UK and elsewhere would be a very welcome step forward.

Surveys of disadvantaged groups ought to be conducted on a systematic basis. They would serve to highlight the extent of sex inequality as well as the effects, and would enable real rather than perceived needs to be addressed. There has to be much more emphasis on women's equality issues locally and regionally; the growing tendency is to legislate and control from a national and nowadays even an international level. While European policies ensure that all Member States should achieve the same levels of equality, they are by nature far removed from local equality issues. In order to ensure that decisions made in the Council of Ministers have impact in Liverpool or Madrid, for instance, governments should appoint commissioners to oversee their implementation.

There are enormous advantages to be had from free exchange of information and experience on gender issues between the Twelve. Most Member States have quite sophisticated feminist movements which are both highly developed and well integrated within the mainstream institutions. Although the main focus of the movements varies from country to country and through time, the overriding aim of each is to combat sex discrimination and sexism in all its forms. Research, policy analysis, development work, demonstration and action-projects can all be achieved on unilateral basis in each country, though they are equally achievable through a multilateral approach. The causes and effects of sex discrimination are broadly the same whether they are endured in Milan, Copenhagen or wherever.

A European programme of action will have far-reaching effects and a profound impact upon the lives of many women. Its effect can be maximized by a promotion of the best equality laws which are currently in place, which in turn can act as role models for other states. National policy which takes a positive stance ought to become international policy. Financial support from the ESF should further be contributed to networking projects between Member States.

The new EC programme – New Opportunities for Women (NOW) – has been developed to focus on training and enterprise creation. Family responsibilities ought to be a priority of the programme, and should be addressed from a male as well as female angle. The programme should aim to operate on as broad a level as possible in order to ensure not only that women become more involved in paid employment but that they are represented in equal numbers with men in the more highly paid professional sectors of the labour market.

Racial Discrimination

In the 1960s there was a great deal of hope and anticipation that the development of new political governing bodies set up to promote equal opportunities for ethnic minorities would have a tremendous impact. In addition to this, it was widely felt that the prevailing social attitudes to race relations would change as a result of the race laws introduced. Political and public opinion about how far these expectations have been met varies considerably.

The impact of any legislation is often heavily influenced and hampered by the economic climate at the time. This is especially pertinent in respect of the Race Relations Acts, which have survived through recession more as a symbol than as a resource which guarantees equality. Persistently high levels of unemployment among ethnic minorities suggest that their equal rights and protection enshrined in the Acts are worth little more than the paper they were written on. The problems with existing legislation on racial discrimination bear a close resemblance to the problems associated with other equality laws. For instance, in the past it has often been assumed that once legislation is enacted, it alone will initiate change and guarantee non-discrimination. As a consequence, insufficient attention has been paid to the need for far wider administrative, economic and political strategies to tackle discrimination; or indeed to the need to develop affirmative-action policy at government or local authority level. In practice, this has meant that anti-discrimination policies have been introduced in a context that has been ill-prepared and poorly organized. It is hardly surprising, therefore, that without the support of a united framework policies have failed to make their intended impact. Perhaps the most pressing need is not just for an improvement in the legislation (as welcome as that would be), but for a substantial reinforcement of political and economic strength and incentives to apply effective equal opportunities policies. In practice, this will only happen if the government voices its commitment to enforce the law. Although successive Labour and Tory governments have made promises to improve and reform the law on racial issues, little has been done in practice. No government has given organizations like the Commission for Racial Equality the power they need to bring about fundamental improvements. In fact, since 1979 the political agenda of the Conservative Party has not included any important initiatives in the field of racial inequality. On the contrary, they have expressed the very opposite intentions by strengthening government control over immigration.

Whether or not one believes that racial discrimination is endemic in society or is merely a prejudice shared by a small number of individuals does not alter the structured institutionalized racism that discriminates against minority populations. Across Europe, housing, education, employment, and social benefits are all unequally distributed on the basis of racial characteristics.

Throughout Europe ethnic minority groups have endured discrimination since their arrival over the latter half of this century. Because of the effects of institutionalized racism, black and Asian people are more likely to be unemployed, to be concentrated in the worst paid and most dangerous jobs and to be patronized by bureaucratic institutions. This situation is not merely exacerbated by token laws but is actively encouraged in some parts of Europe by organized activities of, for example, the National Front in the UK and its more widely supported equivalent in France, *Le Front Nationale*.

What causes or creates social disadvantage? A combination of scapegoating and a general lack of a clear political basis and policy against discrimination goes some way towards offering an explanation. A lack of state intervention in most member countries to manage race relations or to integrate ethnic groups socially and economically into the broader society is also perhaps a cause. Enacting any policy on racial issues has largely been a white-managed experience which has not attempted to address the issues from an ethnic minority perspective. As with all equality issues there is a clear need for realistic future policy to be formulated by the people it affects most; not just treated as another white male bureaucratic exercise. Governments seem to have relied on the assumption that society will ultimately integrate and discrimination be reduced without the need to enact any formal measures to catalyze the process. This has clearly not happened. Furthermore, attempts by minorities to assimilate have not been without their price: loss of identity in exchange for a very superficial and short-lived status of acceptance.

Race relations is a low priority within the EC's Social Charter: there is no official action programme to instigate change. The failure to tackle the root causes of racism and racial discrimination during the past few decades makes it very difficult to anticipate a much brighter future. However, ethnic groups, despite not being given very much help, are by no means helpless in the face of oppression. Increasingly, ethnic minorities are grouping together to give themselves more political strength. Moreover, a growing number of minorities are succeeding in the labour market and in education, despite the discrimination they encounter in the process.

There is an urgent need for national and European parliaments to recognize the dynamic role ethnic minorities have in society and to formalize that role in the framework of clear political strategies to combat discrimination. In addition, there is a need for an independent black political voice represented by an autonomous political party. Throughout the EC, parliaments are essentially white-managed institutions which consequently produce policies which are to affect beneficially a significantly higher number of white lives than black lives. Despite several failed political strategies aimed at assimilation, the recognition that an all-round experience of black lives is very different from the all-round experience of white lives has never been firmly stated. Given the almost exclusively white political power which exists through Europe, whiteness will inevitably affect blackness more than the reverse. A centralized black political party is therefore a prerequisite to enacting successful policies that reflect the real needs and rights of black people. However, since separatist politics have never been popularly received it is unlikely to happen for the time being at least. In race relations as in all other areas of equal opportunities, there are potential benefits to be gained through collaborative work across Europe. Cross-border policy and good race relations practice ought to be encouraged, alongside specific provision in national political and social agendas for non-discriminatory measures. The 1991 Ford Report, drawn up on behalf of the European Parliament's Committee of Inquiry into Racism and Xenophobia, contains over 70 recommendations for Member States to adopt measures to enhance race relations and improve the status of ethnic minorities in their communities. To date, few of the recommendations have been acted upon by Member States. If the report were to be awarded a legally binding status, much progress could be made.

Disability

The World Health Organization (WHO) estimates that out of the 300 million people living in the European Community, 10 per cent are disabled. Furthermore, almost half of the 30 million disabled people are engaged in active employment or are potentially economically active, restricted in their search for work by and large by entrenched prejudice in society about their incapacity for work. It should be noted that in the vast majority of EC states it is, in theory, compulsory to recruit a certain percentage of registered disabled people. The percentage ranges from between 1.6 to 15 per cent among the Twelve. Legal measures in place in the Member States differ considerably in both the standard of provision, and in the degree to which quotas are enforced. In addition, internal discrepancies exist in the availability and standard of local and regional services. There are, however, examples of good practice role-models to emulate. Germany, for example, already has over 600 low-floor buses in operation and half of all new equipment ordered for 1991 was for this type of bus. In Spain, a prototype accessible taxi has been developed and production is forecast to begin operation in the very near future.

Throughout Europe people with disabilities are an extremely disadvantaged and substantial minority group. Chiefly because of the social response and attitude to disability, people in this group are more likely to experience disadvantage in many forms, including housing, employment, education, as well as financial deprivation. In fact, in every major social and economic dimension people with disabilities are unfairly treated in comparison with their non-disabled peers.

Although the effects of deprivation are plain to see, the implications have not yet ever received the full force of government policy. In turn, this has created a very limited arena for public discussion or commitment to disability issues. Very often, discussions have been concentrated on an all-too-limited concept of disability and a narrowly-based approach. This has served to weaken public pressure on governments to introduce radical changes in the status of disabled people. The causes of disadvantage among disabled people stem from a number of things. Lack of adequate legislation, deficiency of enforceable policy, low political commitment, confusion over what direction to take, and the inadequacies of sanctions have characterized political debate on this issue and contributed to the problems of disabled people.

What to do in order to counteract these setbacks and redress the social and economic injustices which confront disabled people has been partly answered by the EC action programme on disability. The EC has made a commitment to all European citizens whose lives are affected by a disability to instigate measures designed to improve overall the existing situation. In time, this should put pressure on or at least encourage national parliaments to firmly establish the rights of disabled people to all social and economic benefits. It is clear, however, that even with legislation in force, more resources have to be channelled into achieving full equality. There is little scope for political apathy if rights are to be effectively established. Since there has been a noticeable tendency to confuse and devalue disability issues, largely by tagging them onto other issues, more people who actually suffer from disabilities should be centrally involved in policy planning and organization of appropriate services. Assessed needs as judged by policymakers are, after all, largely speculative if not formulated with the benefit of experience.

There has been significant progress in some Member States towards increasing the participation rates of disabled workers in the workforce. France has achieved much in terms of its approach to the transport and mobility needs of disabled people. This again highlights the beneficial nature of collaborative work between the Twelve towards counter-discriminatory measures via interchangeable policy and practice.

The EC is also working towards improving the transport provisions for employees with impaired mobility. The general provisions are to be supplemented by training schemes to help workers travel safely to and from places of work; this in turn will be supported by more readily available local information and advice on services. If a proposal for increased mobility is to provide maximum benefits to as many people as possible it should aim to cover the following:

- Such measures should be provided free of charge in order to make them accessible to anyone who is eligible to use such transport. Disabled people's involvement in the labour market is characterized by low pay and inadequate government allowances; therefore only services which are free of charge are acceptable innovations.
- It is crucial that developments aimed at increased transport, accessibility and mobility happen in the very near future. A combination of political and economic will is necessary to ensure that the EC measures will not be unnecessarily delayed. Recommendations and proposals have an unfortunate tendency to remain as such far longer than is actually necessary.

Age Discrimination

Given the concentration of the European workforce in the middle age-groups there are sound economic and political reasons for tackling age discrimination and ageism. Social attitudes to older people are largely based on inaccurate assumptions commonly made about the ageing process. Negative stereotypes prevail throughout Member States; but the action being taken in them to challenge discriminatory practices varies widely. There is also a marked diversity in political approaches to their older citizens, ranging from a legal recognition of their status to a complete overlooking of even their needs.

While the overall ageing of the European population should be viewed as a major benefit of industrialization and wealth, it is often not seen as such. More often the health and social needs of the elderly are regarded as a major drain on the economy. Housing, care, transportation, shelter, health, pensions, employment and retirement have traditionally been treated as a unwelcome expense largely associated with the needs of the elderly. However, although they have been politically regarded as an expensive group to maintain, grossly inadequate funding has been channelled into catering for their needs. As a consequence, in several EC states older people have not received the priority position they require on social agendas and poverty has been the experience of many.

To respond to the needs of elderly people and older workers, the EC has launched an action programme under one of its Decisions. The progress towards the EC Decision in November 1990 to introduce the first EC action programme for older people marks an important first recognition of the needs of older people at EC level. In addition, the EC has designated 1993 as the Year of the Elderly. The aim of the European Year is to raise awareness of issues of ageing and to promote positive images of older people. Within the programme several practical measures are currently being consulted upon and implemented to assist older people throughout Europe. Health and care, as well as employment and re-employment, are issues being addressed. The action programme is, however, limited in its scope. It contains no proposals for new legislation and makes no provision to fund pilot projects. Older people themselves are organizing their own activities through pensioner movements and 'grey' political groups aimed at collectively tackling the problems of discrimination. Political will and coordinated lobbying by older people has focused attention on their needs and gone some way towards successfully challenging public attitudes to the ageing process.

Evidence shows that age-related discrimination occurs in all aspects of life for many older people, which has influenced policymakers to focus attention on the issue. Recent European legislation has put pressure on national parliaments to take action in regard to the needs of the elderly in their communities. Many challenges are posed by an increasingly ageing European population, and it is ultimately up to each Member State to coordinate the issues and initiate clear policy and positive-action measures.

Proposals to alter the status and situation of older people depend on changing attitudes. Traditional stereotypes are negative, inaccurate and only serve to perpetuate myths about ageing. Age discrimination awareness-raising programmes therefore have a central role to play in challenging stereotypes and broadening social perceptions of old age. Like the relatively well-established race and sex equality courses, age is another subject upon which better coverage at all levels in education is required.

The relationship between legislation and attitudes is especially important in respect of elderly people. Public attention is more likely to be focused on an equality issue such as ageing if legal measures to combat prejudice are adopted and enforced. And indirect discrimination against older people ought automatically to lessen in response to increased public awareness of the issues of ageism.

Older people are not an homogeneous group, not least because they may be either employees or retired workers. Therefore, it is important to cater for the diverse needs of both categories and not treat them as a single group. A fairly broad-based 'lifestyle' focus is an important basis on which to frame anti-age-discrimination measures. Whatever method Member States adopt, the central issue is to use legislation to create viable autonomous social roles for older people which maintain the status and financial security previously derived from paid employment. To facilitate this process international and national agendas should address the need for radical changes to educational and leisure structures to promote the public recognition of the crucial role played by older people. A far more widespread attempt at integrating the elderly into existing educational and social frameworks is important: regarding sports, leisure and adult educational activities as patronized by (and therefore, for) people in the younger and middle age-groups is the prevailing norm, and as such serves only to isolate older people rather than make progress towards assimilation.

Unfortunately, with the exception of France the need for legal measures on age discrimination and equality has been overlooked by governments in other EC countries. The resistance on the part of parliaments to enacting specific laws has been mirrored in the labour market. In general, employers have not been obliged, and therefore have not considered it necessary, to incorporate anti-age-discrimination measures within their equal opportunities policies. Legislation is needed as a means of formally setting the agenda for change. Well-researched legal measures serve to highlight areas of inequality in both employment and the wider society. In practice, this enables the root causes of prejudice to be identified, the effects evaluated and appropriate positive action enacted.

A number of specific recommendations are outlined below:

- Discriminatory upper age-limits on all jobs should be removed. It is worth noting that an increasing number of employers throughout Europe are actively recruiting older workers, removing upper age-limits and making a statement on their job advertisements to that effect. As yet, however, the large numbers of older people in long-term unemployment clearly suggests that there is no room for complacency. Far more organizations have a responsibility to enact policy measures which cater specifically for existing older workers and potential employees.
- Recommendations of the grey movement should be widely incorporated into national legislation. Recommendations from 'the horse's mouth' are inevitably far more pertinent than proposals from governing organizations who are essentially sitting in the wings.
- Individual governments should liaise with industrial organizations such as (in the case of the UK) the TUC, CBI and the Institute of Directors, to encourage awareness among employers of the potential of older people and to challenge discrimination.
- In much the same way as Disablement Resettlement Officers exist to give advice and offer help to workers with disabilities, the Department of Employment should fund the appointment of 'age officers' to offer appropriate advice to older workers. Such officers should work alongside other equality personnel to ensure greater coverage of the issues and stricter adherence to the legislation.
- National governments ought to act as role models in their function as employers. They should allow increased choice to older workers and offer greater flexibility and more incentives based on individuals' wishes.
- Employers should include older workers on their equal opportunities committee to help establish policy which reflects their needs. Large organizations which employ several hundreds or thousands of workers should have 'age officers' represented on their equal opportunities committee.

- Recruitment campaigns and job advertisements ought to be targeted directly at older people via pensioners' associations.
- Pre-retirement courses should be universally offered and awarded an equal status with the more firmly established vocational guidance courses for younger workers.

Sexuality

The overall situation facing gay men and lesbians living in the European Community is characterized by few rights, little protection and oppressively heterosexist structures. The issues ought to be centrally addressed at EC level if the equality principles and parameters of the Social Charter are to be met by the Twelve.

The world human rights and equality record on homosexuality is overwhelmingly dismal. Globally, long prison sentences up to a maximum sentence of capital punishment for homosexual acts are not unheard of, though thankfully rarely enforced. National attitudes towards homosexuality range from regarding it as an unnatural lifestyle which is tolerated so long as it is not publicly displayed; as a bourgeois and western perversion; to a phenomenon to be blotted out by a lack of legal recognition of its very existence. Despite the prevalence of such attitudes, lesbian and gay lifestyles are flourishing throughout most countries. Fortunately, most EC countries are (relatively) relaxed towards same-sex partners – albeit universally lacking the political will to encourage and commit themselves to full homosexual equality.

The Single European Market will have an economic and social effect on most groups. Ultimately, the laws dictate what an individual may do, or, in contrast, what s/he may not do. The problems faced by lesbians and gays would be partly solved by the adoption of anti-discrimination legislation and equal rights laws. These are necessary measures towards setting an agenda for change. Legal measures formed in part by lesbians and gays would address the needs from a far wider and more enlightened angle than that of standard bureaucracy.

Numerous organizations exist through Europe which are directly involved in examining the economic and employment situation of gays and lesbians. European support for future collaborative work is essential. A number of measures are recommended below for incorporation into action plans on homosexual equality:

- An accurate assessment, via formalized surveys, of the legal and social status of lesbians and gays throughout the Twelve and within employment is crucial in order for a comparative analysis of circumstances to be undertaken. The most progressive policies and practices ought to be universally adopted.
- Non-discriminatory measures on the basis of sexuality should be implemented in the Equal Treatment laws under the auspices of the Social Charter. It is a conspicuous and revealing omission on the part of governments to decriminalize homosexuality, for instance, and then not enact measures to provide it with legal status.
- The Commission's own employment policies, literature and employment rights ought to reflect positive images of gays and lesbians and assert their full equality rights.
- Europe-wide legal recognition of same-sex partnerships is an essential prerequisite to implementing any other equality right.
- A re-definition of the concept of 'family' and the laws on eligibility for leave for family reasons is needed to incorporate relationships which because of legal, social and religious prohibitions and constraints cannot exist in traditional family structures – 'home' would better reflect the circumstances of a wider range of lifestyles.

Summary

Although there is clearly no shortage of political rhetoric right across Europe, it is overwhelmingly evident that legislation has to be drafted extremely carefully if its provision is to be enforceable. Translating rhetoric into practice is fraught with enough difficulties without it being continuously undermined by inadequacies in the legislation.

Shortfalls in equality laws have become increasingly obvious to policymakers as well as those groups whose expectations have not been met. While further amendments and improvements to existing laws are of primary importance, existing legal measures on issues such as ageing and homosexuality have barely scratched the surface of problems of discrimination faced by these groups. The importance of a legal framework within which to identify problems and potential problems, assess needs and forecast provision cannot be overemphasized. While it is true that laws will not change behaviour overnight or alter common beliefs and prevailing negative attitudes, each will persist more strongly without the legal obligations that ultimately only laws can provide.

Awareness-raising, positive-action programmes and training are all very commendable activities in their own right, but lose much of their credibility when lacking in legal support. All courses of action towards equality require the assistance of legislation as the benchmark for policy and practice.

It is clear, though, that while rights must be clearly established by law, that law also needs the support of public opinion and particularly of those people it is intended to serve. In the end, little can be left to administrative or professional 'discretion' if rights and equal opportunities are to be firmly established. In many government policies, the pressing needs of disadvantaged groups are made subservient to the perceived needs of the economy.

Having extolled the virtues of legislation, there is no intention to demolish it or weaken its impact in observing that laws drafted in national parliaments can sometimes be only as useful as pieces of paper on employers' desks covered in words about their commitment to equal opportunities. Laws, policies and statements all have to have the full support of practical measures designed actually to implement them beyond a draft proposal stage. Awareness-raising programmes and training contribute to enlighten people about the issues as well as encourage them to conform with the policy's intention. In order to make everyone aware of his or her obligations under the Acts, employers need to be reminded regularly and firmly about their commitments. Complacency within organizations leads to non-compliance. Since prejudice and discrimination are deeply embedded in our attitudes and social structures, legally obliging employers to comply is one way to ensure that discrimination is replaced by non-discrimination.

The proclaimed equality of, for example, women, via a whole range of equality measures, highlights the divergent relationship between policymakers, laws and employers. When is equality less than equality? There has been a tradition of divergence between legal guarantees for women and how they are honoured in society. All too often, the various codes and constitutions within the Twelve guarantee equality in theory, but in practice on an everyday level, society denies that equality. In some countries, most notably those in Scandinavia, equality for women is given a very high profile; but the governments and parliaments are still dominated by men.

Similar contradictions prevail in relation to many equality issues. Equal pay in employment is perhaps the most notorious contradiction. Despite the existence of laws, equality boards and governing organizations to ensure equal pay between men and women, gross inequalities persist. An overall figure shows that women still only earn about 70 per cent of men's income in the majority of Member States. Hence it is clear that laws are only workable when they are enforceable at every level; without such force they may have little impact on reality.

It has been shown how the usual discriminators – age, race, sex, etc. – are very often interlinked in so far as their causes and effects frequently overlap. Although there have been numerous independent accounts by each governing body on the realities of, for example, sex discrimination or racial discrimination, there has been little homologous theory about discrimination in its widest context. This omission has serious consequences for the adequacy of society in general to cater for cross-boundary or multiple-discrimination. In view of this, there has to be greater theoretical and practical clarity about the interplay of, e.g., racism, sexism and homophobia in politics and society. A comprehensive and accessible organization which seeks to address and handle all the issues would decrease the pressure on governments to manage equality issues and to enable those issues to be integrated into a wider social setting. Currently, each organization is working autonomously towards achieving the same results: combating discrimination and increasing equal opportunities. While admittedly there is a need for each issue to be addressed separately in order to safeguard its importance, there is also room for overlap and a central 'voice' representing equal opportunities to as wide an audience and at as high a level as possible.

Historically, within the area of equality there has been a tendency for practitioners and policymakers to operate and move forward within the same context – but separated by organizational and political structures. Not only does this create an environment where repetition in effort runs unleashed; more importantly, it neglects those parallel issues which are of fundamental importance. Although aspects of these issues have been addressed in the substantive chapters of this guide, we have not as yet developed an overall uniform theoretical framework.

The dynamics of inequality cross historical, social, geographical and political boundaries. Without analyzing the social and political interaction between, for instance, racist or homophobic structures and other social structures in capitalist societies, it becomes problematic to explain how certain types of inequalities develop and shape the institutions in society. Part of the problem has been associated with the lack of dialogue and communication on theory and method between those involved in research on various aspects of the politics of equal opportunities in the UK and throughout the EC, both on a national and multinational basis. At all levels, although it is clear that each issue must be relatively autonomous, there must also be cohesive interplay between them. Furthermore, integrating cross-national comparisons on each issue enables the causes and effects of prejudice and discrimination to be more systematically identified and anti-discrimination measures easier to instigate.

There has been a legal tendency to 'group' equality issues into one category or (even worse) to 'tag' an 'equality right' onto the end of a quite unrelated set of laws. Equality issues have to be translated into autonomous laws in order to gain the public attention and the political priority which they deserve. In addition to this requirement, it is crucial that each issue is represented by a Minister from each Member State to oversee its administration internally and contribute to its international profile in Brussels. It is not sufficient to name a Minister for the Family or Minister of Equal Opportunities. A Ministry for each issue is required, with an interministerial umbrella body to oversee policy and activity. All too often in the past, sex and race issues have received much more political prominence than for instance, age or homosexuality. Further, there is no reason why the Minister representing each issue should not herself be a member of the respective minority group; a registered disabled person, for instance, representing disability issues is far more likely to do so from an instructive and informed stance than a non-disabled person is likely to do.

A Way Forward

The extent to which social structures will progress in relation to equality is dictated largely by political measures. There is an interaction between the way people feel about their society and the institutions of government, the media, employment, education and so on. Structure shapes consciousness as well as the reverse. Stereotyping and social conditioning in turn mould consciousness. In time, changes in popular belief bring about (long overdue) changes in institutions.

The organizations which govern equal opportunities issues have always been under a wide-ranging amount of pressure (both financial and political as well as public) to cater for their needs. Researching areas of need and disadvantage, as well as campaigning for and implementing change, is a formidable task to be undertaken. Minority group members do not in themselves form a cohesive group; therefore it would be impossible to answer to all of their requirements all of the time. In order to reduce the pressures upon such governing organizations and increase their power a number of measures are necessary. These are listed below:

- Increased financial assistance from national governments in order for them to carry out their roles more effectively.
- An increase in government support for positive-action programmes.
- Stricter adherence to the legislation by governments in their own capacity as employers.
- Increasing the power of governing organizations to oversee the working of the legislation, which includes the power to penalize employers who fail in their equality obligations. Ultimately, such power can only be granted by national parliaments.
- A full commitment to all equality issues from national governments in order to put pressure on all organizations to comply with the principles of equality.

Within the context of equal opportunities legislation, definitions ought to be stated more clearly with regard to both their meaning and their implications. This also calls for an increased measure of consistency. Pensions and retirement ages are characteristic issues which have caused confusion, and created inconsistencies and inequalities. Defining relevant phrases, as is the standard practice in the development of an equal opportunities policy, is an equally applicable step for legislators to take. Confusion over what a term or clause actually means is a widespread yet completely avoidable problem. Focusing on definitions which are both clear and concise in their meaning is a paramount step towards raising the issues, and combating the prejudice which causes discrimination.

If all the measures outlined above and throughout this guide are to have even the slightest practical impact, people from disadvantaged groups have to be involved in each stage of the planning and administration of services. They know from their own experiences both what is wrong and what measures are needed to put it right, far better than the policymakers.

The advantages to be gained from collaboration on all equality issues between Member States are enormous. Shared experiences of discrimination help to address the causes more precisely. Too often in the past, policy has been formulated from a very limited and purely academic standpoint. There has been an additional tendency: to view older people, for example, as a homogeneous group, distinguished by dependency, ill health and lack of mobility, with any other need which falls outside such categories being subsequently overlooked.

All equality issues and concepts ought to be broadened to strengthen their overall political and social impact. If developments are to have a lasting effect, public attitudes towards the whole range of equality issues still need to be radically changed. All too often, the services for minority groups reflect their stigmatized and devalued position in society. In the long run, people are more likely to fulfil social obligations to equality if they believe in the reasons for doing so. Clearly, the potential for improvements and change in existing laws and provision is enormous.

Appendix 1

Equal Opportunities Laws and Treaties

Table 1 Sex equality legislation

Legislation	*Summary of provision*	*Governing bodies*
Treaty of Rome (1957)	Provides that men and women should receive equal pay for equal work. (Article 119)	Established four institutions to implement its provisions: European Parliament; European Council of Ministers; European Commission; European Court of Justice
Equal Pay Directive (EC)	Elaborates on the principle and implementation of equal pay, including the concept of 'equal pay for work of equal value'.	As above
Equal Treatment Directive (EC)	Guarantees the principle of equal treatment in access to employment, vocational training and promotion, incorporating the concept of indirect discrimination and positive action.	As above
Social Security Directive (EC)	Relates to the progressive implementation of the principle of equal treatment for men and women in statutory social security schemes.	As above

Table 1 (*cont.*)

Legislation	*Summary of provision*	*Governing bodies*
Occupational Social Security Schemes Directive (EC)	Extends the principle of equal treatment in social security to occupational social security.	As above
Self-Employment Directive (EC)	Relates to the extension of the principle of equal treatment to women who are employers or self- employed or who work wholly or partly with their spouses.	As above
Equal Pay Act 1970 (UK)	Makes it unlawful to discriminate between men and women in terms of payment and other contractual conditions.	Equal Opportunities Commission
Sex Discrimination Act 1975 (UK)	Establishes the role of the Equal Opportunities Commission (EOC). The Act defines two forms of discrimination, direct and indirect, both of which are unlawful. It should be noted that the provisions of the SDA apply equally to discrimination against either sex. The SDA applies to: • Men as well as women. • Part-time as well as full-time workers. • Self-employed people as well as ordinary employees. • Job applicants. • Contract workers. • Partners in a firm, irrespective of the number of partners involved. The SDA makes it unlawful to discriminate on grounds of sex: • In arrangements made for deciding who is offered a job (e.g. in advertising or in interviewing). • In the terms on which a job is offered. • In deciding who is going to be offered the job. • In the benefits and services an employer gives to an employee (e.g. rewards for work, bonus payments, incentive schemes, welfare provision, etc.).	Equal Opportunities Commission

Table 1 (*cont.*)

Legislation	*Summary of provision*	*Governing bodies*
Sex Discrimination Act 1975 (UK) (*cont.*)	• In dismissals, grievances, redundancy, etc. The main exceptions to the SDA are: • Work performed wholly or in the main outside of Great Britain. • Sex discrimination where sex is a 'Genuine Occupational Qualification' (GOQ) for the job or for part of the job, i.e.: • Where physical identity is important for authenticity (e.g. modelling or acting). • To maintain decency or privacy (e.g. some changing room assistants). • Where a job involves the provision of personal services or promotion of education or welfare that are best provided by women (or men).	Equal Opportunities Commission
Equal Pay (Amendment) Act 1983 (UK)	Amendments to the 1970 Equal Pay Act were brought about as a result of proceedings against the UK government by the European Commission. The amendments brought the UK law into line with the Equal Pay Directive and made it possible to claim equal pay for work of equal value. It should be noted that the comparison between jobs under the Act can only be made with members of the opposite sex. Comparisons cannot be made on the basis of post-holders of the same sex.	Equal Opportunities Commission
Sex Discrimination Act 1986 (UK)	Brings UK sex discrimination laws in line with the Equal Treatment Directive. Thus it introduces non-discrimination laws on a much wider scale than the 1975 SDA had. The amendments outlaw discrimination in all organizations whatever their size, and also affect discrimination in retirement ages: from 7 November 1987 employers can no longer set different compulsory retirement ages for men and women in comparable positions.	Equal Opportunities Commission

Table 1 (*cont.*)

Legislation	*Summary of provision*	*Governing bodies*
Employment Act 1989 (UK)	• Narrows the exemption which makes an act of sex discrimination lawful if it is necessary to comply with a statutory requirement; but • Retains the exemption whereby the Act was needed for the special protection of women due to their childbearing capacity (specifically, working with lead or ionising radiation processes). • Removes most of the restrictions on the employment of women and young persons. • Amends the statutory redundancy scheme in order to comply with the requirements of the Equal Treatment Directive. Now both men and women will be entitled to a redundancy payment up to their normal retirement age or up to the age of 65. • Makes it lawful to discriminate in favour of lone parents in respect of training.	Equal Opportunities Commission

Table 2 Race equality legislation

Legislation	*Summary of provision*	*Governing bodies*
Treaty of Rome 1957	Makes it unlawful to discriminate against EC citizens on the grounds of nationality and citizenship.	European Parliament; European Council of Ministers; European Commission; European Court of Justice
Race Relations Act 1965 (UK)	Made it unlawful to discriminate on the grounds of colour, race, national or ethnic origin in certain (quite limited) public places, e.g. restaurants, hotels, etc. Repealed by the RRA 1968.	Race Relations Board
Race Relations Act 1968 (UK)	Extended the 1965 Act into non-discrimination in areas of employment, the provision of services and housing and provision and allocation of accommodation. Repealed by the RRA 1976.	Community Relations Commission
Race Relations Act 1976 (UK)	Currently in force. This Act totally replaces the 1968 Act. Based on the Sex Discrimination Act 1975, it introduces the concept of 'indirect discrimination' to the area of race. It also sets up parameters for the provision of positive action. The RRA 1976 sets up the governing body, the Commission for Racial Equality (CRE) to oversee the working of the Act in practice. Within the context of employment the Act applies to: • Most employers and employees (see exceptions below). • Job applicants. • Contract workers. • Part-time and full-time employees. The RRA makes it unlawful to discriminate on grounds of race:	Commission for Racial Equality

Table 2 (*cont.*)

Legislation	*Summary of provision*	*Governing bodies*
Race Relations Act 1976 (UK) (*cont.*)	• In arrangements made for deciding who is offered a job (e.g. in advertising or in interviewing). • In the terms on which a job is offered. • In deciding who is going to be offered the job. • In the benefits and services an employer gives to an employee (e.g. rewards for work, bonus payments, incentive schemes, welfare provision, etc.). • In dismissals, grievances, redundancy, etc. Exceptions to the RRA are: • Private households. • Racial discrimination where race is a 'Genuine Occupational Qualification' (GOQ); in general, modelling, acting or restaurant work (to provide authenticity). • Positive-action measures.	Commission for Racial Equality
Employment Act 1989 (UK)	Exempts Sikhs from the requirement to wear a safety helmet when on a building site (section 11). Broadens section 37 of the RRA 1976 (which provides for positive action to be taken by training bodies) so that section 37 training can now be provided by anyone. Also, organizations that wish to provide training under the RRA no longer have to get designation from central government to do so.	

Table 3 Disability legislation

Legislation	*Summary of provision*	*Governing bodies*
Disabled Persons (Employment) Acts 1944 and 1958 (UK)	Introduce: • The 3 per cent quota scheme (NB: applies only to those people on the Register of Disabled Persons; registration is voluntary). • The Register of Disabled Persons (some services for the disabled are only open to those people who register). • The keeping of records by employers to show that the provisions of the Act are being complied with. • Designated Employment Schemes by the Secretary of State (at the moment, car park attendant and passenger electric lift attendant).	Placing Assessment and Counselling Teams (PACTs): one team in each of the Employment Service's 60 areas in the UK; Committees for the Employment of Disabled People (CEDPs)
Chronically Sick and Disabled Persons Act 1970 (UK)	The main purpose is to make provision for access to: • Public buildings • Educational establishments and to maintain: • Parking facilities • Provision of signs.	Local authorities – to implement the Act's measure
Chronically Sick and Disabled Persons (Amendment) Act 1976 (UK)	Extends the 1970 Act to cover places of employment.	Local authorities
Companies Act 1985 (UK)	Provides that all companies employing over an average of 250 workers must contain in their Annual Directors' report a policy statement outlining all policies and measures which have been applied in the previous 12 months in respect of the employment, promotion and training of workers with disabilities. It is an offence not to comply with this provision. The Act applies to all workers with disabilities – unlike the Quota scheme, which only applies to those on the Register of Disabled Persons.	Section 235, and Part III of Schedule 7 of the Companies Act 1985 are administered by the Department of Trade and Industry

Table 3 (*cont.*)

Legislation	*Summary of provision*	*Governing bodies*
Disabled Persons Act 1981 (UK)	Under the 1981 Act providers of premises are required to make provision in accordance with the standards set by the Code of Practice for Access for the Disabled in Buildings (BSI). This law also includes highways and places an obligation on highway authorities to 'have regard for the need of disabled and blind persons'.	Department of Employment
Code of Good Practice on the Employment of Disabled People (UK)	Part I: for service managers and directors; outlines the advantages of a good approach to the employment of people with disabilities. It suggests policy objectives and how to achieve them. Part II: to be used as a reference for implementing policy; provides practical advice on recruitment and training, etc. The code is available through job centres or employment offices or from the Disablement Advisory Service or Placing Assessment and Counselling Team (PACT), free of charge.	Department of Employment; Disablement Advisory Service; Placing Assessment and Counselling Team (PACT)
EC Recommendation (OJL86/225/43) 1986	States that suitable measures to 'provide fair opportunities for the disabled people in the field of employment and vocational training' should be undertaken by the 12 Member States. NB: A recommendation has no legally binding effect: it can urge action but not enforce it.	European Commission
EC Proposal for a Directive on Mobility	Part of the Commission's implementation of the Social Charter. Its main aim is to ensure that workers with reduced mobility have access to safe transport to work. A Council Directive has the effect, once adopted, of requiring Member States to enact legislation. The Commission is proposing to introduce this Directive under section 118a of the Single European Act, which means that only a 'qualified majority' vote is needed at the Council of Ministers, and no single member's government will have a veto.	European Commission

Table 4 Age legislation

Legislation	*Summary of provision*	*Governing bodies*
Employment (Age Limits) Bill 1989 (UK) (no further progress on this bill to date)	Proposes the removal of discriminatory upper age limits on job advertisements and vacancies.	Department of Employment
Employment Act 1989 (UK)	• Amends the statutory redundancy scheme so that all employees will be entitled to a redundancy payment up to their normal retiring age or up to the age of 65. • Extends the age limit of employment protection for women to age 65.	Department of Employment

Table 5 Sexuality legislation

Legislation	*Summary of provision*	*Sponsored by*
Homosexual Equality Bill 1990 (UK) (no progress to date)	Seeks to provide the minimum necessary for lesbians and gay men to achieve legal equality with heterosexuals.	Campaign for Homosexual Equality; The National Council for Civil Liberties; The Stonewall Group
Section 28 of the Local Government Act 1988 (UK)	Makes it unlawful for local authorities to 'intentionally promote homosexuality' in any way, and forbids 'the teaching in any maintained school of the acceptability of homosexuality as a pretended family relationship'.	

Table 6 Ex-offenders legislation

Legislation	*Summary of provision*	*Useful organizations*
The Rehabilitation of Offenders Act 1974 (UK)	Anyone who has been convicted of a criminal offence, and received a sentence of not more than 2½ years in prison, benefits as a result of the Act, if s/he is not convicted again during a specified period (the rehabilitation period). If someone who can benefit under the Act is not convicted again during the rehabilitation period, s/he becomes what the Act calls a 'rehabilitated person' and the conviction becomes 'spent'. The convicted person does not have to reveal it or admit its existence in most circumstances.	The Apex Trust; NACRO (National Association for the Care and Resettlement of Offenders)

Table 7 United Nations human rights treaties

Legislation	*Summary of provision*	*Governing bodies*
Universal Declaration of Human Rights (UDHR)	Was adopted by the General Assembly of the UN in 1948. The UDHR states that everyone is entitled to certain basic human rights 'without distinction of any kind, such as race, colour, sex, language, religion, political or other opinion, national or social origin, property, birth or other status'.	United Nations
International Covenant on Civil and Political Rights (ICCPR)	Came into force in 1976. It transformed the original principles of the UDHR into treaty provisions. The ICCPR, when ratified, binds a country to honouring specific human rights. It pledges not to commit such crimes as slavery, torture, denial of free speech, and extrajudicial killings.	United Nations

Table 7 (*cont.*)

Legislation	*Summary of provision*	*Governing bodies*
International Covenant on Economic, Social and Cultural Rights (ICESCR)	Also came into force in 1976. The ICESCR is concerned with broad social and economic questions, and in most instances the guarantees are in the form of 'taking steps towards' the implementation of a particular Article.	United Nations
Convention on the Elimination of All Forms of Discrimination Against Women (also known as the Convention on Equality for Women)	Was adopted by the General Assembly of the UN in 1979. To date, only about a third of UN members have ratified this Convention. Article 8 of the Convention serves to illustrate the amount of progress which still needs to be made: 'Article 8: States parties shall take all appropriate measures to ensure to women, on equal terms with men and without any discrimination, the opportunity to represent their government at the international level and to participate in the work of international organizations.'	United Nations

Appendix 2

Equal Opportunities Glossary – The Meaning Behind the Jargon

Most subject areas or jobs (and equal opportunities is no exception) are characterized by specific phrases and jargon which are unique to the topic in question. Equal opportunities is a subject which is surrounded by both familiar and not quite so familiar phrases. The basic principles of most subjects extend across and are transferable into many others. This is of particular importance and extremely relevant to equal opportunities. Equal opportunities policies and practices (and not forgetting the jargon!) should not be viewed in isolation or seen as an isolated topic which is divorced from all other subjects. Equal opportunities is about treating everyone equally, regardless of their background or lifestyle, in all aspects of their lives. Therefore it is vital to regard these definitions as sharing an equal context – whether in the home, school, office, shop floor or wherever. In order to reinforce this practice, equal opportunities training and awareness-raising should be seen as an integral part of all employment practices and vocational training.

The following phrases are all commonly associated with equal opportunities. The explanations that are provided for each, with particular relevance to the UK, attempt to highlight the meaning in detail as well as the context (where appropriate) in which each may occur.

Advisory, Conciliation and Arbitration Service (**ACAS**)
The role of ACAS is to settle an employment-related dispute before it gets to **industrial tribunal** stage. As soon as a complaint is received by the tribunal a copy is immediately sent to an Advisory, Conciliation and Arbitration Service complaints officer. Neither party has to speak to the ACAS officer. The ACAS officer attempts to arbitrate between the two parties in order to bring about a settlement.

Age of consent
The age of consent laws refer to the minimum age below which sexual activity is illegal. Age limits vary considerably throughout Europe and

differences between age limits for heterosexual and homosexual activity are also commonplace. Similarly, penalties for engaging in underage sex for heterosexuals and homosexuals also vary widely; with the latter subject to much more stringent penalties. In the UK, the threat of 'being caught in the act' has far more serious implications for homosexual activity than heterosexual. Put simply, a man under 21 engaging in gay sex risks spending two years in jail; furthermore, an over-21-year-old having gay sex with an under-21-year-old risks spending five years in prison. How much attention people pay to age of consent laws in practice is obviously difficult to assess. The age of consent laws are essentially out of touch with reality; sexual morality and activity has changed during the past few decades. The law does not act as a deterrent. Interestingly, only one other country in the world has as high an age of consent for gay men as the UK – Bulgaria.

Ageism

Ageism is to do with the social disadvantage and oppression of older people, and is firmly rooted in British society. It is associated with other discriminations. For example an elderly black female handicapped by a disability could well suffer from a combination of oppression grounded in racism, sexism, disablism as well as ageism. Ageism awareness campaigns and positive legislation are essential in counteracting the effects of ageism. The fundamental starting-point is the question of how to raise awareness. Part of the momentum will have to come from older people themselves. Racism and sexism did not become major issues because large groups of white people and men realized their negative feelings towards black people and women: it was these groups themselves who challenged others to face their own prejudiced attitudes and the discriminatory consequences of them.

Assimilation and separatism

To divide these two definitions would be to confuse, as they are so inextricably linked. The arguments for and against each will be familiar to minority groups in many cultures. Put simply, the argument or difference is between the assimilationists, who believe in joining the establishment, and the separatists, who say that as a minority member you should stay outside.

It is important to note that assimilationism can and does have two quite different forms. In most, if not all, minority groups, there are those people who (for whatever reason) pay little regard to their oppression and attempt to fit into society as unquestioningly as, for example, a white, able-bodied, middle-class heterosexual male may be expected to do. In contrast, some assimilationists wholly recognize the oppressive nature of their position within the establishment, but choose nevertheless to join 'it', and by doing so, agree by and large to its norms. Their general acceptance of the

Establishment's priorities leads to a sense of progress when and if a positive acknowledgement is received from within the corridors of power.

In general, separatism is about questioning the values and ethics of the Establishment which seeks to exclude minority groups in so many ways. As a result of this the separatist chooses to stay outside the norms of the Establishment, and to argue at street level for change and radical improvements in his or her position.

Bisexuality

Bisexuality is about the potential for being sexually or romantically involved with members of either sex. In the context of sexuality, it is crucial to remember that terms such as bisexual, homosexual, heterosexual are merely a set of labels, created in the main by a heterosexist and homophobic society. Such labels serve to alienate, divide and in turn discriminate on the basis of difference; and in their bid to categorize, deny individual uniqueness.

Contract compliance

Contract compliance is about attaching conditions to contracts in order to promote socially desirable ends. It originated in America as a form of positive or affirmative action in the pursuit of increased equal opportunities. In the US, where such provisions exist they aim to ensure that employers brought into work on government-sponsored projects adhere closely to the equal opportunities clauses laid down. In practice, this has meant that whenever an equal opportunities policy calls for non-discrimination action towards a particular group, the employer also has to apply these non-discriminatory conditions, whether in recruitment, training, promotion or any fringe benefit. Contract compliance is nothing new in the UK; yet historically it has presented major challenges as well as opportunities for employers and politicians nationally and locally. Within the UK it has most frequently been associated with the construction industry, and somewhat less with engineering projects. In the recent past many (particularly Labour-controlled) local authorities have agreed to give contracts for building development work only to companies which agree to comply with the equal opportunities provisions in force. The path has not always been smooth in the implementation of such contracts; in fact overall it has been regarded as a contentious issue. The controversy has largely been based on the clear distinction between actually enforcing such contracts such by law, and making voluntary arrangements at the employer's discretion. An alternative theme which has been proposed is the promotion of employment schemes which (in contrast to contract compliance) do not lay down that disadvantaged minorities must be employed through contracts – but do nevertheless state that recruitment should be targeted at and drawn from local communities as far as possible. In practice this ought to mean that government contracts in, for instance, parts of Birmingham or Bolton should foster employment among ethnic minorities who constitute a substantial minority population in such areas. Further criticism of contract compliance has focused on the fact that such schemes do very little to counteract the root causes and effects of discrimination found within the labour market and the wider society. Questions about both the advantages and disadvantages of contract compliance continue to be raised from a political and economic angle.

Designated Employment Schemes

The Secretary of State for Employment has the power to designate an employment; that is, to reserve further entry into particular jobs for registered disabled people. Currently only two employments have been designated in this way: car park attendant and passenger electric-lift attendant are both designated areas of work.

Disability allowances

In April 1992, the UK government announced a number of changes to existing disability allowances, and new benefits have been introduced. The three new benefits are called the Disability Living Allowance, the Disability Working Allowance and Attendance Allowance.

Disability Living Allowance is replacing the previous attendance allowance for people disabled before the age of 65. It is also replacing mobility allowance for people of all ages. Attendance allowance will continue for people whose care needs first arise after the age of 65.

The Disability Working Allowance is an earnings top-up which will help those getting long-term sickness benefits to make the difficult transition back into work, provided they are working at least 16 hours per week. When Disability Working Allowance is fully established it is estimated that 50,000 disabled people will benefit from it at any one time. According to the Minister for Disabled People, the new allowance will give disabled people an important new opportunity to live and work independently in the community.

Disability Working Allowance is a new tax-free social security benefit to help people who:

- Have an illness or disability which puts them at a disadvantage in getting a job and
- Are starting to work or are already working.

Disability Working Allowance was introduced in April 1992. A claim pack is available from post offices or social security offices, or the freephone benefit enquiry line on 0800 882200.

The third new allowance introduced in April 1992 is called Attendance Allowance. If an individual aged 65 or over needs help with personal care because of an illness or disability, he or she could be entitled to Attendance Allowance.

Disablism

Disablism has developed through a similar social process as **racism** and **sexism**. It occurs as a result of the combined effects of prejudice and discrimination experienced by people with disabilities. A person with a visible handicap is constantly at the mercy of society's attitudes towards disability. The attitudes which dominate any group usually reflect the ideas of the most powerful and influential groups; but are nevertheless accepted by almost everyone else without argument. Where the assumptions made about people with disabilities are negative they lead to disablism. Disablism both creates and perpetuates prejudices about the nature and experience of disability. It is a depressing and widely held view that a person handicapped in some way by a disability is somehow inferior to an able-bodied person. This sad reality is reflected most strongly in the world of work. All too often applicants with disabilities are overlooked in favour of able-bodied recruits. The provision of special placements and schemes specifically for employees with disabilities goes some way towards challenging and redressing the situation. However, until such time as this group are absorbed as far as possible into mainstream employment and education the prejudice will undoubtedly continue.

Discrimination

Both the Sex Discrimination Act and the Race Relations Act recognize two types of discrimination:

Direct discrimination This type of discrimination is generally easy to identify, as it is 'direct' or obvious, as its name implies. It consists of an explicit statement or act which lays down different treatment of people according to their sex or marital status. For instance, within the realms of sex discrimination, a contract of employment or agreement might state that 'the annual holiday entitlement for men is five weeks and for women four weeks', or 'management training will be available for unmarried staff only who have completed eight months service with the company.' Both of these statements are prime examples of direct discrimination.

Within the context of racial discrimination, direct racial discrimination arises where a person treats another person less favourably on racial grounds than he treats or would treat, someone else. Racial grounds means any of the following grounds: colour, race, nationality (including citizenship) or ethnic or national origins.

Indirect discrimination This type of discrimination is much less obvious than that described above, and is very often characterized by subtle and ambiguous actions and statements, which can be easily and deliberately misinterpreted and misleading. Within the terms of the Sex

Discrimination Act this occurs where an unjustifiable requirement or condition is applied equally to both sexes; or to married or single people of the same sex, but will have a disproportionately adverse effect on one sex or on married people. For example, an employer might state that a minimum of 15 years' uninterrupted service is required before an individual will be considered for promotion. This situation could well discriminate against women, who are much more likely to have had time out of the workforce to rear children or look after elderly or sick relatives.

Indirect racial discrimination consists of treatment which may be described as equal in a formal sense, as between all racial groups; but in its effect discriminates against a particular racial group. For example, a company advertises a vacancy in the local newspaper and states that 'perfect written and spoken English are required in this job.' This could discriminate against people who had recently arrived in Britain from a non-English-speaking country. In the vast majority of cases a person with much less than perfect English could do the job completely satisfactorily. Similarly, a requirement to wear a uniform which consists of a skirt would discriminate against Muslim women as they would not be able to do this without contravening their religious codes.

Unfortunately, there are very many cases of indirect racial and sex discrimination, many of which are overlooked or pass unnoticed. Indirect racial discrimination is often aimed at a specific racial group, and has a very damaging and negative effect on its target group. Indirect acts or statements of discrimination should never be overlooked or allowed to happen freely. It is important to be aware of what constitutes an act of indirect discrimination, in order to ensure that even the most cleverly worded intention is not overlooked or ignored.

Double discrimination

Double discrimination refers to extended discrimination which occurs due to the interplay between two (or more) discriminating factors, and it often brings class distinction into the equation. The interrelationship between, for example, sex and race is easy to identify. Double discrimination is about two discriminators working together or socially linked such as to render an individual more likely to experience discrimination. In housing, for instance, it might be argued that there is a severe housing shortage and the working class comes off worst, yet black and Asian members of the working class are particularly hard hit because of the added problem of racial discrimination in the process of allocating and distributing accommodation. Many people from ethnic minority groups have successfully breached the class division, but have still not been accepted by the majority on an equal basis with their white counterparts. So long as any type of discrimination persists there will always be individuals and groups more prone to endure the effects of discrimination simply because they are, for example, female and black, gay and disabled or Asian and elderly. Indeed, whatever the combination, to the wider society they represent dual targets for prejudice and discrimination.

Equality

Equality is the end result of good equal opportunities policy and practice. Equality is achieved when everyone, regardless of the group to which they belong or the lifestyle they have, is treated in the same way. Fair treatment extends beyond even the best policy to include all services within and outside the workplace; it is about everybody receiving an equal status without prejudice or discrimination.

One of the greatest obstacles to achieving equality of opportunity and the greatest single cause of inaction is the common response 'We don't have a problem.' People seem to react defensively when it is suggested that there is a need for change, feeling that their judgement and skills are being called into question. Such responses are quite unnecessary since responsibility for ending discrimination lies far beyond any individual or group: like anything, it inevitably reflects society's values. It is a collective responsibility and can be collectively put right.

Equality clause

An equality clause is a provision relating to terms of pay or conditions of a contract under which a woman is employed. The Equal Pay Act 1970 (as amended by the Equal Pay (Amendment) Regulations 1983) operates by automatically inserting an equality clause directly or indirectly (i.e. by means of a collective agreement) in the terms of women's contracts of employment.

Ethnicity

In the use of ethnicity as a means of labelling people, two tendencies and assumptions have become apparent. The first is to regard ethnicity as an exclusive attribute of minority groups. In Britain, for example, the English have traditionally regarded the Scots, Irish, Punjabis, Afro-Caribbeans, Chinese, etc., as sub-groups with readily identifiable characteristics. Curiously, however, the English have not regarded themselves as an ethnic group, because being the dominant group within the population, no direct pressure has been put on them to ask what makes them distinctive. However, if a member of the dominant population visits another country and is placed, perhaps for the first time, in a minority status the issue of ethnicity is more likely to be addressed. Because it takes it for granted as the norm, the dominant group usually identifies itself by the name of the country. Hence a white person born and bred in Norwich would define herself as English; she may be less inclined to refer to her Sikh neighbour as English.

The second tendency has been the assumption that while racial groups are distinguished (and distinct) by their physical appearance, ethnic groups are identified by other characteristics; for example, language, shared history, religion, customs, etc. This tendency has led to ethnic groups being regarded as sub-groups of racial groups. For instance, French-, Italian-, and Irish-Americans may be regarded as ethnic subdivisions of the whole racial group called White Americans. Problems arise when appearance creates social divisiveness and certain dominant cultures are seen as superior to smaller sub-cultures. Furthermore, it is worth noting that there is a tendency for minority members to define themselves differently (and more accurately) from the way the dominant group defines them. For example, in the UK, many immigrants from the Indian sub-continent are referred to as Pakistanis regardless of which part of the sub-continent they are from.

Evaluation
Evaluation is generally the process that follows on from a **monitoring** programme. The data and figures which have been collected during the monitoring process often reveal inequalities in the workplace. It may be that the statistics reveal a higher number of white people gaining promotion than black people; or a larger percentage of men in managerial positions than women. The purpose of evaluation is to put right any imbalance in the workforce where there is evidence that a minority group (or indeed any group) is disadvantaged. Evaluation relies upon a strategic approach where everyone becomes party to the plan to change and improve. Evaluation enables corrective action to take place by highlighting areas which require **positive-action** programmes or improvements in equal opportunities practice. Chapter 3, which looks at strategies to increase the effect of equal opportunities policies and programmes, examines methods of evaluation in more detail.

Feminism
Throughout history women have been treated less favourably than men; and even today the situation, on close inspection, is not that much improved. In our current government there only two female ministers to represent over 50 per cent of the population who are women. Women occupy more of the low paid jobs than men and are scantly represented in management positions. Women own less than 1 per cent of the total property in the world.

With these dismal figures in mind the case for feminism is strengthened. Feminism embodies the belief that men and women are equal, but that women have been held back or oppressed throughout our history. The women's liberation movement is sometimes also referred to as feminism. A feminist is a person (female or male) who strives towards achieving equality for women by giving women the same rights as men in law, and by putting pressure on government to improve and update legislation. Nationally and locally feminists are active in improving the way women are treated and viewed by society, and in advancing the availability of equal opportunities for women in all aspects of life.

Genuine Occupational Qualification (GOQ)
As referred to in chapter 2, a GOQ by law covers situations when discrimination is allowed and acceptable. Under the terms of the Sex Discrimination Act, being a man or a woman is a GOQ for a job only where:

1 The essential nature of the job calls for a man or calls for a woman for reasons of physical form (excluding physical strength or stamina) for example, modelling; or in acting or stage performances, for reasons of authenticity. For example, Hamlet is more realistically performed by a man, as Desdemona is by a woman.
2 The job needs to be held by a man or by a woman to preserve decency and privacy; for example the job of changing room assistant in a lingerie department may require a woman. Advertisements for/employers of nurses and nursing assistants can also claim a GOQ for the same reasons.

Other GOQs in relation to sex discrimination include employment which is mainly held outside of the United Kingdom, or a job which is one of two to be held by a married couple (for example, housekeepers for a stately home). In general, very few other exceptions can be claimed. An organization which offers a service such as employment, or other facilities and services should approach the Equal Opportunities Commission for advice on whether a GOQ can be claimed. The Commission will advise organizations on when it is considered appropriate to do so.

Similar provisions exist within the guidelines of the Race Relations Act, for the purposes of privacy or authenticity. For example, a Chinese or Indian restaurant may wish to recruit Chinese or Indian waiting staff in order to provide a more authentic atmosphere. Similarly, a GOQ may be claimed if the job involves modelling where the person's physical appearance is important: for example, in an advertisement for cosmetics especially for black skin. Advertisements in the national press sometimes include the term GOQ for particular jobs. For example, an Asian Women's Hostel seeking to recruit an Asian female whose mother tongue is Gujerati would include within the advertisement a statement to the effect that the post has a GOQ exemption from the provisions of the Sex Discrimination and Race Relations Acts.

Ghetto
Any group of like-minded people who associate together in large numbers is often referred to as a 'ghetto'. Since the beginning of time people (and animals) have shown a tendency to group together to create safe environments. It is probably, therefore, built into human nature to group and to mix with people who feel, think and live in a similar way to oneself. So a ghetto is inhabited in the main by one race or group.

The Jews of Venice lived near to a foundry or Geto. Subsequently the word ghetto came into more general use, first being applied to cities other than Venice, and, later, to races other than the Jews. Still later, it has been applied to groups which are united on the basis of cultural cohesion.

Ghettos are partly the product of prejudice. They grow because members of a minority group find more security in one another's company than in isolation. An advantage of the ghetto is the ability for individuals from minority groups to mix and gain mutual support. In contrast, one major disadvantage of the ghetto is that it does little to assist non-minority groups to begin to understand how other people live; and thus contributes little to combating prejudice in wider society.

Grey power

Grey power is the general term referring to the organized structure of older people grouping together to give themselves a collective political and economic voice. Variations on the phrase include grey movement, pensioner movement or simply the Greys. The grey movement has developed in response to political and social agendas which discriminate against older people. Political groups of the over-50s are a fairly recent development in most European countries, but are already well established in the US as well as parts of Australia. In America, the Grey Panthers have both a powerful and increasingly influential voice – and proved themselves such when they successfully overturned the Reagan administration's intention to reduce the social security budget. The group is part of the Association of Retired Persons which is represented across the United States; it currently has over 20 million members. In Western Australia there is a grey-power registered political party which in 1988 polled 6 per cent of the votes in state elections. Within the EC Member States the grey movement is also growing, albeit at a more gradual pace. Germany is the probable leader in European politics for older people. A new political party, the Greys, has entered the spectrum, and fought in the West German parliamentary elections in 1990. Throughout Scandinavia the movement is also gaining rapid support. Central policy issues among the various grey groups are closely related and include health, pensions, finance, ageism, and the rights of older workers as well as pensioners.

Heterosexism

Heterosexism as an attitude has been around for as long as the human race has, but as a term in its own right it is relatively new. It has been coined to describe an attitude of mind or way of thinking that categorizes, and then unfairly dismisses, a group of (different) people as inferior and not sharing as valid a status as the main group because of their sexuality. Heterosexism is institutionalized in our laws, religions, media and indeed in our everyday language. Perhaps the most influential forums for the words and images of heterosexism are television, radio and newspapers, as well as the majority of published fiction. Their combined effect is to reinforce heterosexism and portray it as the norm; and as such, anything else as deviant and abnormal. Lesbians and gay men have been almost entirely excluded from representation, particularly in programme development and media presentation. Wider heterosexism at work can take many forms, from deliberately not employing lesbians and gay men to harassment and dismissal.

Heterosexuality

Since plenty has already been written about homosexuality, what about the opposite form of sexuality and lifestyle – heterosexuality? Heterosexuality is sexual activity between male and female partners; it is assumed to be the norm for behaviour. Children are on the whole expected to grow up to be heterosexual and to pursue teenage fantasies and relationships to that end. One in every ten people is homosexual; by definition, therefore the rest are heterosexual or bisexual. However, the situation is not clear-cut on two levels. First, figures are not generally as reliable or accurate as they could be, not least because the subject is as complex as human behaviour is. Second, it is not simple to categorize human beings and their activities as there is clearly a degree of overlap in behaviour. The causes of heterosexuality and homosexuality have been the subject of much debate for years – though the questions have most often been asked about the latter, since it has been regarded as the exception, rather than the rule. A combination of chemical, emotional and environmental factors probably goes some way towards creating heterosexuality. Equally, however, peer-group pressure as well as social conditioning from the cradle onwards are very strong influencing factors.

Homophobia

Several dictionaries offer several definitions of homophobia, all of which reach the same conclusions, albeit through a variety of approaches. Basically it is a combination of prejudice and discrimination aimed at homosexuals. Phobia means an irrational and excessive fear, for example, hydrophobia (fear of water). So alternatively, homophobia could simply be said to be society's dislike and fear of homosexuals. This fear incorporates ignorance, which we have already seen manifests itself in prejudice towards a particular group. If that were the complete definition of homophobia, many people would argue that since all of us harbour prejudices to a certain extent, let us therefore accept homophobia complacently. However, there are lessons to be learnt from leaving things too much to work themselves out; the most repugnant one being the massive prejudice and subsequent acts of discrimination that have ensued.

The realities of homophobia in society make it impossible for two men or two women who are partners to display even the mildest form of physical affection towards each other in public. In the UK, it has been known on several occasions for a homosexual couple to be prosecuted for showing affection in the street. In contrast, imagine how often we are confronted in public by heterosexual displays of affection, since these face no such threat of prosecution. In much the same way as ethnic minority groups have formed their own communities in order to avoid prejudice and discrimination, the gay community have opened bars, clubs and support groups in order that they may avoid the homophobic responses of the public and of the law-enforcement organizations.

Industrial tribunal (IT)
An industrial tribunal is an informal hearing which deals with employment matters. The tribunal panel is made up of a chairperson who is qualified in law, and two lay persons. In the case of a race tribunal it is essential that one of the panel should have up-to-date knowledge of the law on racial discrimination. The people who sit on tribunals are appointed by the Department of Employment; individuals have no right to get the panel members changed. There is no legal aid available for tribunals. While industrial tribunals were originally set up for people to represent themselves, the fact of the matter is that this can involve great expense. In practice, it is important to be represented by someone with a knowledge of the law; you may need the money to pay for a solicitor. In the case of sex discrimination, a trade union, law centres, advice bureaux or the Equal Opportunities Commission can represent you. For a race tribunal you can get representation from these groups or from the Commission for Racial Equality.

Masculinity
Masculinity means all kinds of things to all kinds of people. The traditional stereotypes of what constitutes masculinity are at last beginning to be challenged. Historically, to be masculine has meant to be large, aggressive, dominant, powerful, logical, analytical, strong, etc. In contrast, to be feminine has implied that one is passive, accepting, caring, weak, polite, well-groomed and all sorts of other adjectives that added together create a 'ladylike' image of feminine. In the past men (or women) who have deviated from the stereotype have been regarded with suspicion and contempt. For a man to be accepting and passive has not been regarded as acceptable or standard behaviour. Therefore, a combination of social pressure and peer-group pressure to conform has perpetuated the popular image of masculinity.

Lesbians, feminists, gay men and anti-sexist heterosexual men have gradually challenged and eroded the myths surrounding masculinity. They have focused attention on the latent feminine characteristics of men which have been previously suppressed. Furthermore, they have extended the concept of masculinity by highlighting the fundamental flaws in its common imagery. Masculinity means both more and less than the traditional stereotype of the all-powerful, successful dominant male. The old shame and embarrassment associated with males displaying female characteristics is slowly dying with the recognition that characteristics are not, and should not be, gender based.

Maternity leave *see* **Statutory Maternity Pay**

Minority

Small groups which are nationally or racially based within larger groups are referred to as 'minorities'. The physical characteristics, language, speech, dress or costume – or a combination of these factors – of minorities such as Asians or Afro-Caribbeans in contemporary Britain may make them readily identifiable. But equally, groups of Scots or Irish in England are regarded as minorities. In countries like Britain and America (both multi-racial and multinational communities) a person may not be conscious of being in a minority in one part of the country, but be conscious of his or her minority status in another part. Minorities have always been subject to prejudice and various forms of discrimination by the majority. Minority groups are often described and labelled with sweeping generalizations and stereotypes. Even such inoffensive and (by usual standards) praiseworthy acts as hard work and perseverance may be interpreted as threatening when performed by a minority group: sociologists have demonstrated how working hard for long hours is positively to be admired when applied to most people (especially the famous or national heros), but when applied to a minority group member – for example, the Jew – the same characteristics are quite often scorned. In this, and in several other ways minority groups suffer at the hands of the majority.

Misogyny

Misogyny is the intense dislike of women by men. A misogynist is a woman-hater; the word is derived from Greek, *misein*, meaning hate, *misos*, meaning hatred, and *gune*, meaning woman. Such hatred is often manifested in the verbal and physical abuse of women. The causes of misogyny are likely to be an interaction of a number of factors. An individual's upbringing, emotional and psychological disposition, educational achievements, status in employment, etc., each continue to produce behavioural traits in adults. One school of thought is that misogyny is entirely to do with the psychological difficulties boys have in becoming men, with a fear of being controlled by women.

The low status of women in the workplace (highlighted by their lower pay, poorer access to vocational training and promotion, lower grade jobs, etc.) is a form of institutionalized misogyny which keeps women in subordinate positions to men. Misogynistic beliefs culminate in attitudes that demean women's bodies and abilities.

Mobility

Many people both in and out of employment suffer from reduced mobility. Mobility in the context of equal opportunities refers to transport problems associated with a whole range of different types of disability, including both physical and mental disabilities which may mean a carer or travel companion is necessary. Mobility is also about accessibility – access to both means of transport and public buildings. In order to facilitate this, all new buildings and new vehicles should be designed to accommodate people with reduced mobility. In addition all existing transport and buildings ought to be progressively adapted to achieve the same. In practice this means that minimum standards and requirements have to be in force. All EC Member States should therefore ensure that they have the legislation in place to implement basic standards for organizations and manufacturers to adhere to.

Monitoring

Monitoring and **evaluation** are difficult to separate. When an organization sets up an equal opportunities policy and working party, one of the duties of the latter is to ensure that the policy is actually working. Monitoring is about collecting statistics, figures, information and research analysis in order to evaluate and ascertain what effect the policy is actually having. It is the process of checking the relative position of women to men, married people to single people, black to white, able-bodied to disabled people within an organization, for the purposes of ensuring the equal opportunities policy is effective.

Monitoring can be carried out using a variety of methods depending on the size of the organization and the amount of time available to be allocated to it. Methods include handing out questionnaires and forms, interviewing, assessing the results of job advertisements, and reviewing application forms and other selection methods. Monitoring includes the widespread and thorough assessment of recruitment methods, and **evaluation** of that material with an analysis of factors such as the numbers of applicants with regard to ethnic origin, sex, sex orientation, disability and ex-offenders. Regular review of recruitment practices should be the norm if monitoring is to be effective. Surveys of the ethnic origin of the existing workforce alongside an analysis of the complete workforce profile can be used to monitor progress in the implementation of the equal opportunities policy. The same types of surveys can be used to analyse numbers of all minority groups within a workforce. The results of these surveys or monitoring processes should help determine the need for further initiatives or positive-action campaigns. The statistical information gathered should be used as an aid in training to encourage objectivity in selection methods, recruitment and promotional processes. Successful monitoring methods are examined in further detail in chapter 3.

Moral majority

Views and beliefs (supposedly) held by most people characterize an imaginary group known as the 'moral majority'. How the perceived majority apparently thinks and acts is reinforced daily by the media. Essentially, however, how people think, behave or potentially would do so in a given situation is almost impossible to assess with any degree of accuracy. The projection of the existence of this 'moral majority' both creates and reinforces stereotypes; and has a negative tendency to categorize conformists and isolate non-conformists.

National Assistance Act

The National Assistance Act was passed in 1948, three years after the end of the Second World War. It was introduced as a means of ensuring that the accommodation needs of people in need of care because of age, disability or infirmity are met. Their lack of the most appropriate accommodation might be due to a number of reasons; for example homelessness or the unsuitability of current housing in meeting their needs. For instance, a person with reduced mobility or impaired vision would be severely restricted if housed on the ninth floor of a block of flats; even more so if the block did not contain a lift. Any person of any age may apply to his or her local council for assistance in securing suitable accommodation. In general, the homes are either owned by or run by the local councils. The central government lays down the minimum charge that a council may request, and above that the local authority assesses what an individual should be charged. The system obviously leads to wide fluctuations and discrepancies in affordable services from area to area and person to person. A person in one local authority with exactly the same needs as an individual in a different authority may be unable to benefit from the provisions under the Act simply because s/he cannot afford to. Again a degree of consistency is necessary if all people who are entitled to benefit are to be treated equally.

Nationalism

Nationalism is about Britishness, Frenchness, Irishness, etc. It generally refers to and attempts to summarize the national feelings of the majority population towards their country, culture, beliefs, lifestyles, achievements and uniqueness. A nationalist shows an exaggerated pride in his or her country, the effects of which may spill over into an exaggeration of its positive image and an understatement of its negative image and traditions. In addition, extreme nationalists generally wish to maintain a specific order and social mix in their country. This might mean a desire to keep their country inhabited by particular groups only – usually groups which belong to the same racial, cultural, religious and ethnic group as themselves. Throughout the last decade in France, and earlier in the UK, waves of nationalist feeling led to the formation of groups whose collective aim was to extol the virtues of, for instance, 'Britishness' while simultaneously undermining the status of any group of citizens that fell outside of their definitions and categories.

Negative terminology

Everyday English language usage is riddled with negative terminology. Negative terminology is misleading and ultimately discriminatory in effect. Examples of negative racial language include 'whiter than white', 'blackmail', 'black mark', 'accident black spot'. Black is associated with that which is bad and creates a negative image, whereas white is seen as good and as such produces a positive image. In order to counteract prejudice, negative terminology should be avoided. Derogatory and negative language is also commonplace when referring to homosexuals; 'queer', 'puff', 'shirt-lifter' and 'lezzie' are insulting and only serve to perpetuate society's homophobia.

Orange Badge Scheme

The Orange Badge Scheme allows an exemption from standard parking restrictions for some disabled people. It allows people who display an Orange Badge to park a car (in which they have been either a driver or a passenger) in the following circumstances: at parking metres free of charge for an unlimited time period; on yellow lines for up to two hours; and indefinitely in zones where parking is generally restricted to particular times. The badges are issued by local councils, who are permitted to make only a nominal charge for them. Three main groups of people qualify: registered blind persons; those in receipt of mobility allowance or supplement; and people who are suffering from a permanent or semi-permanent disability which causes problems walking. In addition, children aged two or above may benefit from the scheme if they satisfy any of these conditions.

Parental leave

Parental leave is a period of leave granted to individuals in order to care for a child. In general it is available to either parent who is employed by the company. The leave is usually granted after the maternity leave period has expired. A European Commission proposal for a Directive on parental leave and leave for family reasons was introduced in 1986 at the time the European Council approved the second Community action programme on the promotion of equal opportunities for women (1986–1990). Progress on this front has been slow, however, with the proposed Directive no nearer coming into force now than it was in 1986. There are wide variations in the provision of parental leave both within the UK and between each EC member country. The UK does not guarantee any statutory right to parental leave. In contrast, most other countries do provide at least a few rights, though the amount and form varies from country to country. In fact, wide variations exist in national provisions on many related issues including: length of parental leave entitlements, the time period within which the leave must be taken; and the period of leave granted per child. Despite the overall lack and inadequacy of legal measures on parental rights there is a gradual tendency for a growing number of employers to organize their own affairs internally with respect to their employees' rights as parents. Nowadays employers with a commitment to equal opportunities are increasingly recognizing the importance of granting leave to their staff for childcare reasons. However, there is still a very long way to go throughout all Member States before parental leave is awarded the seriousness it deserves. Parental rights are essential, but they do need to be supplemented by quite radical changes in the organization and culture of the workplace. Traditions die hard; the lifelong conditioning of men and women to their roles defies overnight solutions. Equally, stereotypes have a tendency to persist – 'Women with children are unreliable' is an often heard assumption which presupposes that women are the sole carers in the home. A combination of legislation, collective agreements, and management awareness is necessary to address the relationship between employment and family responsibilities. Local equal opportunities policies supported by national legislation can go some way towards incorporating parental rights as a crucial component of policies. Laws, policies and codes of practice have to recognize and commit themselves to individuals' career prospects and childcare arrangements.

Paternity leave

Paternity leave is the right of fathers to paid time off work around the time of the birth of their children. It ranges in its provision both within the UK and within the EC Member States. About two days' leave is commonly granted by an increasing number of organizations, but this is generally arranged by collective agreements rather than by statutory right. Some European countries offer far more rights to fathers than the UK; in fact the UK is one of the least generous providers in regard to paternity rights. Denmark leads the EC in its provision, which is both relatively generous and more flexible than most other comparable systems.

The right to paternity leave is a measure of a country's or an employer's commitment to increase men's participation in family responsibilities. If leave entitlements coupled with more flexible working arrangements are only available to (and therefore used by) women, this will perpetuate female inequality. Employers and national parliaments should make explicit and detailed policy commitments and guidelines which recognize the importance of increasing men's involvement in the care of young children; and review existing policies in the workforce which may be incompatible with the objectives of paternity rights. As is the case with all equality issues, governments have a central and dual role to play. The most pressing need is for a change in legislation which incorporates family policy in its broadest sense; not merely restricting policy to maternal provision. Secondly, governments as employers should act as role models in their own levels of provision to fathers as well as mothers. In addition, they should actively encourage other employers to emulate them by providing special support and incentives to companies who comply with paternity leave rights. The development of employment policies that are responsive to the needs of workers with family responsibilities requires a combination of legal measures, collective agreements and company workplace initiatives. There needs to be a structured framework at all levels – international, national and local – involving managers, trade unions, equal opportunities representatives and all those directly concerned with childcare and employment, to propose recommendations as well as monitor and review developments.

Pornography

Women and children are the primary victims of pornography. Pornography is the most obvious example of legalized sex discrimination that exists in most countries world-wide. Whether there is a proven link between availability of pornography and sexual crime has been a subject of much debate since the Obscene Publications Act of 1959 emerged. One opinion is that rapes and indecent assaults increasingly involve behaviour that defendants have read about and are in consequence encouraged to try: as a result, pornography contributes to sexual violence against women and children. Another school of thought believes that there is no correlation between pornography and sexual violence.

Most so-called liberal democratic countries have an abundance of pornography, which is available through as many 'reputable' as disreputable outlets. Perhaps one of the negative side-effects of the process of liberalization and freedom is the rapid growth in the pornography industry that accompanies it. In many countries the pornography industry is as visible as, for instance, the cigarette industry, and indeed enjoys a much higher public profile than many other industries. Contradictions abound – in several countries religious festivals are conducted in the midst of hustlers trading their porn. Statues of Our Lady are carried along in processions flanked on all sides by pornography.

The abolition of censorship in the UK with the emergence of the Obscene Publications Act in 1959 coincided a short time afterwards with the enormous boom in pornography. While those involved got rich, women were subject to degradation of the most obscene kind. As well as being sexually degrading pornography also validates violence against women, and strengthens oppression. Suffice to say that any country which boasts about its commitment to human rights and equality should seriously address issues like pornography as a major obstacle to achieving such equality.

Positive action

Positive action is sometimes wrongly referred to as positive discrimination. Both the Sex Discrimination Act and the Race Relations Act make provisions for permitting certain forms of positive action. The purpose of positive action and one of its primary functions is to counteract the effects of past discrimination. Training organizations, employers, trade unions and any similar organization can take action to encourage members of a particular group to take advantage of opportunities for holding particular posts. For example, an organization may presently employ very few black people or very few women in managerial positions. In order to correct this situation the personnel department may lawfully target specific training programmes, for example, at those particular groups. These points ought to be borne in mind about positive action:

- Positive-action measures (whether they are single or ongoing) are about encouragement, not about enforcement.
- It is unlawful to discriminate in favour of one sex or in favour of a particular racial group at the point of recruitment. Selection is still made on the basis of the best person for the job.

Positive action was in the news towards the end of 1990 when the British Broadcasting Corporation (BBC) announced gender targets for 1996. This is an exceptional move. Up until the introduction of the Opportunity 2000 campaign in 1991, the BBC was alone in its attempt to confront the issue head-on; no other British institution, from central government to the most liberal-minded local authority, had publicly committed itself to such a strategy.

The aim behind the BBC's plan is to raise the number of women in senior management from 10 to 30 per cent and in middle management from 18 to 40 per cent. The key word is 'target'. By law the BBC must not use the word 'quota', since this would constitute discrimination against men. In order to further this process the BBC is organizing regular staff monitoring and recruitment schemes such as careers fairs, job sharing, career breaks, and holiday pay schemes for working parents. In addition, in order to help managers in their personnel duties, fair selection training courses are being introduced. Since in 1990, 43 per cent of the BBC's total of 28,000 staff were women, targeting and positive-action drives to recruit and promote more women into management positions represents logical and economic sense coupled with good equal opportunities practice. Since Opportunity 2000 has been launched, it is likely that other employers will become actively involved in positive-action measures to eradicate work-place practices which tend to perpetuate inequality.

Examples of positive action:

ABC Products PLC

> This factory has an equal opportunities policy. Management accordingly proposes to run a special course for female operatives (within our engineering workshop) who wish to become qualified for promotion to Inspector Grade. (Section 48, Sex Discrimination Act)

ECOLYM LTD

> We are one of Europe's largest industrial companies, and have vacancies for Laboratory Technicians at our Midlands Refinery. If you have good GCSE passes in English, Maths and four sciences, why not consider a job in the Chemical Industry.
>
> At present few of our laboratory technicians are women. Applications from women as well as men will be welcome. (Section 48, Sex Discrimination Act)

Prejudice

Webster's Dictionary defines prejudice as 'an unreasonable or unjustifiably adverse opinion without just grounds or sufficient knowledge'. It is clear in this sense that prejudice is associated with stereotypes, since stereotypes are general or sweeping statements produced without adequate knowledge. Prejudiced people often do not sufficiently test out their beliefs against reality; or their minds give them a false view of what reality is – although even what reality is, may in the last analysis be a matter of opinion. Prejudice literally means to prejudge a person, group of people or a situation. They are often judgments which have no sound basis in fact or truth; and by virtue of this lack of knowledge carry with them a high degree of speculative ignorance and prejudice. Prejudice could be said to be the cause of discrimination, or a precipitator to acts of discrimination. Prejudice is the thought-process and discrimination the action that is taken as a consequence of the thought. If we are honest with ourselves, it is probably true that most people harbour prejudices towards or against certain groups of people. Fortunately, however, most prejudgments do not lead to acts of discrimination.

Prejudice, in its most usual forms, is generally targeted at particular groups of people. These groups may change as peoples' prejudices change and are focused elsewhere. Black people, Jews, gays and lesbians and indeed most minority groups suffer from prejudice to various degrees. Prejudice is most commonly aimed at minority groups, and is therefore felt mostly by minority groups. Most minority groups fall prey to society's prejudices, which are voiced daily in all forms of the media. A random selection of tabloid newspapers would provide numerous examples of prejudice.

Why does all this prejudice has to happen – where did vicious acts of discrimination originate? There is no single answer or panacea available to sweep society clean of prejudice and discrimination overnight. It would take volumes to explore the reasons underlying each person's prejudices. What is clear, however, is the very definite relationship between prejudice and discrimination and power and politics: the group that exercises discrimination holds much more power than the group it is discriminating against. Perhaps it is a human weakness in all of us which collectively manifests itself in a desire to own and control power. Whatever the causes, the results are damaging for all of us; and only when we abolish the inevitable inequality that discrimination causes can we call ourselves a democracy and all of us enjoy the benefits which that brings.

The human tendency towards prejudice depends much more on how you think than on what you think. The open mind is receptive to new ideas and welcomes new experiences. In contrast, the closed mind is hidebound by narrow interpretations of life. The open mind is probably less subject to prejudice than the closed. We are all subject to some extent to prejudice; and the attitudes out of which prejudice are born are probably closely related to our upbringing. The attitudes instilled in the mind by parents during early life can be very difficult to change. **Scapegoating**, or trying to shift the blame, can lead to prejudice; when it occurs at societal level in which a number of people share a prejudice, it may be aimed at an individual or, through a stereotype, at a group of people. Similarly, personal inadequacy can lead to prejudice. The person suffering from a deep sense of personal failure may be desperately anxious to identify inferiority in someone else. This enables him or her to find one gratifying thing about himself. Thus hatred and prejudice towards the minority group appears to fulfill a positive role at times of personal insecurity. Such a scenario may well go some way towards temporarily alleviating an individual's personal problems, but is by no means right or effective in society.

Quota: the Quota scheme

The Quota scheme relates to the disability aspect of equal opportunities. It was introduced under the Disabled Persons (Employment) Act 1944. All employers in the UK who have 20 or more employees have a statutory obligation to employ a quota of registered disabled persons. The obligation is to give employment to registered disabled people up to a Quota; that is, a proportion of their total staff. The national figure currently stands at 3 per cent of the working population. It is not an offence to be below quota, but in this situation an employer has a duty to engage suitable registered disabled people if any are available when vacancies arise. An employer who is below quota must not engage anyone other than a registered disabled person without first obtaining a permit to do so from the local job centre.

Historically, the scheme has been fraught with problems, and has often overlooked the central needs of people it was designed to assist. In fact, at times it has been close to being abolished altogether. Problems about Quota are similar in native to those with regard to most equality issues. Non-compliance is commonplace. Prosecutions under the Disabled Persons Act for non-compliance amounted to ten in total in the 36 years from its introduction up until 1980. Furthermore, not even in these ten cases were fines imposed. Overall there has been a marked unwillingness to enforce Quota, particularly in the years between the end of the Second World War and the late 1960s when total unemployment was low, though still relatively high among workers registered as disabled. The weaknesses in enforcing Quota are evident in all kinds of organizations, including not least government departments. The problems with the scheme have been compounded by the lack of encouragement from government for people to register as disabled; therefore a true picture of actual numbers is difficult to ascertain. Clearly, one of the most significant methods to increase compliance would be to apply a levy, fine, charge or any other sanction to organizations which fail to comply. The advantages would be twofold. First, this would increase employment rates among registered disabled people as more employers would set out to put their obligations into practice. Second, it would provide funds from charges which could be channelled into employment schemes for disabled workers, transport design and building modifications.

Racism

Racism is about the actions people take in response to the presence of other races or ethnic groups. The word entered the English language as well as most other European languages in the 1930s. It was first used to identify the belief that race determines culture. The underlying concept was that of race as type or group; and as something divorced from the major population. Its meaning has gone through several changes; from racism as a political form like capitalism, to later being regarded more within the concept of racial prejudice and discrimination. Racism today is generally used on a much more general level and refers to anything connected with racial inequality.

Racial conflict and racism are a symbol of the psychological difficulty people have in tolerating what is different from themselves – in this case the colour of skin. Racism is usually considered to be the process whereby black people are oppressed and discriminated against by white people. Some people may disagree and feel that the reverse may also occasionally be true, and that white people can be victims of racism. A more realistic school of thought believes it is impossible for white people to suffer from racism. Centuries of white power and dominance have resulted in black oppression. Racism has been around for centuries, during which time (in most parts of the world) the white person has been master and the black person has been slave. Racism is manifested in several ways, ranging from physical violence to verbal abuse. In chapter 3 equal opportunities policy and practice which can go some way towards challenging and combating racism are examined.

Records
Employers subject to the **Quota** scheme or having any designated employments are required to keep records as specified in the Disabled Persons (General) Regulations 1945, as amended. These records must be retained for a period of two years.

Refugee(s)
Refugees are usually individuals or (more likely) groups of people who for political or economic reasons have left their country of birth. The political situation has generally meant that their safe return to their home countries would be unlikely. The status of refugees is widely affected by the laws, particularly immigration control laws, in the host country or potential host country. Perhaps because refugees are intended to be only a temporary phenomenon, most immigration laws do not clearly define procedures for handling the arrival of sizeable groups of refugees. This is apparent in the UK laws as much as anywhere else in the EC. Within the UK there has been much debate on the position of refugees since the late 1970s. In 1979, the British government agreed to accept one and a half thousand refugee 'boat people' from Vietnam. In fact, between 1975 and 1982 almost 17,000 boat people were given the right to enter Britain. The situation regarding the boat people was exceptional in that it was regarded as a world-wide problem that required humanitarian action on a world-wide scale. Unfortunately, the British stance has not been quite so sympathetic to the needs of other people fleeing from persecution in their own country. In practice, many refugees in recent years have been assisted far more by black and Asian groups than they have by central government. An increase in global mobility coupled with an increase in violations of basic human rights in many areas suggests the need for legislation and policy to be in place to cope justly with refugees.

Register of Disabled Persons
The Register of Disabled Persons was set up to help disabled men and women get employment. Registration is voluntary, but some of the facilities reserved for disabled people are reserved specifically for those who register. People eligible for registration are those who, on account of injury, disease or congenital deformity are substantially handicapped in getting employment or keeping suitable employment, and whose disability is likely to last at least 12 months. People in employment can apply for registration equally with those who are seeking employment. Registering

as a disabled person is a fairly straightforward procedure. An appointment should be made with a Disablement Resettlement Officer (DRO), based in most local job centres. When an individual is accepted on to the register she or he will be issued with a Certificate of Registration, known as a 'Green Card,' which is valid for a fixed period.

Rehabilitation

Rehabilitation is about re-establishing an individual back in the community or the labour market after a period of absence. It is generally referred to in the context of either disabled workers or ex-offenders. For the former group it is usually an amount of time that is set aside to prepare an individual for re-entry into employment after, for example, an industrial injury. It involves quite formal assessments of a person's level of disability, whether of a congenital or accidental nature. Unfortunately, however, the growth in rehabilitation centres has coincided with the growth in long-term unemployment and poor prospects in the labour market which have hit disabled workers the hardest. Ultimately, therefore, for many disabled workers a period spent at a rehabilitation centre has prepared them brilliantly for returning to work – which in itself has been largely impossible to find.

Offenders and individuals with past offences generally 'undergo' a rehabilitation period; the primary aim of which is to equip them with the necessary skills for re-entry into the world of work.

Rehabilitation period and spent convictions (1975)

The rehabilitation period relates to the Rehabilitation of Offenders Act which came into force on 1 July 1975. If a person is convicted of a criminal offence and receives a sentence of not more than two and a half years in prison and does not commit another offence during a specified time (known as the rehabilitation period) s/he becomes what the Act calls a rehabilitated person. The conviction for the offence committed becomes 'spent' or in practical terms, forgotten. The rehabilitation period varies and depends on the sentence imposed for the original offence; although there are some sentences that carry fixed rehabilitation periods. The exceptions include the following:

1. A sentence of imprisonment or youth custody between six months and two and a half years has a ten-year rehabilitation period.
2. A sentence of imprisonment or youth custody of six months or less has a seven-year period.
3. For a fine or community service order, the period is five years.
4. For an absolute discharge, the period is six months.

All of these rehabilitation periods, except the last one, are halved if the person was under 17 at the time.

A rehabilitated person in possession of a spent conviction can enjoy the many benefits open to his or her non-convicted peer group within the realms of employment, training and housing.

Retraining schemes
The UK government has introduced several initiatives to stimulate the re-employment of certain traditionally disadvantaged groups, most notably women who wish to return to paid employment after spending time in unpaid employment in the home. Similar re-training schemes have been implemented in most other EC Member States, and the majority of them have targeted women as the main beneficiaries. However, there is an increasing need to broaden the client base and focus on other equally disadvantaged groups – for instance, older women. Most areas of employment and recruitment practices are directed at younger people far more than older workers; and there is little evidence of either government- or employer-led changes in this approach. Stereotypes about old age strongly influence employers' perceptions of ageing as incompatible with a capacity for productivity. Unfortunately, advancing age is commonly assumed to be indicative of a general decline in capacity and in the ability to learn new skills.

Scapegoating
Scapegoating means shifting the blame, or finding a scapegoat to carry the burden of responsibility, guilt or dissatisfaction. The scapegoat mechanism is very common and occurs at both a societal as well as an individual level. When it happens on a societal level in which several people share a prejudice, it may be aimed at an individual, or through a stereotype at a group of people. Let us take an example: suppose a man in Bradford loses his job and spends a long time unemployed. As his time without work grows he is very likely to thrust the blame onto a scapegoat, and in an area where there is a relatively high density of ethnic minorities he may blame them for causing his unemployment by taking all the jobs. Furthermore, in this instance his feelings seem to him to be entirely rational even though in reality they bear little resemblance to the employment facts and statistics in the area. Similar sorts of scapegoating happen all around us. Unfortunately, we may rarely be conscious of the tricks our minds are playing on us – but nevertheless should be wary of them.

Segregation
Segregation is generally about separating one group of people (usually the minority) from another group of people (usually the majority). As a rule it refers to segregation on the basis of race or on the basis of disability. There has been a tradition in the UK, particularly within the field of education, for children to be labelled and grouped according to their ability level (either mental or physical ability). This has applied specifically to young people with disabilities, many of whom have in the past been segregated from their non-disabled peers and taught in special schools or in separate groups within mainstream schools. The issue is not just about segregation

within education, but the fact that the attitudes entailed both reflect, and are reflected in, society at large. In reality rather crude divisions between disabled and non-disabled people have gone beyond the school gates at age 16 and permeated employment and training as well as social benefits like housing provision. More recently overwhelming evidence has shown that segregation is not just unnecessary but also incompatible with the fundamental needs of disabled people. Nowadays more people than before are catered for within mainstream provision as part of the general institutional framework. Integration rather than segregation ought to enhance the social development of disabled people, as well as serve to raise the awareness of the issues among non-disabled people. A decline in negative stereotyping and prejudice should accompany integration.

Perhaps the most pernicious example of racial segregation is the apartheid system in South Africa. By the end of the 1950s in South Africa people were segregated on the basis of racial criteria. Most aspects of life have been affected by such enforced segregation including an individual's rights to marriage, education, voting, hospitals, health care, employment, leisure and recreation, etc. Racial segregation still happens elsewhere, but it is not usually supported or reinforced by bureaucratic structures as in South Africa. Let us take an example. New York is one of many American cities which is inhabited in different parts by different groups – either racial, ethnic or national groups. In the past people have shown a tendency to group together in similar cultural groups for a variety of family, social and economic reasons. However, there is an enormous difference between enforced segregation and voluntary segregation. The former undermines even the most basic equality rights; whereas the latter in theory at least does not jeopardize social rights.

People can be indirectly segregated by unfair and unequal employment practices. In many Western countries one is far more likely to find white people in positions of power than black or Asian people. Although in the UK a Race Relations Act in theory protects people from being discriminated against on racial grounds, in practice discrimination very often occurs. In fact, the true picture is often one where white, black and Asian people are occupationally segregated, with a far higher proportion of white people in professional and highly paid employment than black or Asian people. In contrast to the apartheid system this is of course not a *formalized* method of segregation, but nevertheless it does still exist. Both informal and formal types of segregation ultimately contravene any legislation which purports to endorse equality for all citizens.

Severe disablement allowance

One might be forgiven for assuming that this allowance would automatically be paid to all people with severe disabilities. Unfortunately, however, this is not the case. Severe disablement allowance, introduced in 1984, is a tax-exempt weekly payment to mentally or physically disabled people who have been continuously incapable of work for six months, and have not paid sufficient National Insurance contributions to qualify for invalidity or other benefits. Even if an individual satisfies these criteria the claim is not necessarily straightforward. A number of conditions have to be fulfilled in order to prove that you are severely disabled. Problems about the allowance are linked to the problems over definitions of the terms involved; and to the inevitable problems arising out of subjective assessments of an individual's eligibility. On top of all the other clauses attached, the allowance cannot as a rule be paid for the first time after pension age, because it is seen as overlapping with the standard retirement pension.

Sexism

Sexism is the unfair and unequal treatment of women by men. The women's liberation movement which emerged in the 1960s, gradually began to realize that the groups that campaigned for equality for people in general – for example, for racial equality – were still not giving equal treatment to women. In order to correct this situation organized groups were developed to attempt to combat this sexism. A combination of practical measures and government legislation have together made massive headway in society, which has helped to increase public awareness of women's abilities and move towards eliminating sexism.

Sexual harassment

Sexual harassment is unwanted and uncalled for attention paid to someone. In its mildest form it can be displeasing and a nuisance to the person who is suffering from it. In its worst form it can be a dangerous and very disturbing series of events that can lead to severe emotional and mental problems. Although sexual harassment can happen anywhere and to either men or women, it most commonly occurs in the workplace; and it most often is something women are subjected to by men. Very often, if a woman is being sexually harassed at work she can be afraid to make a complaint for a variety of related reasons. The harasser, for instance, may be her boss or her supervisor, or just very popular among his colleagues within the workplace. Alternatively, the woman may be frightened to complain as by doing so she may risk her chances of promotion, or worse still, lose her job. Sexual harassment is a serious issue and therefore needs to be treated with the seriousness it deserves. The issue has to be addressed with all the legal remedies it rightfully merits. It is a social, psychological and legal problem and consequently requires a combination of methods to solve it.

All cases of sexual harassment should be written down as soon as they happen. The harasser should, in the first instance, be politely asked to cease his behaviour. In some cases this will be sufficient for the action to stop. If the harassment continues, all instances should be written down. Wherever possible a witness should be sought to bear testimony to the harasser's behaviour. All of the specific cases which have been written down should be subsequently reported. The most appropriate person to report to varies from one organization to another. Suitable people include representatives from management, trade unions, personnel, equal opportunities working parties or the harasser's immediate manager. If sexual harassment results in a woman having to leave her employment, she can claim Constructive Dismissal under the Employment Protection (Consolidation) Act 1978 as well as claiming under the Sex Discrimination Act. It is important to mention that employers can also be held liable for their employees' actions, unless they can prove that they have taken all practical measures and steps to counter sex discrimination. For instance, if a woman was been sexually harassed and she rightfully informed her employer who did not take it seriously, then she would have a case against her harasser and her employer. Adoption of an equal opportunities policy should help in the handling of such complaints. The guidelines laid down in the policy should ensure that the grievance procedure specifically provides a channel for processing complaints of harassment.

Men who endure harassment should have the same rights of claim and protection as women. It has already been emphasized that the recipients of sexual harassment are generally female. This is because it is related to both power and gender roles. Gays and lesbians are particularly vulnerable to sexual harassment, mainly because they cross traditionally perceived roles of what being male or being female means. In addition, they are doubly prone to its effects since to complain is to make a fairly clear statement about your sexuality. Affirming one's sexuality when it deviates from the perceived norm carries the risk of further harassment, victimization and dismissal. In almost all EC countries there is as yet no anti-discrimination laws for lesbians and gay men, so in general they are without protection.

Clearly, there is an overwhelming need for organizations individually to address the scope and concept of sexual harassment and to apply action which incorporates protection for all men and women regardless of their sexuality. It is worth noting that in mid 1991 the EC adopted a Recommendation and a Code of Practice on the protection of the dignity of men and women at work. The Recommendation is mainly about the prevention of sexual harassment at work; it is a welcome development with far-reaching implications in so far as it treats the issue as a male as well as a female problem. The Code of Practice prepared by the Commission aims to supply practical help and guidelines for employers, trade unions and individual employees about the means of reducing the occurrence of sexual harassment in the workplace. In addition, the guidelines will assist organizations in developing procedures for handling the problem and preventing its recurrence.

Sheltered Placement Scheme (SPS)

Introduced in 1985, the Sheltered Placement Scheme represents an important step forward in providing employment opportunities for people with disabilities. Under the scheme, a person with a disability is employed by a sponsoring organization – a voluntary body or a local authority – and work is provided by a host employer organization. The host organization pays only for the work which the disabled person does, the balance of his or her wage being paid by the sponsoring organization. The main advantage of the scheme is that the disabled person is integrated into a normal working environment, which can facilitate the transition to normal working. Also, it allows the job to be tailored to the disabled person's requirements.

Statutory Maternity Pay

Statutory Maternity Pay (SMP) was introduced in the UK from 6 April 1987. It is payable to employees who meet certain qualifying conditions. Under the old scheme of maternity provision women could receive maternity allowance from the state, and where applicable, maternity pay from their employers. Statutory Maternity Pay combined and replaced these two elements, although women who are not entitled to receive SMP can still qualify for state maternity allowance.

SMP is payable by employers to employees; in order for a pregnant employee to qualify she must:

- Have been continuously employed by her employer for at least 26 weeks (irrespective of the number of hours worked) ending with the fifteenth week before the Expected Week of Confinement (EWC). This fifteenth week is known as the Qualifying Week (QW).
- Have average weekly earnings of not less than the lower earnings limit for the payment of National Insurance contributions.
- Still be pregnant at the eleventh week before the EWC.
- Have stopped working for her employer wholly or partly because of pregnancy.
- Provide her employer with notice of her maternity absence.
- Provide her employer with evidence of her EWC.

Statutory Maternity Pay is one maternity right and is a separate provision from the second right: the entitlement to return to work. A female employee is entitled to take maternity leave at any time after the beginning of the eleventh week before the EWC and return to work afterwards, provided she:

- Has accumulated two years continuous service, being employed for at least 16 hours per week, or five years continuous service, being employed for at least 8 but less than 16 hours a week, by the beginning of the eleventh week before the EWC.
- Is still in employment at that time; in other words still has a contract of employment.
- Tells her employer in writing and at least 21 days before the start of the absence:
  - That she will be absent from work because of pregnancy;
  - That she intends to return to work; and
  - The expected week of confinement (EWC).

A woman has the right to return to work at any time before the end of 29 weeks beginning with the week in which the birth occurred. On her return she must be reinstated in the same kind of job as before and on the same terms and conditions that she enjoyed before. This means that as regards pensions, seniority, holidays and other terms she must be treated the same as previously.

From 1994 pregnant women throughout the European Community will qualify for up to 14 weeks of maternity leave irrespective of their length of service, following adoption of a new EC Directive. In addition, Statutory Maternity Pay (SMP) will have to be set at a level which is at least no lower than payments made for absence through sickness.

Solipsism

In the context of equality, solipsism is essentially tunnel vision which regards everything from a white perspective. It is not necessarily a deliberate attempt to discriminate racially; but rather a non-acceptance of black experience in all its forms. The focus of Western feminism almost exclusively on a white female perspective is a prime example of solipsism. Politicians engage in solipsism when they enact laws which will predominantly affect white persons' lives and do not take into account a black person's social, economic or political life or experience.

Stereotyping

A stereotype is an idea, belief or popularly held view about a particular group of people or situation. The stereotype is based on supposed fact and on imagery or assumptions which have no factual basis. The risks involved in stereotyping are often overlooked. The stereotype or incorrect image that is created is very often a totally distorted and grossly exaggerated overview of a situation or group of people. A stereotype is a generalization about a group of people: for example, the sly and shrewd Jew, the emotional Irishman, the mean Scotsman, the butch or femme lesbian or the limp-wristed gay. Stereotypes of old age are not uncommon; for instance, adjectives like senile, doddering or wrinkled are frequently used in descriptions of older people. We cannot escape generalizations, but we should beware of stereotyping. Stereotypes are invariably based on inadequate evidence, since no single individual has enough concrete evidence to form one. Indeed, very often stereotypes are formed in our early childhood when we are subject to the beliefs and prejudices of our parents and immediate peer group. It is quite possible that all future experiences are then interpreted through the stereotype to which one has been introduced. If one is told that redheads are quick-tempered, one will tend to use occasions when a redhead loses his temper as confirmatory evidence, and will tend to make no mental note at all when redheads behave in a calm and self-controlled way.

It would be incorrect to suggest that stereotypes are always completely false. The members of one minority group may indeed work hard; perhaps in order to combat the discrimination in society at large from which they suffer. Members of another minority may be lazy, possibly because they have been robbed of all incentive by those who have denied them the opportunities which would have come with equal status.

But stereotypes equally are misleading. For example, in the early eighteenth century the Englishman was regarded as revolutionary and the Frenchman as stable and solid. Stereotypes are unreliable and potentially damaging; in order to achieve true equality it would be better to avoid using them in everyday language and terminology.

Time off for family responsibilities

The right to leave from work for family reasons varies considerably both nationally and regionally throughout the whole of the EC. In general it is informal in nature and quite arbitrary. Reasons for which leave is usually granted vary considerably from country to country. Furthermore, some countries offer leave as a statutory right, while others rely on collective agreements to be locally arranged and spasmodically enforced. The UK legislation provides for no statutory rights for this type of leave; but there is evidence which suggests that an increasing number of companies are making their own verbal and written arrangements internally.

Eligible reasons for family leave include bereavements, family weddings, illness of a child, visits to children's schools, first Holy Communion and wedding anniversaries. As a general rule time off is allowed on each occasion that the circumstances arise. Therefore coming from a large family automatically gives you more right to leave. An exception to this is Greek law which places an upper limit on the total number of days off for family reasons. It is worth noting that most arrangements in the EC Member States about family leave discriminate in essence against gay and lesbian families who are not recognized as such under the majority of national laws. Interestingly the EC draft Directive on parental leave and leave for family reasons which was introduced in 1986 provides for specific circumstances which should be considered as justifying time off; these are: illness of a spouse, death of a close relative, wedding of a child and illness of a child (or the person caring for the child). However, confusion has often arisen about just what constitutes a close relative; so there is a clear need for a precise definition on the category of relatives the Directive will address if it becomes law. The proposed Directive is no nearer coming into force now than it was in 1986. In the UK both the current government and employers consider legislation on this issue to be inappropriate and believe that parental and family leave should be left to voluntary or collective agreements between employers and employees. In practice, this creates gross inequalities in provision.

Victimization

The Sex Discrimination Act and the Race Relations Act both include and define victimization as a completely separate form of discrimination. Victimization arises where, in any of the situations to which the Acts apply (education, training, employment, goods and services) a person (the discriminator) treats another person (the person victimized) less favourably than he or she treats other people, with the grounds for this unequal treatment based solely on the fact that the victim has asserted, or intends to assert, his or her rights under the terms of the Acts.

Xenophobia

In a similar fashion to **racism**, xenophobia has undergone a few changes in emphasis with regard to its definition. Unlike racism, however, xenophobia is not really a very widely used expression. It is essentially an extreme dislike of foreigners – and is therefore related to the concept of **misogyny** (extreme dislike of women). Relatively speaking, if prejudice indicates a dislike, then xenophobia indicates a hatred. Human nature being what it is, wherever different groups of people are geographically or socially brought together mild forms of xenophobia are almost bound to exist. The increase in multi-culturalism, coupled with the impact of the Single European Market and greater mobility, should serve to temper xenophobia. Challenging any irrational belief contributes towards increasing acceptance and tolerance.

Appendix 3

Governing Bodies, Organizations and their Roles

This appendix looks at organizations and services relating to equal opportunities issues. The availability of services, information and practical help in achieving equal opportunities varies widely depending on the type of help required. It is undoubtedly evident by now that the legislation and policymaking on, for instance, sex discrimination or disability far outweighs (though it is still grossly inadequate) that which is available on homosexuality or age. The same situation is reflected in the services that these groups are offered. In addition to advisory services and governing organizations, this appendix also addresses specific schemes which are available to provide practical help. In general these types of scheme are geared towards disability and ex-offenders.

Sex Discrimination

The Equal Opportunities Commission (EOC)

The introduction of the Sex Discrimination Act in 1975 highlighted the need for a public body to be set up by the government to prevent people being treated unfairly because of their sex, and – in the area of employment – to prevent discrimination occurring against married people. The Act therefore established an Equal Opportunities Commission with powers to monitor compliance with the legislation.

The aim of the Equal Opportunities Commission is to create equal opportunities for women and men in all aspects of life. Particular emphasis is placed on the following aspects:

- Employment: this includes recruitment and selection, promotion and demotion and transfer.
- Education and training: this includes access to educational opportunities at all levels and all subject areas. It addresses the issues of equal access to training facilities.

- Consumer rights: This applies to equal access to consumer rights. For example, credit from banks or building societies should be offered and supplied on the same terms to both married and single people, male or female.
- Welfare benefits: Similarly, all welfare benefits and advice are, or should be, offered to both sexes equally. In the past married women have received significantly fewer welfare benefits than married men.

The Commission also has an advisory and persuasive role. Through this role it is empowered to investigate areas where men and women are being treated unfairly, and advise organizations as appropriate. This can involve close liaison with management to correct the unequal practice, and help in introducing an effective equal opportunities policy and programme of action. The EOC has the expertise to advise both small and large organizations on all kinds of issues relating to sex discrimination, marriage discrimination and equal pay.

The Commission is run by up to 15 men and women who are appointed by the Home Secretary. These people are called commissioners. Together, they combine their knowledge, experience and expertise to approve, direct and carry out the Commission's policy.

The Equal Opportunities Commission may conduct formal investigations, ask for and compel evidence and examine documents belonging to an organization. Such documents may include contracts of employment, job descriptions and pension policies. The EOC may also serve non-discriminatory notices to bodies known or suspected of committing acts of discrimination (a non-discriminatory notice requires the person on whom it is served not to contravene specified provisions of the Act). Other activities in which it may become involved include seeking injunctions against employers guilty of discriminatory practices and supporting action in the courts by the aggrieved persons.

Everyone has responsibility to ensure the availability of equal opportunities. If you come across any case or examples of sex discrimination, inform the Equal Opportunities Commission; they are qualified to offer advice and guidance to remedy the situation. At the same time inform your local Member of Parliament, trade union, staff association or club, or indeed any organization to which you belong. The more people who are kept informed and up to date on cases of sex discrimination, the faster public opinion will change for the better and oppression will decrease. Public opinion influences government and in the long run improves the chances of parliamentary changes for the better.

The UK Federation of Business and Professional Women (BPW)

The federation is a world-wide network of professional women who seek to encourage all women to achieve their full potential in employment. The UK branches of BPW have successfully lobbied Parliament and the EC on several issues including equal opportunities laws, the inadequacy of the legislation safeguarding part-time workers, age discrimination issues, childcare, tax relief for childcare, and equalization of state pensions for women and men. The aims of the federation are:

- To encourage and train women to take an active role in public life and decision-making at all levels.
- To evaluate changing work patterns and press for improvements in education and training.
- To seek full equality between women and men.
- To undertake studies about the problems common to business and professional women in Europe and throughout the world, and to apply the results of such research in wider policymaking.

European Women's Management Development Network (EWMD)

The network was established in 1984 under the guidance of the European Foundation for Management Development (EFMD). The organization is committed to promoting women in management to their maximum potential. It seeks to change and combat workplace attitudes, cultures and structures that have traditionally oppressed women; and to facilitate women's achievements as managers. The network is represented in most EC Member States as well as other European countries.

European Network of Women's Studies (ENWS)

The European Network of Women's Studies was originally set up by the Dutch Ministry of Education and Science in 1989; it is cooordinated by a senior official at the Dutch Ministry of Education. Each EC Member State is represented by a national contact; these representatives meet in Europe twice a year. Recently, the Committee of Ministers of the Council of Europe have approved the ENWS. Its objectives are to stimulate and support research in women's studies and to apply the results of research in all sections of policy making. Currently, there is much interest from the network in positive-action measures designed to increase women's employment in the more traditional male areas from which they have previously been excluded. The UK network is a national association for women's studies in Britain. The steering body arranges conferences, holds meetings and liaises between related organizations to promote feminist research and teaching.

Useful addresses

Business and Professional Women (BPW)
Head Office
23 Ansdell Street
Kensington
London W8 5BN

Equal Opportunities Commission (EOC)
Overseas House
Quay Street
Manchester M3 3HN

European Women's Management Development Network (EWMDN)
c/o European Foundation for Management Development
Rue Washington 40
B-1050 Brussels
Belgium

International Working Group on Women and the Family
c/o A Woman's Place
Hungerford House
Victoria Embankment
London WC2

National Council for Civil Liberties (NCCL)
Women's Rights Unit
21 Tabard Street
London SE1

National Women's Aid Federation
374 Featherstone Street
London WC1

Opportunity 2000 (for further information)
Business in the Community (BITC)
5 Cleveland Place
London SW1Y 6JJ

Rights of Women (ROW)
52/54 Featherstone Street
London EC1 8RT

Women Against Sexual Harassment (WASH)
242 Pentonville Road
London N1 9UN

Women's Royal Voluntary Service (WRVS)
17 Old Park Lane
London W1Y 4AJ

Women's Studies Network (UK) Association
WYCROW
University of Bradford
Bradford
West Yorkshire BD7 1 DP
Part of the European Network of Women's Studies (ENWS)

AIDS and HIV

There are several organizations throughout the UK designed to assist people who have AIDS or who are HIV-positive. There are also 50 AIDS helplines located throughout the country which offer local telephone advice and information, and act as a signposting service to local support groups. The National AIDS Helpline offers free 24-hour advice and information. Tel: (0800) 567 123.

Terrence Higgins Trust

The Terrence Higgins Trust is the largest and longest-running organization in the UK dealing with AIDS and HIV infection. The Trust has both paid and voluntary workers who offer among other things a support group for people affected by AIDS. They also offer 'buddying', whereby an individual is allocated a particular support worker. Counselling and information services are also provided.

Health Education Authority (HEA)

The Health Education Authority produces booklets on HIV and AIDS. Most are available free of charge.

Body Positive Groups (BP)

There are a growing number of Body Positive (BP) groups in the UK. The London office can supply names and addresses of regional BP offices. Body Positive offers advice to people with AIDS or HIV. They hold a national conference each year.

Useful addresses

Body Positive (London)
51b Philbeach Gardens
London SW5 9EB

Health Education Authority (HEA)
Hamilton House,
Mabledon Place
London WC1H 9TX

Terrence Higgins Trust
52–54 Grays Inn Road
London WC1X 8JU

Racial Discrimination

Commission for Racial Equality (CRE)

The prime responsibility for making the Race Relations Act work belongs with the Commission for Racial Equality. The commission has a chairperson and 14 members, who are appointed by the Home Secretary. The various racial minority groups are substantially represented in its composition.

The main duties of the Commission are:

- To work towards the elimination of discrimination.
- To promote equality of opportunity and good relationships between racial groups.
- To keep under review the working of the Act, and to draw up suggestions for change if required.

The law cannot produce complete racial harmony, but it can remove some of the causes of grievance and prejudice. Since 1976, when the Race Relations Act was passed, the number of blatant cases of direct discrimination has undoubtedly been reduced. However, recent studies have shown that the Act has done very little towards preventing indirect discrimination. It was shown earlier that this type of discrimination is much less easy to identify, and therefore much more difficult for the aggrieved individual to provide concrete evidence about. As a result of this, it is essential that all of us act as 'watchdogs' for incidents of racial discrimination. Indirect discrimination can manifest itself in very subtle and insidious ways, which makes it almost impossible for an individual to instigate a complaint of discrimination.

Advice on the employment provisions of the Race Relations Act is available from the Commission for Racial Equality and also from the following organizations:

- The Advisory, Concilliation and Arbitration Service (ACAS)
- The Race Relations Employment Advisory Service (RREAS) of the Department of Employment.

Regional offices of these organizations can be found below, and also Thomson's directories, the Yellow Pages or through Directory Enquiries.

Runnymede Trust

The Runnymede Trust is a non-party-political race relations research organization. The Trust has a long-standing interest in the participation of ethnic minority members in party politics at national and local levels. They conduct research and carry out surveys of minority involvement both as candidates and voters, as well as campaigners and party workers. In addition, they research attitudes to various institutions and behaviour as well as ethnic minority activity in the wider society. Their most recent survey conducted in association with National Opinion Polls (NOP) researched the attitudes of a representative quota of white, Asian and Afro-Caribbean people. The survey's findings fell into five main categories of attitudes: race discrimination, immigration, racial attitudes, political party support, and attitudes to how many ethnic minority members are actually living in the UK. Research papers and the results of surveys are published by the Trust.

Industrial tribunals

Application should initially be sent to the Secretary to the Tribunals at the Central Office of Industrial Tribunals (COIT) of which there are three. Once an application has been received and registered by COIT, the Secretary then delegates it to the relevant Regional Office of Industrial Tribunals, which thereafter has total charge of it.

England and Wales: 93 Ebury Bridge Road
London SW1

Scotland: St Andrew's House
141 West Nile Street
Glasgow G1 2RU

Northern Ireland: Bedford House
16–22 Bedford Street
Belfast BT2 7NR

Race Relations Employment Advisory Service (RREAS)

The RREAS aims to provide assistance to employers in the implementation and adaptation of equal opportunities policies and practice, placing emphasis on race issues. The service is appointed by the Department of Employment and teams are located across the following five regional offices.

London: Room G17
11 Belgrave Road
London SW1V 1RB

West Midlands: Fourteenth Floor
Cumberland House
200 Broad Street
Birmingham B15 1TD

East Midlands: 102 Lower Parliament Street
Nottingham NG1 1EH

Northwest: Room 713
Sunley Tower
Piccadilly Plaza
Manchester M60 7JS

Yorkshire and Humberside: Room 317
City House
New Station Street
Leeds LS1 4JH

Useful addresses

Commission for Racial Equality, Head Office
Elliot House
10–12 Allington Street
London SW1E 5EH

The Runnymede Trust
11 Princelet Street
London E1 6QH

Black Rights – Britain's First Black Law Centre
221 Seven Sisters Road
London N4
(next to Finsbury Park Tube Station)

Disability

Reorganization of services

In 1991, the UK government announced a major reorganization of the three services it provides for people with disabilities: the Disablement Advisory Service (DAS), the Employment Rehabilitation Service (ERS) and the Disablement Resettlement Officer (DRO). Integrated teams called PACTs (Placing Assessment and Counselling Teams) are to be formed to take on all the present functions of DROs, DAS and the ERS teams. The aim is to provide a 'one-stop shop' for employers and people with disabilities seeking information, advice or assistance. There is at least one team in each of the Employment Service's 60 areas in Great Britain. Until they are all fully operational the first point of contact for PACTs is the Disablement Advisory Service through the Job Centre.

Disablement Advisory Service (DAS)

The Disablement Advisory Service exists in most large towns and cities in the United Kingdom. The service was set up in 1983. There are over 70 DAS teams covering all parts of the country. They can provide information and advice to individuals and groups on most matters relating to disability. The service helps employers of all sizes and in all branches of industry and commerce to adopt and implement good policies and practices in relation to the employment of people with disabilities. Its advisory role includes practical help on matters such as the recruitment, selection and retention of registered disabled people. The service also provides up-to-date information on the unique schemes available to overcome difficulties faced by people with special needs and their potential employers. It also acts as a signposting body directing people to other organizations for specific help on specific handicaps.

At every employment office or job centre a Disablement Resettlement Officer (DRO) is available to advise disabled men and women, and to help them secure suitable employment. The officer can also help in matters relating to registering as a disabled person. In addition to helping individual disabled people, the disablement resettlement officer can advise employers on recruiting disabled people and making the full use of the services of disabled people.

There are a number of grants which are available to assist employees and employers to coordinate the policy and practice towards workers with disabilities. For detailed information on cash grants in particular areas and for particular disabilities, the Disablement Advisory Service is the usual source of help. Financial assistance is available for the following:

- Job introduction scheme: This is available for employers who wish to take on a person with a disability for a trial period. The Employment Service can make a cash contribution towards the salary during the trial period.

- Adaptations to premises and supplying equipment: Grants are available to employers to recruit or retain a particular person with a disability. For example, if an existing employee loses a leg in a traffic accident and requires a wheelchair; although the building previously had no wheelchair access, a grant could be awarded to pay for a wheelchair ramp and toilet facilities.
- Fares to work scheme: This grant is payable to certain severely disabled people who have to use a taxi to get to work. A grant of up to 75 per cent of the total cost is available.
- Personal reader service: Financial help is available in order to recruit or retrain a blind or partially blind person. The cash goes towards employing a part-time reader. Applications should be made direct to the Royal National Institute for the Blind (RNIB), or via the local job centre.

There is other financial help available, so the four schemes listed above do not provide a complete picture. Further help can be found locally as part of a fund-raising or sponsorship appeal. Alternatively, national institutes for specific disabilities can supply further information.

Other help is available – such as loans for special tools or equipment, assessments and recommendations for workers who become disabled, and the design and manufacture of equipment to help individuals with disabilities overcome their handicap at work. Again, further information on these and other types of practical help is available through the Disablement Advisory Service.

The service can also provide information on the provision of work for severely disabled people. The sheltered placement scheme (SPS) is one such example. This scheme enables employers to provide opportunities for these people to work in their organization.

There are hundreds of groups which deal with the disabled. For more information contact the Disability Alliance:

The Disability Alliance
25 Denmark Street
London WC2H 8NJ

The Disablement Advisory Service can be a useful local source.

Information about different disabilities and their effects on and relationship to employment can all be found in one comprehensive guide, produced by Woodhead Faulkner in conjunction with the Royal Association for Disability and Rehabilitation (RADAR). The employer's guide can be purchased from RADAR:

Royal Association for Disability and Rehabilitation (RADAR)
25 Mortimer Street
London 21N 8AB

The Employers' Forum on Disability

The Employers' Forum on Disability is the only employers' organization in the UK concerned exclusively with promoting the employment of people with disabilities. Membership is open to any employer wanting to make it easier to recruit, train and develop disabled employees. The Forum operates in association with The Prince of Wale's Advisory Group on Disability, and Business in the Community (BITC)

Employers Forum on Disability
5 Cleveland Place
London SW1Y 6JJ.

Disabled People's International (DPI)

The British Council of Organizations of Disabled People (BCODP) is the British branch of Disabled People's International. DPI is a world-wide organization which consists of over 80 groups controlled entirely by disabled people.

British Council of Organizations of Disabled People (BCODP)
St Mary's Church
Greenland Street
Woolwich
London SE18 5AR

Addresses of the Offices of Opportunities for People with Disabilities

Head office:	1 Bank Buildings Princes Street London EC2R 8EU
Birmingham:	The Gate House Wellhead Lane Birmingham B42 2SY
Crawley:	Room 3/3B Beehive Building Gatwick Airport South Gatwick, Crawley RH6 OLA
London:	41 Chiswell St London EC1Y 4SD
Wirral:	Quest International Bromborough Port Wirral Merseyside L62 4SU
Brentwood:	Brentwood Community Agency Essex Way Brentwood Essex CM13 3AX

Hove:	SEEBOARD Grand Avenue Hove East Sussex BN3 2LS
Manchester:	Norweb Hathersage Rd Manchester M13 OEH
Bristol:	Cadbury's Building Somerdale Keynsham Bristol BS18 2AU
Leicester:	3rd Floor, Insurance House 125–129 Vaughan Way Leicester LE1 4SB
Sheffield:	Neepsend PLC 3 Lancaster Street Sheffield S3 8AQ

For information and advice about employing people with specific disabilities contact the following organizations.

Blindness:	Royal National Institute for the Blind (RNIB) 224–228 Great Portland Street London W1N 6AA
Deafness and partial hearing:	The Royal National Institute for the Deaf (RNID) 105 Gower Street London WC1E 6AH
Cerebral palsy:	The Spastics Society 16 Fitzroy Square London W1P 5H
Severe disablement:	Sheltered Employment Procurement and Consultancy Services (SEPACS) c/o The Employment Service Steel City House Moorfoot Sheffield S1 4PQ
	Remploy Limited 415 Edgeware Road Cricklewood London NW2 6LR

Mental illness: The National Association for Mental Health (MIND)
22 Harley Street
London W1N 2ED

Mental Handicap: The Royal Society for Mentally Handicapped Children and Adults (MENCAP)
The Pathway Employment Service
169A City Road
Cardiff CF2 3JB

Age Discrimination

Age Concern

As there are no statutory safeguards to protect the rights of older people, there is therefore no governing body as such. Age Concern is a registered charity and depends on public support. The organization is actively involved in a wide range of activities, not least of which is its role in research and training. For example, it is involved in organizing and conducting awareness campaigns towards countering ageism. It also acts as an important information-provider for older people and people who work with or care for them. Locally, it seeks to enhance the quality of life and provide services tailored to meet local needs. As well as providing information and advice, the service is also engaged in day care, transportation schemes, and clubs for the elderly. In many areas specialist facilities for physically and mentally frail old people are also available.

Eurolink Age

Eurolink Age is a Europe-wide network concerned with older people and age-related issues. It is now into its tenth year in operation as a non-profit-making body. It was formed as a means of ensuring that consideration of the interests of older European citizens was prioritized on the European Commission's political and social agendas. The organization works closely with a wide variety of EC institutions in order to bring age-related issues to the attention of the policymakers, and to ensure that appropriate action is taken to cater for the growing number of elderly people in the Community. The organization draws membership and interest from a broad range including older peoples' organizations, trade unions, social welfare groups, national and European politicians and medical practitioners. Formal links have also been established between Eurolink Age, the United Nations and the World Health Organization. Eurolink Age produce a bulletin three times a year in both English and French.

The Pre-Retirement Association

The Pre-Retirement Association (PRA) is a non-profit-making and non-party-political organization that has, among other activities, been running retirement preparation seminars nationwide for over 25 years. Courses are conducted for small groups on a daily or a week-long basis. Issues covered include finance, health, time management and leisure, etc. The organization also has a resource centre with a wide range of information on many aspects of ageing.

Forum on the Rights of Elderly People to Education (FREE)

FREE is an information network open to anyone interested in education and older people. It produces a quarterly information bulletin giving details of initiatives, research and publications on leisure education for older people. FREE is coordinated by the education and leisure officer of Age Concern England.

Useful addresses

Age Concern – England
Astral House
1268 London Road
London SW16 4EJ

Age Concern – Scotland
54A Fountainbridge
Edinburgh EH3 9PT

Age Concern – Wales
4th Floor
1 Cathedral Road
Cardiff CF1 9SD

Age Concern – Northern Ireland
6 Lower Crescent
Belfast BT7 1NR

FREE
Education and Leisure Officer
Age Concern England
1268 London Road
London SW16 4EJ

The Pre-Retirement Association (PRA)
19 Undine Street
London SW17 8PP

Lesbian and Gay Rights

The Campaign for Homosexual Equality (CHE)

The Campaign for Homosexual Equality was set up in 1969 as a successor to the North West Homosexual Law Reform Committee. It is a voluntary organization which is working to change the laws and attitudes which prejudice and discriminate against lesbians, bisexuals and gay men. In the 1970s it was Manchester-based, and is now located in London. The CHE established the momentum and initial impetus for the setting up of other related organizations; most notably Friend, the nationwide counselling service for gay people.

Stonewall Group

The Stonewall Group was formed in 1989 and is London-based. Its principal aims are to achieve full equality and full public and social acceptance for lesbians and gay men. The group has an equal representation of gays and lesbians. Stonewall's activities are wide-ranging and include political lobbying in the UK and European parliaments.

LAGER (Lesbian and Gay Employment Rights)

LAGER was set up in 1984 and is a London-based voluntary organization. Its fundamental aim is to challenge discrimination against lesbians and gay men. It is most closely concerned with ensuring equal opportunities for homosexuals in employment and seeking employment. The organization's services are broadly twofold. First, it offers advice and information to lesbian and gay men as well as training for those that are unemployed. Second, it offers consultancy and training to other organizations on all aspects of homosexuality – from drafting a good equal opportunities policy to show how discrimination can be avoided, to providing advice on employment contracts and recruitment. LAGER is the only such organization in the country.

Around Britain there are several groups and organizations which are specifically for homosexual men and women. In addition to social clubs there are many others including professional groups, religious and special-interest clubs and societies. To find out about these groups one of the most thorough sources is *Gay Times*, which is published monthly. Another source of information is the London Gay and Lesbian Switchboard – telephone 071 837 7324 (24 hours).

Useful addresses

Campaign for Homosexual Equality (CHE)
PO Box 342
London WC1X ODU

Lesbian and Gay Employment Rights (LAGER)
St Margaret's House
Bethnal Green
London E2 9PL

The Stonewall Group
2 Greycoat Place
Westminster
London SW1P 1SB

Black Lesbian and Gay Centre
Annex B
Tottenham Town Hall
Town Hall Approach Road
London N15 4RX

Ex-offenders

National Association for the Care and Resettlement of Offenders (NACRO)

NACRO has existed sinced 1966 and is a registered charity; it is the successor to the National Association of Discharged Prisoners' Aid Societies (NADPAS). The organization promotes the care and resettlement of offenders and ex-offenders in the community. It assists the victims of crime and involves all of the community in the prevention of crime. Activities include running training programmes and educational projects for people at risk of becoming involved in crime. The project liaises with external employers and groups to help increase the job opportunities for these young people. By building up a network of contacts in the world of work the association has had a great deal of success in placing young people in employment. This has the additional bonus of not only proving to the young people their own worth, but of improving their worth and image in the eyes of many employers. Further practical assistance is the provision of housing for people considered at need. These combined activities help to develop more effective ways of dealing with crime than the more traditional punishment procedures that have existed in the past.

In conjunction with its direct role in helping young people, the association also has many other initiatives. Foremost among these is its role as a research organization and information-provider for people interested in and concerned about crime-related issues and offenders. Training sessions are held for the latter by experts from NACRO. The research and recommendations developed by NACRO help contribute to the formation of crime policy; which, in time, helps in the prevention of crime.

The association also has a welfare role which has continued to grow for the last hundred years since NADPAS began operating. The main aim is to provide help for prisoners' families by setting aside money for grants and financial assistance. Nationally, it receives about 40 requests a week for monetary help. Assistance is requested by individuals via the social services, probation service, citizens advice bureaux and prisoners' wives groups. Of course, other groups and individuals can approach the fund independently if they wish.

NACRO is funded by the government, principally via grants from the Home Office, though other government departments can and do contribute. Other sources of financial aid include local authorities, private companies, agencies (for example, the Training Agency), and donations from individual supporters.

Nationally and locally there are several schemes and occasional grants awarded to offenders, past offenders and their families. These vary from the provision of educational and training courses or schemes, to recreational and leisure initiatives.

In addition, housing projects and accommodation may be available through the following organizations:

- National Association of Voluntary Hostels (NAVH).
- Stonham Housing Association.
- National Association for the Care and Resettlement of Offenders (NACRO).

The Local Probation service or welfare department can direct people who are interested in these groups and wish to know if they run a project in a particular area.

Ex-offenders and their families are also entitled in certain circumstances to financial help. This is made available and administered through welfare funds, which are almost exclusively under the auspices of NACRO. Recognized welfare organizations may apply on an individual's behalf. Other cash help is also availabale for some educational courses through, for example, the financial award scheme undertaken by NACRO.

There are several groups dealing with this issue; some are national and others are available at a local level. Many groups deal with specific areas, such as housing or education or the provision of job clubs; but they all share the common interest – that of looking after the needs of this group. Listed below are some of the better known national organizations:

National Association for the Care and Resettlement of Offenders (NACRO)
Head Office
169 Clapham Road
London SW9 OPU

Apex Trust
Brixton Hill Place
London SW2 1HJ

National Education Advisory Service
c/o NACRO
567A Barlow Moor Road
Chorlton
Manchester M21 1AF

New Careers Training Agency (Employment Training)
c/o NACRO
54 Bradford Street
Birmingham B5 6HS

New Careers Training Agency (Youth Training)
c/o NACRO
Fourth Floor
Clarence House
Darlington Street
Wolverhampton
West Midlands WV1 4ND

Human Rights

United Nations (UN)

The United Nations Organization was established in 1945, just after the end of the Second World War. Its principal aims were to attempt to maintain peace throughout the world and to foster good relationships between all nations. Its Charter was signed by 50 countries. The main ambitions of the Charter were to ensure that all members states were to be treated as equals, to work towards long-term peace and to settle as amicably as possible any tensions which may arise. Its headquarters are in New York and all members sit in the General Assembly.

The National Council for Civil Liberties (NCCL) and The Civil Liberties Trust

The National Council for Civil Liberties (abbreviated to Liberty) was formed in 1934. It is an independent and non-party-political organization which campaigns to defend existing civil liberties, as well as amend and improve inadequacies in current liberties when necessary. It is funded by members, donations and publication sales, and includes a network of 17 groups. It has a paid staff team.

The Civil Liberties Trust is Liberty's sister organization, and was set up in 1963. It was formerly called the Cobden Trust and is a registered charity. Its main role is to undertake research and educational work on all civil liberties matters. Both organizations are based in London.

Amnesty International

Amnesty International is a world-wide non-political organization which works for the release of prisoners of conscience: men, women and children who are detained in countries all over the world for their beliefs. It was founded in 1961, as a result of an appeal by a British lawyer who had become increasingly concerned about the number of prisoners throughout the world who had been deprived of their liberty for no greater reason than that of openly expressing their beliefs. There are now Amnesty sections in over 40 countries. Their headquarters is in London. Local groups have been established throughout the UK and new members are welcome at any meeting. Members may 'specialize' in particular human rights issues which interest them: abolition of the death sentence, release of women prisoners, child torture, etc.

Useful addresses

Amnesty International
5 Roberts Place
off Bowling Green Lane
London EC1R OEJ

Civil Liberties Trust
21 Tabard Street
London SE1 4LA

National Council for Civil Liberties (NCCL)
21 Tabard Street
London SE1 4LA

The Law Centres Federation
Duchess House
Warren Street
London
(They will give you your local Law Centre address which gives free legal advice.)

National Association of Citizens' Advice Bureaux (NACAB)
Middleton House
115–123 Pentonville Road
London N1 9LZ

Appendix 4

UK Representatives on EC Equality Networks

Advisory Committee on Equal Opportunities between Men and Women

Mrs J Foster
Chairperson
Equal Opportunities Commission
Overseas House
Quay Street
Manchester M3 3HN

Working Group on Equal Opportunities in Education

Mr Michael Richardson
Teachers Branch 2
Department of Education and Science
Room 4/8
Elizabeth House
York Road
London SE1 7PH

Women in Public Service Steering Committee

Mrs Sue Collins
Head of Equal Opportunities Division
Office of the Minister for the Civil Service
Horseguards Road
London SW1P 3AL

Working Group on Vocational Training for Women (IRIS)

Mr John Sharman
Equal Opportunities Commission

Overseas House
Quay Street
Manchester M3 3HN

Ms Jane Evans
Department of Employment
Caxton House
Tothill Street
London SW1

Network on Women in Local Employment Initiatives

Ms Kennedetta Ayemoba
Economic Development Unit
Birmingham City Council
Broad Street
Birmingham B1 2NA

Expert Group on 'Women in the Labour Force'

Dr Elizabeth Garnsey
7 Clare Road
Cambridge CB3 9HN

Group of the Consultants Promoting Positive Actions in Industry

Mr Robin Chater
1 Ham Cottages
Ickleton Road
Wantage
Oxon OX12 9JA

Childcare Network

Mr Peter Moss
Thomas Coram Research Unit
University of London
Institute of Education
41 Brunswick Square
London WC1N 1AZ

Index